THE GERMAN NAVY IN WORLD WAR TWO

Edward P. Von der Porten

Foreword by Grand Admiral Karl Dönitz

BALLANTINE BOOKS • NEW YORK

SBN 345-24133-9-150

This edition published by arrangement with
Thomas Y. Crowell Company

First Printing: August, 1974

Printed in the United States of America

BALLANTINE BOOKS
A Division of Random House, Inc.
201 East 50th Street, New York, N.Y. 10022
Simultaneously published by
Ballantine Books, Ltd., Toronto Canada

Dedicated to the memory
of my grandfather,
Paul M. Von der Porten,
physician, author, historian
of Hamburg and New York 1879–1964.
He applied history to life.

Acknowledgements

FORMER German naval officers have given generously of their time in granting interviews, reading the manuscript at various stages of its development, and answering questions. Their aid provided valuable information and colourful detail, and it corrected a variety of errors. I am deeply indebted to Grand Admiral Karl Dönitz, General-Admiral Wilhelm Marschall, Admiral Werner Fuchs, Admiral Theodor Krancke, Vice-Admiral Gerhard Wagner, Vice-Admiral Edward Wegener, Vice-Admiral Friedrich Ruge, Rear-Admiral Eberhard Godt, Rear-Admiral Hans Meyer, Captain Gerhard Junack, and Dr Jürgen Rohwer.

Lieutenant (jg) Donald Hansen, USNR, and Mrs Clarence Phillippi read the manuscript. Mrs Richard Bigelow helped proof it. Their many hours of labour created a far more readable book than it would otherwise have been.

My wife, Saryl, helped make possible the travel connected with the research, made many sacrifices to enable me to carry on the work, and typed and proofed the final version. Without her aid, the task would never have been completed. I trust it justifies her hopes.

The facts of the German Navy's story are, I believe, substantially correct; their weighting and interpretation are entirely my responsibility.

Contents

List of Illustrations

Foreword

THE book *The German Navy in World War II* by Edward P. Von der Porten presents in its broad view an accurate, clear, and vivid picture of German naval strategy.

The political and the military leadership of Germany – reared in continental concepts, and caught in them – did not recognize the decisive importance of the naval war to grand strategy. This lack of understanding was one of the fundamental reasons for the political and strategic errors committed by the German State and war commands.

I hope this excellent book receives wide circulation.

May the information contained therein contribute to the preservation of peace in the world.

Dönitz
Grossadmiral a. D.

Introduction

WARFARE has often been treated as a phenomenon sharply separated from the broad movements of history: as a grand adventure, a mystical test of personal or national virility, a chessboard for monarchs, a senseless contest secretly controlled by economics, or the supreme irrationality of mankind. Each point of view reflects an aspect of the truth, but accepting any one alone would relegate the study of war to technicians, antiquarians, or moral philosophers. The nineteenth-century concepts of victory – of destruction of the opponents' war-making capability and will – are also inadequate, if not foolish, analyses of mechanism and method, not of true strategy. Our violent century, with its capacity for mass destruction far in excess of any previously known, demands that war be seen in its dynamic relationships to long-range national and world objectives.

In this light, a study of the theoretical and actual strategy and tactics employed by the weakest branch of one of the world's most aggressive régimes, the Navy of Nazi Germany, may suggest concepts valuable in the even more terrifying milieu and for the far more critical decisions of the Atomic Age. The German Navy of 1919–45 was an example of the military organization pure and simple, whose only real concern was creating a power system to place at the disposal of the State. That Navy was smaller than most of its contemporaries, so its problems stood out in exceptionally bold relief; its victories and defeats remain relatively uncomplicated for clear analysis.

It is customary to divide studies of military affairs into three broad categories: grand strategy, strategy, and tactics.

Grand strategy is the combined planning of political, economic, and military organizations towards basically political ends, and in this sense is the most integrated form of national planning to further the interests and enhance the position of the nation in the world setting. As will be seen, Germany under Hitler possessed no such planning system except as it existed in the mind of Hitler himself.

Strategy is the art of using the elements of power to reach national goals in the international arena with a minimum of risk and loss. It consists of the development of material, the planning for possible alternatives, and the ordering of the forces at the command's disposal in order to place them in the most advantageous position prior to actual contact with an enemy.

Tactics refers to the disposition and manoeuvring of forces during combat.

This study examines the theoretical strategic plans of the German Navy, the means which were at its disposal, the forces which modified the strategy, and the actual strategy adopted as the trend of events and the influence of the personalities involved changed the theoretical strategy. Grand strategy, whenever flashes of it can be ascertained, is of particular interest, although it would be a vain search to expect a consistent one in Nazi Germany. Much of the study is taken up by naval strategy, a strategy often strangely isolated from contemporary events – isolated not only from developments in Allied Italy or soon-defeated France, but even from the other German Armed Forces and from the High Command. The results of this strategic fragmentation will be apparent.

Strategy results in action, and tactics modifies the theoretical base on which it rests. The battles selected for intensive treatment are those which forced changes in strategy, influenced the thinking of the German military or political leadership, or have an intrinsic interest for other reasons. Many of the capital-ship actions were influential in the strategic sphere, but submarine actions were often elements in broad campaigns in which individual events were not decisive. The relatively few submarine combat narratives, then, do not reflect a lack of appreciation of the submarines' influence in the war.

Grand Admirals Erich Raeder and Karl Dönitz were the dominating naval figures of the period. In a different fashion, Hermann Göring spoke for the Air Force. Overshadowing all was the figure of Adolf Hitler, who arrogated the military positions of Commander-in-Chief of the Army and Commander-in-Chief of the Armed Forces to himself in addition to his political power as Supreme War Lord. Hitler's and Göring's ideas are analysed only as they apply to naval strategy, and politics is ignored except where it impinges directly on strategy.

German terms, with the exception of Oberkommando der Wehrmacht (OKW), which has no meaningful English equivalent, have been translated into English in order to avoid confusion and to prevent as much as possible an emotional reaction to certain words.

Chapter 1

THE NEW NAVY

New ships and new strategies June 1919–September 1939

THE battleship *Friedrich der Grosse*, which had been the flagship of the Imperial High Seas Fleet in the titanic Battle of Jutland, hoisted her ensign in the alien harbour of Scapa Flow – home of Great Britain's Grand Fleet in the war that had ended seven months before. Throughout the anchorage, German flags rose to the mastheads of seventy-three other warships. No cannon rendered a salute, none shouted anger or defiance; yet the *Friedrich der Grosse* was sinking. Near the German Fleet, ships flying Great Britain's proud white ensign lay quietly at rest. As the *Friedrich der Grosse* settled, the battle cruiser *Von der Tann* rolled more and more sluggishly as compartment after compartment flooded. She had fought at Dogger Bank and throughout the bloody chaos of Jutland, sinking the *Indefatigable* of Vice-Admiral Sir David Beatty's battle cruiser line and then duelling with the Grand Fleet's battleships until every gun had been shot out; but she had kept her place in the line. That had been in 1916, three years before. In the calm midday of June 21st, 1919, she finally sank – not torn by enemy shells but scuttled by her own crew as a final defiant act, cheating the Allies of the spoils of war. Around her sank the other great ships of the Kaiser's Fleet: the battleship *Bayern*, which had been incomplete at the time of Jutland and had never fought Germany's enemies; the *König*, which had led the battle line into the thick of the Grand Fleet's concentrated salvoes; twelve other veteran capital ships; eight light cruisers; and fifty destroyers. The British, reacting far too late, fired vengefully as the German crews left their sinking ships.

The magnificent despair of Scapa Flow helped to still the memories of the red, early November days of the Kiel Mutinies, when the German sailors' refusal to sail had set off the revolt that ended World War I. It nullified the grim internment ceremony of November 21st, in which the Fleet had sailed into captivity between the lines of British ships and then had been ordered by Admiral Beatty to lower its flags. That day in Scapa Flow marked the beginning of a new German Navy, one that was to derive its spirit from the old. The scuttlings and surrenders were followed immediately by plans for rebuilding – although the immediate prospects were not good.

After the scuttlings and the toll of extra shipping exacted by the victorious Allies as a consequence, the Navy was left with only eight obsolescent pre-dreadnought battleships, eight old light cruisers, and thirty-two equally useless destroyers and torpedo boats. Not even that small number could be kept in service under the provisions of the Treaty of Versailles, which limited the Weimar Republic to six of the old battleships, six light cruisers, twelve destroyers, and some supporting light craft. Through other provisions in the Treaty, the Allies sought to ensure that the German Navy would remain a coast-defence force, small in both the number and the sizes of ships. The Treaty permitted battleship and cruiser replacements after they were twenty years old; but the battleships' replacements were to be cruiser-size ships of 10,000 tons with the 11-inch guns of small battleships, and the cruisers' replacements were to be 6,000-ton light cruisers with 6-inch guns. Other replacements were also permitted, but the destroyers were limited to a very low 800 tons, and the torpedo boats to 200 tons. No aircraft, aircraft carriers, nor submarines were permitted.

As with the other Armed Services, the Navy's personnel

also were limited. Fifteen thousand officers and men were permitted, the men to be on twelve-year and the officers on twenty-five-year enlistments.

Throughout the period of the Weimar Republic, the Navy could not build even to the Treaty limits. With budget limitations as a restriction, it began to organize, from the very beginning, in skeletal form. Civilians were assigned to the technical and research work, so that the largest possible group of officers could be retained towards the goal of future expansion. As early as 1921 the division of the ships into two fleets, or squadrons, was in effect, even though reactivation of old ships was not complete until 1925. Despite the antiquated ships, all sorts of problems were worked out for future use concerning such operations as minesweeping, coding, code-breaking, and long-range radio communications.

Meanwhile, the battle of the budget was fought each year as the Navy struggled to obtain funds from a reluctant Reichstag. The Navy commonly overcharged for budgeted items, and the extra money was used for unauthorized activities. Those 'black funds' were dissolved in 1928; but many preparatory operations continued in one guise or another, with the secret authorization of the Government. The Navy negotiated for the building of fast banana freighters, for eventual use as auxiliary cruisers; planned for the use of trawlers as minesweepers; chartered commercial planes for anti-aircraft practice; arranged civilian pilot training for prospective naval officers; and supervised the design and building of prototype naval aircraft and aircraft radio systems. Those activities, and many other minor ones, violated the official budget and the Treaty of Versailles, but they served to keep up the skills of a cadre of officers who were to use those skills when the opportunity came again.

The submarine, which had been the Allies' running wound in the Great War, was handled somewhat differently. The Navy, in July of 1922, acquired an interest in a Dutch design company in The Hague that employed some of the best German submarine designers. That group bridged the gap until 1935, when some of its latest designs for foreign countries served as the basis for the first new German submarine models.

In the meantime, the Navy proceeded with other building programmes in keeping with the Treaty. From 1925 to 1928 two small groups of 800-ton torpedo boats were built. The first light cruiser, the *Emden*, was constructed, and was used thereafter for training and to 'show the flag' around the world.

The Twenties were much more than years of slow building: they were years of intellectual ferment, inside and outside the Navy. The Great War was analysed by minds sharpened by vivid memories of national disaster. A Minister of Defence was designated to be Commander-in-Chief of all the Armed Forces, and his staff was to draw up a unified military strategy for the first time in German history. The need for such plans was a clear lesson of the Great War, but integration was so slow that the Army and Navy retained considerable autonomy for another decade. At first, planning was oriented towards possible problems with the newly reconstituted neighbouring country of Poland. The Navy's role was seen as supporter of the Army or as a partner allied in a localized war. The power to defend the Baltic entrances to prevent the junction of the French and Polish Fleets was an early goal. Practical men like Admiral Paul Behncke, the Navy's Commander-in-Chief during the years 1920–24, and Rear-Admiral Erich Raeder, a rising naval officer, believed that the Navy had to concentrate on such tasks, which were within the Navy's immediate potential but which echoed the concept of the very limited role assigned to the early Imperial Navy.

Others' concepts ranged further afield, questioning all accepted ideas. Vice-Admiral Wolfgang Wegener tore apart the strategy under which the Imperial Navy had fought World War I. To his mind, the concentration on the idea of battle, which had dominated late Imperial Navy thinking was a faulty reading of the international naval 'bible', *The Influence of Sea Power upon History* by the American Rear-Admiral Alfred Thayer Mahan. Mahan had stressed battle to contest sea lanes; but the German Grand Admiral Alfred von Tirpitz had stressed battle in what was essentially his strategic world, the North Sea. When the British had refused battle on the German terms and had instituted indirect blockade at the North Sea exits, the short-range German High Seas Fleet had been powerless to affect the outcome of World War I. As early as February 1915, Wegener had urged capture of the French west coast and movement of the German Fleet there, where it could have threatened the vital British Gibraltar and North Atlantic trade routes. Such a threat would have brought battle and decision.

Wegener's book *The Naval Strategy of the World War*, published in 1926, emphasized and enlarged on those views. Great Britain, he said, was historically hostile to any expansive European power, so a renascent Germany would inevitably have to fight Britain. In order to do so successfully, Germany would have to become an oceanic power. That required the creation of a large, balanced fleet; the acquisition of bases, such as those in western Norway and France, that led to the critical North Atlantic arena; and finally, decision by battle on the trade routes. Were she to fail to create such a basis of naval power, Germany would have to enter an alliance powerful enough to challenge the British at sea; for Britain controlled Europe's trade routes. Even such a Continent versus maritime-empire power pattern would be insufficient if the United States were hostile. In fact, in Wegener's view, alliance with the United States seemed the surest security for Germany's future. Because neither constructing a dominant Navy nor arranging alliances was feasible, the conclusion was implicit in Wegener's thesis that German irredentist or expansionist hopes could lead only to disaster.

Admiral Wegener's ideas did not become a new gospel for German naval leaders. To some they were too radical, too broad, or too distant for serious concern; to others they furnished theoretical support for more specialized solutions to the problems of future German naval power. Wegener's ideas, and those of his contemporaries, ensured that the rising young officers of the new German Navy would have a broader intellectual background than their Imperial Navy predecessors; however, a reluctance to emphasize the political effects of sea power (for instance, the submarine's effect on American entry into World War I) kept German strategic thinking from being as broad as it might otherwise have become. Many officers found grand strategic thinking interesting, but seemingly irrelevant to their practical task of building a small Navy from practically nothing. Repeatedly, however, in the nineteen years left to the new Navy, the Wegener ideas were to be echoed in its operational plans.

In 1928, the last year of Admiral Hans Zenker's leadership, the practical problems of German strategy came very clearly to the fore. The oldest of the battleships was ready for replacement, and the new design became a storm centre. To Admiral Zenker's staff the choice was clear. Building a slow, heavily armoured, 10,000-ton monitor for coast defence and use in the Bay of Danzig would signify a return to the ignominious status of the Prussian Navy, by making the new Navy once again a minor adjunct to the land forces. The alternative – building a unit useful to an offensive, oceangoing Navy within the limits of the Versailles Treaty – posed a very difficult problem, however. Its nature would proclaim the ship's purpose no matter how much its proponents tried to explain its functions in terms of Baltic convoy duty. The Reichstag was violently split because of the ship's probable effect on world opinion and because of its expense. Finally, however, the *Deutschland* – a remarkable unit in every way – was approved.

Officially designated as displacing 10,000 tons, she actually was 1,700 tons over that limit, even though all-welded construction was used to save weight. Her armour was light; her six main battery guns were the 11-inch size stipulated by the Treaty, and her all-diesel drive gave her an operating range of 21,500 miles and a top speed of 28 knots. The intention of the Treaty makers had been completely thwarted. The extra tonnage, it was later claimed, merely added to the defensive qualities of the ship in the form of extra compartmentation and armour but all warships are compromises among the characteristics of speed, weaponry, passive defence, and endurance, so greater size usually produces more powerful ships. It is ironic that the German ships then being built were to engage ships that were built within the strict limits of the Washington Treaty of 1922 – a naval limitation treaty that had not included or mentioned Germany. Those enemy units would include 'treaty cruisers' like HMS *Exeter*, with her six 8-inch guns, which Captain Hans Langsdorff in the *Graf Spee* shot to pieces in the Battle of the River Plate.

The *Deutschland* was designed as a high-seas raider, more powerful than any ship faster than herself except three British battle cruisers. In the event of war with France, she and her sisters were expected to force the French to use most of their Fleet for escort duty, in order to free the Baltic and North Seas and the North Atlantic routes north of Scotland for German shipping. She could also be used in other situations, such as a war in which Germany had allies. The idea of building ships that would not be limited to special purposes, and the idea of powerful, long-range raiders foreshadowed the Naval Staff's Z-Plan of 1938–39 and the course of World War II.*

The *Deutschland* gave the Germans control of the Baltic and caused quite a stir abroad. There was an immediate reaction in France, where the *Dunkerque*-class battle cruisers were built in answer to the threat. Later, even the United States responded to them with the *Alaska*-class battle cruisers of World War II.

Complementing the *Deutschlands* was a system of supply

* The classification of those three ships – the *Deutschland, Admiral Scheer*, and *Admiral Graf Spee* – has caused so much confusion that they will be referred to simply as the *Deutschlands*.

for them and other potential raiders on the high seas. As early as 1927 an effort was made to contact former members of the World War I overseas supply organization. By 1931 the system was again well organized. It was to be used only in benevolent neutral countries, and consisted of agents who were members of steamship companies abroad. They were to arrange the loading of German merchant ships with supplies for the raiders on signal from Berlin and to see that those ships put to sea, to meet the raiders in remote areas.

In the fall of 1928 the experienced, competent Admiral Raeder was appointed Commander-in-Chief of the German Navy. His was the heritage of the Imperial Navy: training in sail and steam; duty on the flagship of the 'Sailor Prince', Rear-Admiral Prince Heinrich of Prussia, in the Far Eastern squadron and in the North Sea battle line; study at the Naval War College; frequent travel; and editing and writing for the German naval journal and annual. Each new post had brought him into contact with more of the men who were to determine the world's maritime future – men such as Grand Admiral Tirpitz, the creator of the High Seas Fleet; Admiral Sir John Jellicoe, who was to command the British Grand Fleet at Jutland; and most of the German officers who were to distinguish themselves in World War I. Service on the Kaiser's yacht had given him a close view of the highest social and political circles.

Raeder's reputation was made during World War I. In sortie after sortie and in the two great battles of Dogger Bank and Jutland, he had stood on the flat bridges of the battle cruisers *Seydlitz* and *Lützow* as Chief of Staff to Vice-Admiral Franz von Hipper, informing and advising the great naval officer and watching the world's two greatest Fleets dual for mastery of the seas. At Jutland he had seen the *Lützow* torn by ten major shell hits and a torpedo. With Admiral Hipper he had shifted from the crippled flagship, first to a torpedo boat, while water cascaded about them from British salvoes, and then to another battle cruiser in order to resume command of the scouting forces. After the war Raeder had held a succession of posts – most of them administrative, but with interludes of historical study and sea command – and had risen steadily in rank in the small but growing Navy that was dominated by the heroes of Jutland.

Admiral Raeder was a stiff disciplinarian, an intense worker, and an extremely practical thinker. He applied himself vigorously to the development of the Navy, and saw that task, together with the building of a competent officer corps and well-trained and disciplined crews, as his main responsibilities. He countenanced the violation of the Treaty of Versailles and the secret preparations, feeling that they were minor infractions and necessary to improve what he considered a very weak position. He supported a limited role for the Navy, in keeping with its limited strength. Despite his historical studies of the German raiders of World War I, the Admiral at first opposed the raider design of the *Deutschland* because high-seas raiding seemed irrelevant to the Navy's role; but he accepted her and arranged for more of the type when she proved practical and versatile. The Wegener thesis he rejected on the ground that Germany would never again fight Great Britain.

Although personally somewhat formal and distant, Raeder listened to others' ideas and could accept frank talk, especially on a person-to-person basis. A sense of insecurity, however, intruded on his relations with most people outside his small official circle. This manifested itself in requests not to repeat items discussed 'under four eyes' and in a sensitivity to criticism, which he apparently interpreted, unjustifiably, as a challenge to his authority. He also tended to keep close control of operations, limiting the initiative of the officers in the sea commands by detailed instructions and closely criticizing their conduct of operations when they returned. In all this the High Seas Fleet influence is apparent, modified little because he lacked close contact with other navies, governments, and peoples after World War I.

Raeder had the unusual opportunity of directing a modern navy for fifteen years, from its early stages of building to its use in combat. His planning and organization were very good; it was his misfortune that war came too soon. Through good times and adversities he held the German Navy to high standards, kept it out of politics, and prevented interference by outside forces with its personnel or organization. He was even able to keep out the Nazi Party and to maintain the chaplain corps and normal religious services.

The years from 1928 to 1933 were busy ones for Raeder and his Navy. New ships, including modern 6,000-ton light cruisers, were built. Some were fitted with diesels in addition to their main steam turbines, in order to increase their range. In 1932 a five-year construction programme was planned and approved by the Minister of Defence. It included destroyers, torpedo boats, motor torpedo boats, and basic organization for aircraft and submarines, which were to be set up by 1933. In the case of the submarines, the planning was under the guise of an anti-submarine school. Experiments were made with mines, minesweeping techniques, new minesweepers, and new torpedo boats, and electronics research leading to the development of radar was begun. The armaments industry was encouraged to find foreign markets in order to keep up its skills and production capacity. Private firms also developed naval catapults, aerial torpedoes, and guns for aircraft. Finally, North Sea naval manoeuvres were held, directed towards defence in local wars at first, then against France or Russia. The 'task force' idea of grouping ships for specific purposes was developed at that time. No exercise was ever held with the assumption of Great Britain as a possible enemy.

In 1933 Adolf Hitler became Reichs Chancellor. A few days after his accession to power, Raeder had his first conference with him. Hitler's strategic ideas were continental, founded on Sir Halford Mackinder's Heartland Theory – which envisioned a power base built upon the land mass of eastern Europe and western Asia. From the first, however, he seemed to understand and agree with Raeder's ideas. They agreed that the basis of the Navy's strategic planning was to be peace with Great Britain secured by recognition of Britain's naval superiority, which she needed because of her position as a world colonial and maritime power. Hitler suggested that an agreed ratio of strength was to be negotiated if possible. Russia was the arch-enemy of Germany and Europe, said Hitler; war with England was out of the question.

Raeder and many other naval leaders were impressed by Hitler's leadership and peaceful accomplishments, although their attitudes exhibited a notable ambivalence that most of them never resolved during Hitler's lifetime. For none of the new Navy's higher officers, who had grown up in the grandeur of the Imperial Navy system, could be comfortable socially with the domineering Austrian ex-corporal, whose conferences were essentially self-centred monologues. Not that he was always crude: his language was uneducated, but he had a remarkable gift for suiting his speech to his audience and a knack for showing disarming personal kindness. To Raeder he was formally correct and polite, meeting Raeder's idea of the proper relationship between the Navy's leader and the head of Government. Hitler's ruthlessness, injustice, and brutality did not show themselves clearly at first and the mass atrocities, a development of the war years, were hidden by Hitler's methods of dividing power and by the enormous wartime pressures, which kept everyone in authority tightly tied to his own limited responsibilities. The peculiarities of Hitler's decision-making process, in which he demanded objective presentations but rejected those that did not suit his preconceptions, were balanced by his obvious successes in foreign affairs and later in military ventures. His strength lay in the political and psychological fields. He had the ability to take advantage of opportunities even if normal military preparations and safeguards were not complete. He did not make detailed, long-term plans, however. His successes covered many weaknesses, such as his tendency to reserve judgement while seemingly agreeing to a proposal and his failure to coordinate the many Government departments that were concerned with a single problem.

The most important factor in the Navy's relation to Hitler was that it remained non-political, as both wished. Only slowly did the disadvantages of that position become clear, as the Navy found itself badly handicapped in its struggles with the other Services – particularly the Air Force, with the politically powerful Hermann Göring at its head.

The first result of functioning under the new régime was a new five-year naval building programme, based on the Treaty of Versailles. Personnel were increased, however, so that by 1935 the number was three times that permitted by the Treaty. Building up to the Treaty limits was planned for the first time.

To the Ministry of Defence in Hitler's first Cabinet came General Werner von Blomberg, as Defence Minister and Commander-in-Chief of the German Armed Forces. His organization, the Oberkommando der Wehrmacht (OKW), was intended to draw up a unified military strategy and to coordinate the operations of the existing two (later three) branches of the Armed Forces. A combined operations staff was to be added to the OKW later. This would have given Germany a fully developed, unified command structure for the first time.

The chain of command was quickly upset, however, by the creation of the German Air Ministry, under Hermann Göring. The new branch, though theoretically the equal of the Ministry of Defence, was in practice its superior because of the position of Göring in the Nazi hierarchy. Göring immediately began to create a secret Air Force and attempted to take over the undercover Army and Navy Air Forces as its nucleus.

Göring's plans set off a bitter battle over aerial strategy. The Navy said it needed a separate air arm, trained in operations over the sea and equipped with aircraft for that purpose. Göring was an extreme air-power advocate – probably without much real understanding of the implications of that position. He believed in a radical form of the single Air Force, to the point that all air operations except warship float-plane flights were to be controlled by that branch. Even those few naval planes were to be developed and supplied by the Air Force. His objects in war were air superiority and strategic attack, and he placed little value on cooperation with the other Services. There were to be exceptions to his singlemindedness, as in parts of the blitzkriegs of 1939–41; but they were more rare than it seemed to observers on the Allied side. The needs for weapons, trained personnel, codes, and communications for the special tasks of the other Services were slighted or ignored. The feud was just beginning.

Partly in hopes that the terms of the Treaty of Versailles might be modified, Raeder began planning in 1934 for larger ships. It was time to build two more of the '10,000-ton' *Deutschlands*. Three had already been built and were considered successful, but Raeder wanted to make the next two larger and more powerful by the addition of a third triple 11-inch gun turret. Hitler did not wish to upset foreign powers by an action so overtly contrary to the Treaty of Versailles, so he told Raeder to plan for a ship with more armour and compartmentation; those plans could later be altered to include the extra turret. Tonnage might go up to 25,000 tons that way.

Raiders were much in the Navy's mind at that time, and secret preparations were made for converting four fast merchantmen into auxiliary cruisers. The necessary guns could not be obtained from the Army, however, and the project was dropped after some unpleasant exchanges; but the planning continued.

Submarine construction came closer and closer to realization in 1934 and early 1935. A Turkish and a Finnish submarine designed by the Dutch design bureau served as the last steps before German construction. The

Finnish vessel was partly designed in Germany, and was used for trials by the Germans before being turned over to the Finnish Navy. It became the prototype for the first German coastal submarine series: the 250-ton *U1* through *U24*. The Turkish craft became the prototype for the *U25* and *U26*, the first oceangoing submarines. Parts for the *U1* through *U24* were ordered and prepared outside Germany. Raeder suggested that it might be desirable to assemble six of those submarines in November 1934, so that they would be ready in case of trouble over the re-establishment of the Armed Forces. Hitler rejected the idea, but parts were brought in secretly in early 1935 when a great change in the prospects of the German Armed Forces was expected as a result of Hitler's more aggressive policies.

In March 1935 Hitler broke the bonds of the Treaty of Versailles openly. He announced the official establishment of the Air Force under Göring as the third branch of the War Ministry. Göring also kept his post as Air Minister. Naval aviation was forced to concede to Göring, to some extent, when the Air Force was formed. According to an agreement reached during that year, the Navy was to operate and control a Naval Aviation Branch of the Air Force in time of war. That organization contained naval officers transferred to the Air Force for that purpose. In return, Göring promised to supply sixty-two squadrons with 700 aircraft to the organization by 1942 and to maintain its ground facilities and supply system. The arrangement looked reasonable on the surface – but it failed to quiet the fears of those who knew Göring. The Navy Air Force, characterized as 'excellent' at that time by Raeder, began its decline with that reorganization.

In June 1935, as a gesture of good will on the part of the British and as an ostensible confirmation of German intentions to respect Great Britain's worldwide commitments despite the breaking of the Treaty of Versailles three months earlier, an Anglo-German Naval Treaty was drawn up. From a fleet of three *Deutschlands*, six light cruisers, and twelve torpedo boats, the Germans were permitted to reach 35 per cent of the strength of the world's greatest sea power. The new Treaty allowed them five battleships, five heavy cruisers, eleven light cruisers, two aircraft carriers, and sixty-four destroyers – with increases above that total when Britain increased her Fleet. Submarines were permitted again, up to 45 per cent of the British tonnage (or approximately forty-five units at that time), with an escape clause that permitted building to 100 per cent after notifying the British and at the expense of other ship categories. A German concession was the limitation of battleship size to 35,000 tons (the physical limit of the Panama Canal), which was the same restriction the British used and which had been established by the Washington Treaty. By agreeing to the London Submarine Protocol of September 3rd, 1936, the Germans also agreed that their submarines were to adhere strictly to prize law, which provided for the safety of merchant ship passengers and crews in time of war. Neither the battleship tonnage limit nor prize law was adhered to in the long run, although the German Navy attempted to follow prize law at the beginning of World War II, until the development of the war at sea made such attempts impossible.

Within the Germany Navy the Treaty was hailed as a masterpiece, both by those who thought war with Great Britain would occur and by those who believed it would not. As Hitler explained the Treaty, Germany would develop a closer rapport with Britain by acknowledging her dominance at sea. Germany would avoid a naval armaments race, which she could not win and which would just alarm Britain. Raeder and other high-ranking leaders of the Navy concurred with this view; until the very outbreak of war, Raeder himself believed that Hitler's ambitions were confined to the Continent and that peace with Great Britain could be maintained for a long time. At the same time, the new Treaty was praised by those officers who felt that war with Great Britain was sure to come. In the event of war, this group reasoned, British strength would be over-extended by involvement with Italy and perhaps

Japan, as well as by the need to provide cover for convoys. As a result Germany might achieve parity with Britain in the North Sea. That conclusion, however, depended upon the twin assumptions that, first, war would not break out until after Germany had completed the building programme permitted in the new Treaty and, second, that the German battleships would be newer and more powerful than their British counterparts.

On June 28th, 1935, eleven days after the signing of the Treaty, *U1* was commissioned in Kiel. The mysterious, heavily guarded sheds that had been erected in 1934 were opened to reveal the first new German submarines. By January of 1936, eleven other small submarines were in commission; all had been under construction before the Treaty.

The first submarine flotilla – composed of three 250-ton coastal-type craft and named the Weddigen Flotilla, after a 1914 submarine hero – was placed under the command of Captain Karl Dönitz on September 28th, 1935. Other submarines were being used for training. Within a year of the London Treaty, twenty-four small submarines had been built.

Any appreciation of the submarine in the inter-war years and in World War II requires an understanding of exactly what it was. The word 'submarine' is itself a misnomer. 'Submersible' would be a much better term; but 'submarine' is the traditional one. Until close to the end of World War II the submarine was basically a surface craft. It found its quarry on the surface, tracked it on the surface, attacked and escaped on the surface. It was fast; it could see, but only rarely be seen; and it had a choice of weapons when engaged on the surface. The submarine submerged only to avert danger or to make an attack in daylight (which was not the usual attack time). Below, it sacrificed speed and, to some extent, security because Asdic (the British equivalent of Sonar) could pick it up.

By 1935 the submarine had been improved considerably since its last employment in 1918. It could operate noiselessly; could stay underwater longer, using more efficient batteries; could fire torpedoes without giving away its position, using wakeless electric torpedoes and suppressing the water swell when launching them; and could destroy ships more effectively, using torpedoes that were exploded under the ship's keel by magnetic firing devices. Improved radios made entirely new tactical and even strategic plans possible.

Karl Dönitz was the ideal choice as Commander of the new Submarine Service. He had a broad understanding, gained in Navy assignments, of naval affairs on an international scale. Those assignments had included wartime service aboard the light cruiser *Breslau*, whose famed dash through the Mediterranean to Constantinople with the battle cruiser *Goeben* in 1914 brought Turkey into World War I. After the war he had continued to broaden his knowledge with surface-ship assignments, culminating in command of the light cruiser *Emden* on a training cruise in the Atlantic and Indian Oceans. However, it was his two years' service on submarines during the Great War that had determined his future. So decisive had been the impact of his submarine experience that Dönitz based his decision to remain in the Navy in 1919 on the assurance that the submarine Service would be re-established. The sixteen-year wait for that development merely sharpened his plans for the new submarine tactics and strategy. When the moment came, in 1935, that he could stand in the conning tower and take the tiny *U1* to sea, his mind held the complete picture of the way great fleets of oceangoing submarines would threaten the existence of the world's greatest maritime empire.

Something equally important was complete in Dönitz at the same time. Assimilating the mixed heritage of surface-ship formality and submarine intimacy, Dönitz had developed a brevity and incisiveness of speech and command that he balanced with a personal concern for each of his men. In the war room or in the mandatory conferences with his commanders when they returned from cruises,

Dönitz's attitude was one of careful attention to all the facts and suggestions. He also asked searching questions that brooked no evasion of awkward facts. When he set aside the pressures of conference or war room, Dönitz invited his officers in for relaxed luncheons or dinners at which a tone of lighthearted banter and *camaraderie* prevailed. Those informal gatherings most sharply illustrated the personality differences between Dönitz and the rather austere and authoritarian Raeder.

Dönitz realized that no country could be defeated by the *guerre de course* – uncoordinated raiding of commercial shipping. He accepted the commerce raider of World War I, the submarine, without basic changes; but he planned to use it in radically new ways. With the goal of 'tonnage war' – that is, maximum enemy tonnage losses per submarine per day at sea – always clearly in mind, he chose the North Atlantic as the only decisive theatre, and planned to meet massed convoy escorts there with 'controlled operations' designed to bring massed attackers to the convoys by radio command. In the first group-attack exercises Dönitz experimented with a group commander, to direct attacks from a submarine in the combat area. Later, when the efficiency of radio control from his own headquarters ashore was proved, he abandoned that idea and substituted the method in which the first submarine to find a convoy became a radio beacon submarine, leading others to the target while Dönitz changed the submarine dispositions to bring the greatest possible number of boats to the scene of the action. Once in contact with the convoy, the submarines operated independently at night on the surface, much in the manner of torpedo boats. They disengaged before dawn and ran ahead so as to be massed for the following night's attack. So realistic was the training for those attacks that the first casualty occurred as early as November 1936, when *U18* was rammed and sunk by an escort vessel as it tried to break through the escort ring to attack its target at close range.

Dönitz's tactics required many 'eyes' to locate convoys,

so he wanted as many medium-size submarines as possible. He felt that they would also be less vulnerable and more manoeuvreable than larger submarines. His superiors in the Naval Staff, however, felt it would be more profitable to build some larger craft – up to 2,000 tons – for use in distant oceans as submarine cruisers, with guns up to 6-inch calibre as the main attack weapons. Some Naval Staff officers even wished to eliminate the submarines' radios, contending that they were of more danger than value. In the debates the raider concept clashed with the idea of tonnage war. The question as to the best use of the tonnage allowed by the Anglo-German Treaty caused a two-year delay in construction. Finally the submarine cruisers were dropped from the programme.

In 1935 a greatly expanded shipbuilding programme was planned, in line with the new limits and based on construction capacity and experience. Its goal was the 35-per cent ratio with Great Britain by 1944 or 1945. The first step was the building of the two expanded *Deutschlands* with a third turret. When completed, those two small battleships, or battle cruisers, displaced 31,800 tons (as against their announced 26,000 tons). Their nine 11-inch guns were light in comparison with those of other countries' battleships, but their armour was fairly heavy. Their range of 10,000 miles at 19 knots, with top speed of 32 knots, was considerable. Each ship had a heavy secondary battery, composed of twelve 5.9-inch guns and numerous anti-aircraft guns.

Both members of that pair (the *Scharnhorst* and *Gneisenau*) and of the next pair built (the *Bismarck* and *Tirpitz*) used very high-pressure superheated steam-turbine drive. Large diesel engines would have been preferable; but to wait for their development would have delayed construction of the battleships for too long.

In three oversize heavy cruisers that were ordered at the same time, the change to turbines restricted the range so that they were not very useful in the Atlantic. The sixteen destroyers of the same programme were also too short-ranged, for the same reason. Twenty-eight submarines and numerous minor craft also were ordered. With the advent of conscription, the number of midshipmen was increased and reserve officers were trained for the rapidly growing Fleet.

The 1936 building programme was featured by the beginning of the last two battleships – the *Bismarck* and the *Tirpitz* – designed with conventional power plants. Although Hitler wanted 80,000-ton battleships with 20- or 21-inch guns, Raeder and his staff were able to show him that 16-inch guns were the largest for which there would be any need, and that ships designed to mount such weapons would be both cheaper and more practical in terms of harbour depths and docking facilities. The *Bismarck* and *Tirpitz* were of 41,700 and 42,900 tons, respectively, each with eight 15-inch guns – designed to compare favourably with the best French and British models. Their announced tonnage, to keep up appearances, was 35,000 tons. The ships had a very powerful secondary armament of twelve 5.9-inch guns and more than forty anti-aircraft guns, all with a rapid rate of fire. They had excellent compartmentation, very heavy armour, the best Zeiss optical range finders, and precision controls. They could do nearly 31 knots and had an 8,000-mile range. The designers had produced the world's most powerful battleships. They intended that the next ones would be more powerful still.

Shore facilities developed very rapidly. An electric-acoustic torpedo plant and submarine engine development plant were put into operation. Many private shipyards were working for the Navy by that time on conventional construction. Included in that category was the first combination oiler-supply ship, with the very fast speed of 21 knots.

Foreign affairs concerned the Navy very little in those years. All aggressive actions were strictly land-based operations. From the Rhineland move of 1936 until well into

1938 the European crises found the Navy on the alert basis in case of interference by outside powers, but with most of its leaders still quite sure that no war was coming. The American Neutrality Act of 1937, proclaiming abandonment of neutral rights, must have encouraged that attitude, as did the Anglo-German Naval Agreement of that year. The latter (a supplement to the 1935 Treaty) is a curious thing, unless it is explained simply as a German attempt to convince the British of sincerity. The main provision was a reaffirmation of the 35,000-ton limit on battleships – which the Germans had already broken. Another feature was a provision for reporting any deviations that might become necessary because of the actions of a third power. All construction was to be reported. (Raeder's later justifications for not reporting deviations were that the Germans did not wish to be accused of starting an arms race and that extra tonnage was for added defensive features. It was a strange proceeding.)

By 1937 the submarines were engaged in practice exercises based on a possible war with France, in which they would have attacked the North Africa–Provence convoy route. They showed their potential in the war games. They 'destroyed' a well-protected convoy in the Baltic under directions from Kiel, and later operated in the Atlantic and off the coast of Spain. Dönitz was becoming convinced that war with Britain could not long be delayed, and he pressed Raeder to concentrate on submarines; but Raeder discounted the possibility of war. Hitler had said that there would be none. Raeder also seems to have thought that German submarines might not have much chance against British anti-submarine techniques.

On November 5th, 1937, Hitler made the first announcement to the War Minister, the Foreign Minister, and the heads of the three Armed Services that his plans could not be fulfilled peacefully. While several of them were outspoken in their opposition and were consequently forced out of office, Raeder seems to have been little affected. His reaction to Hitler's speeches, he said, was that they were often contradictory because designed to gain an end – in this case, perhaps, the resignation of the men who opposed him. Hitler had told Raeder that the speeches were to create an impression and to stimulate action, not to be taken literally. He also had Hitler's assurance that Czechoslovakia had been written off by the British and that war with Great Britain would not come; at most a local conflict seems to have been expected. Naval operations studies were still directed towards possible trouble with France, Poland, or Russia.

Hitler's next moves were to appoint himself War Minister and to redefine the relationships of the OKW with the three Services. The OKW, under General Wilhelm Keitel, was to 'coordinate' the assignments of the three services and provide 'tactical' support; that is, it was to coordinate industry, economics, manpower, and the like, and in addition was to serve as a working advisory staff to Hitler. Hitler was to discuss the situation with, and issue orders to, the heads of all four departments. In practice, any one of the Armed Forces could often protest OKW decisions to Hitler and have them countermanded – although this was most difficult for Raeder, who had less influence with Hitler than his counterparts.

In another vital field, that of allocation of scarce resources, the German Navy had no standing at all. Not only was the Navy the least-favoured Service because of Germany's long land frontiers, which forced her leaders to emphasize the Army and Air Force for defensive strategy, but in addition the entire War Ministry was disposed against it. Hitler and Keitel stood up for the Army, while Göring furthered the Air Force cause. It was Göring who, as Deputy for the Four Year Plan, issued orders to the Ministries of Economics, Finance, and Transportation in matters concerning the Armed Forces. Little wonder that under such a system even submarines had relatively low priorities. The best that could usually be obtained by the Navy was an order from Hitler to Keitel to see what could be done about a particular problem; usually nothing was done.

Various reasons account for the inefficient command structure that developed under Hitler's leadership. Part of the explanation lies in the basic problem of any dictator: that of preventing any group, especially one of the Armed Forces, from becoming too powerful. Coupling that motive with the suspicious nature which Hitler exhibited partly acounts for his downgrading of the old military High Command. Such a process is cumulative, however. If no replacements can be found, the dictator will find himself taking over more and more of the functions than he can handle adequately – as happened to Hitler and Göring.

The elimination of leadership creates a vacuum, which is filled by men who have not had adequate experience and training to appreciate the need for expert advice and expert organization. Göring's naïve acceptance of the most radical air-power theories, for instance, had no check because his position depended not on his military skills but on his political reliability. Perhaps education in a broad sense might have made a difference, but Germany was not a country in which education laid stress on such concepts as sea power.

While politics in one sense is a part of any governmental system, in a new dictatorship (which has a tendency to be unstable structurally) the attempt of each leader to obtain more power at the expense of others throws personal motives into greater prominence than in most other systems. It also creates isolated power blocs that react violently to each other. A corollary to that is the suppression of initiative in the lower echelons, which are politically alien to the group in power. Political infiltration adds to the insecurity, and consequently lowered efficiency, of the lower echelons.

All those factors – political appointments, fragmentation of authority, educational deficiencies, excessive personal power – influenced the German command structure.

During good times the inner tensions were not too evident; adversity brought out all the weaknesses.

At the end of May 1938 Hitler told Raeder for the first time that he expected Great Britain to be one of Germany's enemies at some time in the future. He wanted a speeding up of work on the two battleships *Bismarck* and *Tirpitz*, preparation for more battleship construction, and planning for submarine parity with Great Britain. A plan to build 129 submarines by 1943 or 1944 was drawn up. Dönitz protested that such a programme was insufficient because it assumed that there would be no war soon – a very dangerous assumption to make. Raeder and almost all his staff felt the Navy should adhere to the concept of the balanced fleet. He was still confident that Hitler would not start a war within the next few years, and he felt that a change in the building programme would be taken as a hostile act.

In December 1938 Hitler invoked the escape clause of the Anglo-German Naval Treaty, using Russian submarine building as the reason. At a conference in Berlin, Admiral Andrew Cunningham was informed of the action and was asked the sanction to build two more heavy cruisers, in order to bring German strength to the five allowed by the Treaty and also to match Russian construction. Both requests were granted.

The 1938 Army General Staff war plans were drawn up for a war that included Great Britain. The Navy declared itself unready to fulfil even the limited role for which it was cast in the war plans. According to the plans, the Navy was expected just to tie down British surface units and harass the British Fleet while the Army and Air Force made the decisive moves.

In September of 1938 a naval committee was constituted, under Captain Hellmuth Heye, to make recommendations for an increased shipbuilding programme and to make a strategic reappraisal of Germany's position for a potential war with Great Britain. As basic assumptions, the committee members agreed that colonies, naval communications, and secure access to the oceans were needed if Germany was to become a world power. Such aspirations were expected to lead to war with Britain and France, and eventually to involve one-half to two-thirds of the world. Since Germany could not support such a war effort, the committee's function was to design plans that would provide the greatest possible sea power within Germany's economic potential. That meant development of a force to wage economic war against Britain's shipping lanes, thereby helping to win a limited European war by crippling Britain.

The first step was to gather all the ideas presented by exponents of various strategies and to reduce them to the terms of the forces required for their execution. Those ideas apparently included Dönitz's requests for large numbers of submarines – requests which reached a figure of 300 submarines after the 1938–9 winter manoeuvres. However, neither Dönitz nor any member of his staff was asked to contribute to or participate in the committee's work – an indication of the surface-fleet orientation of the Naval Staff. The first total of ships required, called the X-Plan, was impossibly high; so it was reduced by Rear-Admiral Werner Fuchs, Raeder's Chief of Construction, to accord with Germany's shipbuilding potential. The resulting Y-Plan was subjected to much comment but few modifications, and finally emerged as two alternative Z-Plans. Raeder stayed out of the violent strategic, tactical, and personal conflicts that developed during the committee's deliberations, but when they were resolved he took Fuchs with him and presented the two plans to Hitler for his decision.

One of the plans emphasized submarines, armed merchant cruisers, and *Deutschlands.* It would have been quick, cheap, and one-sided. The other plan was for a balanced, well-armed fleet for offensive use against British naval forces and shipping. That one was slow, expensive – and quite promising. Hitler assured Raeder that there would be time for building and chose the second plan, insisting that each unit in it be more powerful than any corresponding unit in enemy fleets.

Hitler gave the Z-Plan precedence over all other construction projects in January 1939. With Fuchs in charge of the construction programme, a goal was set for delivery of large battleships within six years, as compared with the original eight-to-ten-year estimate.

The core of the fleet was to consist of the four battleships then built or under construction and, in addition, six superbattleships, each displacing 56,200 tons and mounting eight 16-inch guns. The programme also included twelve small battleships of 20,000 tons, each with 12-inch guns; four aircraft carriers of from 19,000 to 27,000 tons; the three *Deutschlands*; five heavy cruisers; forty-four light cruisers; sixty-eight destroyers; ninety torpedo boats; and 249 submarines, which ranged in size from coastal types to submarine cruisers. Completion was hoped for by 1948. All the new surface units were to be capable of at least 29 knots with either all-diesel or mixed diesel-and-steam-turbine propulsion and with great operational range and endurance. They were to be the finest ships of their classes ever built. As much secrecy about their characteristics as possible was to be maintained, to prevent British countermoves.

The strategic concepts behind the use of the planned fleet combined several of the usual choices of operations open to a commander-in-chief. First, commerce warfare would begin with minelaying by destroyers, with submarine attacks at the approaches to the British Isles, and with the *Deutschlands*, small battleships, light and heavy cruisers, secret raiders, and submarine cruisers scattered across the oceans. Second, a fleet composed of old battleships would form a 'fleet-in-being' in the North Sea to tie down British capital ships. Third, when the British had over-extended themselves by scattering their slow forces to protect the convoys and hunt down the raiders, the main fleet, in two sections, would go to sea to destroy convoys and escorts. Each section would be composed of three superbattleships, one aircraft carrier, several light cruisers, and several destroyers. In such a plan all elements of the fleet would be used to their maximum potential because they could be given information and directions by radio from Berlin. The strongest argument of all was that the battle groups would enjoy the offensive advantage of the raider and yet be able to strike telling blows. Unhindered by defensive commitments, that would be a most formidable threat; if Germany could gain allies to tie down even more of the British Fleet, it might be decisive.

In terms of grand strategy, the Z-Plan was a throwback to the go-it-alone attitude of the Kaiser's diplomacy in relation to the other western European sea powers. It reflected the risky idea of victory with one great blow that was the core of the pre-World War I Schlieffen Plan for victory on land. Original as the Z-Plan was in many respects, and as thoroughly as its formulators had grasped the idea of long-range warships for dominance in the Atlantic, the 'Dispersion Strategy' (as it may be called) presented a number of unresolved problems. First, it assumed that there would be no war with Great Britain before 1944 at the earliest – because concentration on building a balanced fleet would have at least five years of weakness before a reasonable number of heavy ships could be ready. Second, the Z-Plan assumed that it would be possible to outbuild Britain for a short time, allowing for the obsolescent nature of the existing British capital ships; and it implied that war would come during the 1944–8 period – before the British could regain a decisive capital-ship lead.

Many people, including Dönitz and some high-ranking members of the Naval Staff, did not believe Britain would remain neutral in the event of further German aggression; but Raeder, much influenced by Hitler, accepted his assurances that political arrangements would keep Britain quiet. Hitler asserted that a strong German Fleet would make it dangerous for Britain to go to war and would encourage a German-British rapprochement. The desire both to threaten and to seek accommodation is an interesting illustration of Hitler's curious love-hate attitude towards Great Britain. It represented a poor reading of the British spirit – a misreading encouraged by the weak Chamberlain leadership. It repeated the error that had been made by Admiral Tirpitz forty years earlier.

All of the ideas discounted a series of practical problems. The Z-Plan assumed that the British would not increase their capital-ship construction significantly for some years, and that they would have no allies with large navies. (The latter consideration was founded, in part, on a projection of 'America First' sentiment far into the future – despite the obviously hostile attitude of the naval-minded Franklin D. Roosevelt administration.) Geography also was a permanent limiting factor: the narrow access routes to the Atlantic represented a problem that could only get worse as air-search range and methods improved, while the problem of finding bases for ships damaged in the Atlantic could not be fully solved even by seizure (considered unlikely at the time) of French bases. The largest French dry dock – the Normandie Dock at St-Nazaire – was too small to hold the Z-Plan battleships, and all the French bases were close to British air bases.

Tactically, the British could have decided against dispersing their forces and concentrated for decisive battle instead, at the expense of a damaging but temporary halt to their convoys. Hindsight indicates that the Z-Plan fleet was weak in aircraft carriers; but that could have been corrected, as experience with the first carrier would have shown their value. The strong orientation towards gunnery in the plan – extending even to the heavily armed aircraft carriers and the twenty-seven submarine cruisers; but that is not surprising, considering the state of naval warfare in 1939 and the severe weather limitations imposed on the operations of existing aircraft in the North Sea and North Atlantic theatres of operations.

Whether it was feasible or not, the Dispersion Strategy of the Z-Plan was a startling combination of the ideas of the *guerre de course* (commerce war) and the fleet-in-being. It aimed at the decisive form of naval war: command of the sea. To Germany, denial of the sea to Great Britain equalled command for Germany; German trade could be dispensed with, but British trade could not. What the Dispersion Strategy did was to pose questions that were to be vital to the Western sea powers in the soon-to-dawn Atomic Age: such questions as concentration of the battle line for maximum power versus dispersion for convoy escort requirements; vulnerability of scattered warships to locally superior enemies versus control of vital sea lanes; security by concentration of major fleet units against submarine and air attack versus security by dispersion to baffle enemy search systems; and passive defence of convoys, bases, and fleet formations versus more active defence by focal-area patrol or long-range blockade. All those naval problems had been resolved for three centuries by use of massed battle lines, blockade, and convoys; German naval strategists reopened them all.

A few minor modifications were incorporated into the Z-Plan in early 1939. The twelve small battleships were eliminated in favour of three battle cruisers of 32,300 tons with six 15-inch guns each. A table of priorities was worked out, which emphasized the battleships (because of the time taken to construct them) and the submarines, which were to serve as a stopgap. That part of the programme was to be completed by 1943. Raeder considered Hitler's acceptance of the programme to be a guarantee that no war with Britain would be started soon.

Dönitz and the submarine staff considered the entire Z-Plan hopeless on the grounds that the British would not remain quiescent so long and that only submarines (supplemented by relatively inexpensive and therefore expendable raiders like the *Deutschlands*) would have a real opportunity in the Atlantic. To those men, massed submarines were instruments of sea power sufficient to deny sea lanes to their enemies.

To the Z-Plan organizers, on the other hand, submarines

were raiders forming only a part of a much larger sea-power structure. They feared to put too much emphasis on a single weapon system that might be countered effectively by new anti-submarine weapons or search systems – as the submarine's more primitive predecessor had been countered in 1917–18. British reaction to a sudden change in submarine construction was expected to be quite hostile; that served as a political brake to the Naval Staff officers. They also had to take into consideration Hitler's predilection for battleships. He was fascinated by technology and by symbols of power, going so far as to memorize masses of technical detail from the ship identification manuals and then to parade his knowledge – to the acute embarrassment of Raeder, who did not memorize such trivia but tried to talk grand strategy to Hitler. In such circumstances any attempt to shift the naval building programme to submarine construction, to the exclusion of capital ships, would have been doomed to failure.

By the spring of 1939 the submarine had evolved into two primary types: the 770-ton VII C medium-size fleet type and the 1,120-ton IX C long-range fleet type. In manoeuvres carried out in late 1938 and early 1939 in the Baltic and Atlantic, tactical command was exercised from shore headquarters, with local tactical command in the hands of senior commanders afloat. The manoeuvres were very successful. In January Dönitz said he needed 300 submarines to make his tactics decisive. Raeder still believed there would be no war soon; but in the summer he approved the raising of the Z-Plan total to 300, after witnessing the July Baltic submarine exercises.

That was far from a complete victory for Dönitz, whose strategic concepts required that 75 per cent of the submarines be medium-size fleet types and the rest mostly long-range fleet types. He envisioned no heavy-gun submarine cruisers and no new small, coastal types. Raeder, on the other hand, simply increased the number of units while retaining the prior Z-Plan proportions of 15 per cent submarine cruisers, 27 per cent long-range fleet type, 42 per cent medium-size fleet type, and 16 per cent coastal type.

While Dönitz was gaining an increase in his submarine fleet size, he was accepting a low-priority status for experimental work on a method of highspeed propulsion for a true submarine (that is, one that would operate primarily below the surface) – the Walter hydrogen-peroxide gas turbine. The immediate need for increasing conventional warship construction and the complexities involved in creating such a radical propulsion system discouraged its rapid development. Also, one of Dönitz's strategic ideas, that of stationing some submarines abroad permanently, was rejected in those same midsummer weeks.

Planning was complicated in the spring of 1939 by another disagreement with the Air Force. As early as 1937 Göring had begun talking about taking over operating control of the Naval Operations Branch of the Air Force in time of war. In January of 1939 Göring was able to force a revision of the 1935 agreement. In a joint statement after conferences, Raeder and Göring announced the formation of a new post: that of General of the Air Force with the Commander-in-Chief, Navy. The Air Force took over aerial minelaying (with Navy consultation), aerial attacks on enemy ships at sea, aerial reconnaissance for prospective naval actions, and the provision of aircraft for naval engagements on request. The Navy retained reconnaissance duties and tactical control during naval engagements. For those purposes the Air Force was to provide nine long-range reconnaissance squadrons, eighteen multipurpose squadrons, twelve carrier-borne squadrons, and two shipboard squadrons of catapult aircraft. The Air Force was to use thirteen bomber wings for naval purposes. All aircraft were to be built to naval specifications. A serious division of command had been created – which was to become worse as the Air Force became deeply involved in the many tasks of World War II.

Foreign affairs seemed still to influence naval planning very little at that time. Hitler's aggressive moves seemed to be balanced by peaceful statements and diplomatic manoeuvring. The speech about peace at the time of the *Bismarck*'s launch in February 1939 contrasted strangely with the seizure of Memel from Lithuania in March, in which the Navy had a role. In April the Anglo-German Naval Treaty was abrogated by Hitler, without consulting Raeder. That senseless and provocative act was read by many naval readers as a clear indication that war with Great Britain was imminent; but Raeder, while surprised and troubled, was again reassured by Hitler, and there was no change in the building programme. The Italian invasion of Albania in April, followed by the British-Turkish Mutual Aid Declaration, was countered by the 'Pact of Steel', the negotiations for which included comments that indicated Italy's unpreparedness for war until 1942.

Hitler's warlike speech to his officers on May 23rd was not regarded very seriously by Raeder because of its many inconsistencies and Hitler's private assurances that the British would not go to war over the Polish Corridor. Through the spring and early summer Raeder kept reminding Hitler that Britain had to be kept out of the European struggles – and Hitler kept assuring him that this would be done. In Hitler's speech to his officers of August 22nd, he seemed to have carried off another *coup*: he announced the Soviet-German Non-Aggression Pact and told the commanders that England and France were expected to remain quiescent while Poland was isolated. Raeder believed anew that there would be no immediate war, although he warned Hitler that the British might not back down in renewed crises.

Meanwhile the usual planning was done to put the Fleet on an alert status and to send the ships to sea. That was nothing new.

Chapter 2

THE FIRST BATTLES

War against the coalition September 1939–April 1940

Suddenly the war came. On September 1st, 1939, German forces struck Poland; and France and Great Britain entered the conflict two days later. 'The surface forces . . . can do no more than show that they know how to die gallantly . . .' wrote Grand Admiral Erich Raeder* as all his hopes and plans collapsed. That gloomy prophecy was not the basis for German action, however; and once the initial shock had worn off, Raeder and his staff prepared to wage a very active war.

The naval organization required little change to shift to a wartime basis. Under Raeder the Naval Operations Staff was concerned with strategic and operational planning, and had direct control of raiders and their intelligence and supply systems. Below the headquarters organization were the operations commands, Group East and Group West, which had authority over naval operations and were charged with the safety of coastal waters. Because most of the larger ships operated in the North Sea, the Commander-in-Chief of the Fleet was subordinated to Group West; but during important operations Raeder tended to become deeply involved, leading to some overlapping of authority and consequently some friction, especially early in the war. Dönitz, promoted to Rear-Admiral in October, was Flag Officer of Submarines, a position

* Memorandum of September 3rd, 1939, in 'Führer Conferences on Naval Affairs', *Brassey's Naval Annual: 1948*, pp 37–8.

subject only to the control of general directives of the Naval Operations Staff. The use of separate codes by submarines, which forced surface ships to contact nearby submarines via Berlin, was the only major disadvantage of the system.

On the first day of hostilities against Great Britain, Raeder met with his staff in order to revise Navy plans to fit the new situation. He settled on what was, in effect, a much-reduced Z-Plan. The *Deutschland*-class raiders, two of which were already at sea, were to attack Allied merchant shipping, while the two small battleships were to remain in the North Sea – where their presence would hold down British battle cruisers and battleships, thus reducing possible opposition to the raiders. The Air Force and a minefield (called the West Wall) in the German Bight were to discourage Allied forays into German waters along the North Sea coast and into the Skagerrak trade routes. Short raids into the Norway-Shetlands area and the Iceland Passages were also contemplated, to force the British to keep their forces spread.

The surface forces were not expected to win control of the seas from the British even by attrition, which had been the concept of World War I. They were instead to disrupt enemy communications, depending on surprise and daring against the supposedly orthodox and conservative British. Attacks against the weak spots in the extended British communications network were to be tempered by tactical caution. To obtain maximum returns from their limited forces, German officers were to avoid battle unless absolutely necessary to further the basic object, that of a trade war.

The battleships were not to be kept in home waters to conserve them; they were simply unable to operate with reasonable hope of success in the key area to the west and south-west of England known as the Western Approaches. The 2,000-mile distance to be traversed was part of the problem: first, far north through the Norway-Shetlands narrows; then south through the narrows on either side of

Iceland. The distance involved meant that the battleships would have required tankers in the Atlantic to operate for any length of time. Also, while it was considered practicable to get the ships out into that area, it was felt that getting them back again through an aroused British Navy would be very difficult. Because Germany lacked repair bases on the Atlantic coasts, even relatively minor damage might result in the loss of a ship. For those reasons the battleships were restricted to active operations as far as the Iceland Passages – a daring plan, considering that the much more powerful but short-range High Seas Fleet had not ventured so far from home in World War I.

The basic purpose of sending out the long-range *Deutschlands* was not really the destruction of shipping; that was only a desirable by-product. The main purpose was to cut the effective shipping of the British Empire by indirect means. One *Deutschland* on the high seas would force the British and French to escort convoys with battleships, which in turn would require extra destroyers as escorts. The shortage of both would force a much longer turn-around time because convoys would have to be larger. The normal loss of efficiency characteristic of convoyed shipping, because of reduced speed and temporary overcrowding of harbour facilities followed by empty harbours, would be multiplied by the need for larger convoys. At the same time much shipping would have to go unescorted, making it an easy target for all forces. The more areas a raider could appear in, the more shipping efficiency would decline.

That strategy considered Great Britain the chief naval opponent. It assumed that land operations would not change conditions rapidly – an idea not shared by Hitler but subscribed to by most Army men. The Navy was determined to wage an active war, and not to hold back its forces for any hypothetical case that might arise later or as a bargaining point at a peace conference. With very limited resources and a situation that changed constantly and often quite fundamentally, there was little choice but to build, plan, and act as immediate necessity dictated. The consequences of such a policy in a long war were evident. While attempts to rectify coming material shortages could be made, the extension of the conflict soon made allocation of resources too unpredictable to allow true long-range development.

The heavy forces were to be supplemented by every other weapon suited to attacks on commercial shipping. The submarine was recognized as the main offensive weapon in the long run; but since there were so few submarines, operations would have to commence with mine-laying by all forces and with attacks by aeroplanes and disguised merchant raiders as well as submarines. Dönitz stated the matter succinctly in a memorandum on the first day of the war: 'With twenty-two boats and a prospective increase of one to two boats a month I am incapable of undertaking efficacious measures against England.'* Submarines in quantity, with trained crews, would not be ready for two years. The German Naval High Command needed two years' worth of stopgaps.

The German Fleet in 1939 consisted of the two small battleships *Scharnhorst* and *Gneisenau*; the three *Deutschlands* – the *Deutschland* herself, the *Admiral Scheer*, and the *Admiral Graf Spee*; the two heavy cruisers *Admiral Hipper* and *Blücher*; six light cruisers; thirty-four destroyers and torpedo boats; and fifty-seven submarines. Of the submarines, only the twenty-two oceangoing units were ready for operations in the Western Approaches. The two powerful battleships *Bismarck* and *Tirpitz* and another heavy cruiser, the *Prinz Eugen*, were still being built and would not soon be ready.

Against them the British had fifteen battleships and battle cruisers, six aircraft carriers, and fifty-nine light and heavy cruisers. Many of their ships were old, and most were slower than the equivalent German units. The French Fleet contained seven battleships and battle crui-

* C. D. Bekker, *Defeat at Sea*, p 9. (The 'twenty-two boats' were oceangoing types.)

sers, two aircraft carriers, and nineteen light and heavy cruisers. They were relatively new ships, notable for their speed, gunnery, and communications. They were, however, vulnerable to submarine and aerial attack.

No German building programme could match the Allied power and the resources behind it. On the first day of the war Raeder completely reorganized the naval building programme to face that fact. Only the two nearly complete battleships and the cruiser were to be completed. Construction of the two Z-Plan battleships was suspended, as was work on one nearly complete aircraft carrier and another still on the building ways. That meant that no replacements larger than destroyers would be available, and that many risks would thereby be unacceptable.

The only programme possible was a submarine building programme, which was to be accelerated to a rate of twenty to thirty a month. Dönitz's memorandum of September 1st, 1939, stated a need for ninety submarines on station in the North Atlantic; that meant that 300 were needed overall. Materials for 300 were available, but for the first year only the pre-war schedule of two deliveries per month could be expected. The VII C became the basic design. The Naval Ship Department had centralized control of submarine building, and quickly arranged work schedules and dispersal. In November the first orders were placed. Faced with the problems of expediting construction and allocating materials, the Department did practically no experimental work.

The Naval Aviation Branch at that time consisted of fourteen long-range, multi-purpose squadrons plus one shipboard catapult aircraft squadron – out of forty-one promised squadrons. Six of the promised thirteen Air Force bomber wings were available for use over the ocean, but since the Air Force used its own grid squares, codes, and radio wavelengths, cooperation between the aircraft and ships was difficult. To make things worse, a major retooling of the aircraft industry at that time left out new naval types. The omission seems to have been another move by Göring to squeeze out Naval Aviation.

The Navy wanted offensive aerial warfare conducted with emphasis on mines and on aerial torpedoes, which it was developing. Göring, however, believed that bombs were the most effective weapons against ships. Nevertheless no policy was consistently followed by the Air Force.

By the time the British and French entered the war to aid Poland, on September 3rd, 1939, the German Navy had only light forces deployed in the Polish theatre of operations. Six Polish submarines and three destroyers escaped from the Germans, while the rest of the ships remained rather inactive – with the exception of a minelayer that laid her mines without removing the safeties! Two German pre-dreadnought battleships, normally used as training ships, and some minesweepers cooperated with the Army and secured the Baltic entrances. All major warships had already gone to the North Sea.

On August 25th, a week before the beginning of the war, German ships abroad had been given instructions to run for home ports. The British were preoccupied with raiders, and the Germans used Murmansk as a refuelling stop for some ships which crossed the Atlantic in far-northern latitudes before running down the neutral Norwegian coast; so almost one hundred ships, totalling 500,000 tons, reached Germany, many with valuable cargoes. Some were intercepted; but most of those were scuttled by their crews. More than 300 ships remained in neutral harbours.

The British, as expected, imposed a blockade at the beginning of the war. Beginning with a comprehensive contraband list, the British extended their controls until by the end of November 1939 all German exports, even in neutral ships, were treated as contraband. Neutral cargoes were checked in the neutral ports to give the British tight control of the trade, and certificates were given to shipmasters so they would not have to go to British ports for inspection – a procedure that would have exposed them to danger from mines and aerial attack. The blockade did not damage the German economy as much as in World War I because trade with Russia and eastern Europe was undisturbed and much stockpiling had been done. The sensitive area was the iron-ore traffic with Norway and Sweden. Each year eleven million tons of iron ore were sent, via the Baltic in summer and through neutral waters along the Norwegian coast in winter, to feed German industry. The Baltic route was secure unless the Allies invaded neutral Norway and Sweden; but the Norwegian coast route was open to attack, if the British were willing to break international law. That situation was to have profound consequences.

The German Navy expected the British to use the tested methods of World War I to deal with the submarine menace; and so they did. British merchantmen came under Admiralty orders even before the beginning of the war. They were instructed to report attacks by radio, to avoid search by taking evasive action, to use gunfire and depth charges against submarines if equipped to do so, and to ram if possible. Evasive routing and armament were used by the fastest ships, while convoys were organized for slower shipping. There were very few escorts, and convoying cut shipping efficiency by 25 to 40 per cent; but convoyed ships did have a better chance to get through. Submarines could not use their deck guns on escorted ships, so their very limited torpedo supplies were used up quickly.

One British device of which the Germans knew few details was Asdic, or underwater sound echo ranging. Its effective use, however, required skill and persistence. Two or three British escorts were generally necessary to locate a submarine accurately. One of them then had to run over the submarine's position to drop depth charges; all of them had to re-establish Asdic contact as the depth-charge disturbance dissipated. Usually the process had to be repeated, often for hour after hour.

The British had too few escorts to form any groups or

maintain attacks for long periods of time. By September 26th, 1939, however, the British were able to announce that all their ships would soon be armed. A limited and not very effective air search system also was instituted by the British, but usually their aircraft merely forced the submarines to submerge temporarily. The British moves created a situation in which German observance of prize law became more and more difficult.

Owing to the very small number of oceangoing submarines available, the German Navy from the very beginning began using its ships to lay mines. It was a combined operation: destroyers and other surface craft laid defensive minefields along the German coast, while submarines mined British harbour approaches. Later in the year, when the nights were longer, surface ships were used also to lay mines in British waters. The surface craft laid mixed moored-contact and ground-magnetic minefields, while the submarines used only the ground-magnetic type. The moored-contact mine was anchored at a fixed distance from the surface and was set off by direct contact with a ship. The cable connecting the mine to its anchor was its weak point, because minesweeping devices could snag the mine cable, cut it, and free the mine to come to the surface, where it could be destroyed by gunfire. The ground-magnetic mine lay on the seabed in shallow water and was set off when a ship's steel hull interfered with the earth's magnetic field. The shock waves from the explosion were expected to break the ship's back. The ground-magnetic mine was particularly effective, and the Germans believed that it would not be countered soon.

As Hitler's hope for a settlement with the French dimmed, they too were subjected to mine warfare, from September 23rd, on. Raeder had been pressing for aerial minelaying even if large numbers of mines were not available, and in November a few sorties were reluctantly flown. For once the Air Force was right: the air drops were not accurate, and the British recovered two mines in the Thames shallows. By the time large numbers of aerial magnetic mines were ready in 1940, the British had devised sweep methods.

All in all, mine warfare, which was continued as a regular policy, was quite successful during the first six months of the war. Despite Air Force indifference and the limited capacity of the small submarines (which could carry only six to eight mines each), the British lost 114 merchant ships totalling nearly 400,000 tons, plus two destroyers and fifteen minesweepers. The battleship *Nelson*, two cruisers, and two destroyers were damaged. The indirect results were considerable, for the British had to divert many potential escort vessels to mine clearance duties, while neutrals were discouraged to some extent from the British trade by mine danger. The port of Liverpool, in fact, was temporarily closed by the British for that reason. German losses were two submarines; two destroyers, accidentally sunk by one of their own aircraft; and damage to two light cruisers by the British submarine *Salmon* while they were covering an offensive minelaying sortie by five destroyers. The losses were considered moderate. Analysing the operations, the Naval High Command was unhappy only with the failure of the Air Force to contribute more to the effort, especially in distant areas not easily reached by ships.

All available submarines had been sent to sea before war broke out, and they received the news by radio on September 3rd. Lieutenant-Commander Fritz-Ludwig Lemp in *U30*, like the rest of the twenty-one submarine commanders in the Atlantic, found no enemies on the first day of war. Not until well after sunset did a ship appear. She was blacked out, zigzagging, and off the normal shipping routes. Lemp identified her as a British auxiliary cruiser – that is, a large merchant ship armed as a patrol or escort vessel – and proceeded to attack. Only after the first torpedo struck was the truth apparent: the stricken passenger liner *Athenia*, with more than 1,400 persons aboard, was sending an SOS. Four ships, including two destroyers, immediately answered the call – while *U30* hastened away, not even reporting the attack because of Lemp's desire not to break radio silence. Not many steaming hours away, the German liner *Bremen* heard the SOS. She might have been the accidental victim, or the saviour of the *Athenia*'s people; but the grim necessity of war kept her to her course and away from the scene where, in midmorning, with rescue ships gathered around, the *Athenia* pointed her bow to the sky and plunged into the Atlantic deeps. One hundred and twenty men, women, and children died with her.

'Atrocity!' screamed the Allied Press. 'Churchill's sabotage!' retorted Dr Joseph Goebbels, charging that the British sank the *Athenia* to create a new round of 'German Terror' stories like the Great War's exaggerated 'Rape of Belgium' tales. Raeder and Dönitz knew nothing at first. Hitler reacted by ordering that no passenger liner was to be attacked under any circumstances.

U30 returned to base later in September. Only then did Dönitz have the truth – but Goebbels would not be stilled. Instead of a candid admission of error, he continued to trumpet the transparent 'sabotage' charge. Moreover, to compound the deception, Dönitz was ordered to have the offending page of *U30*'s war diary replaced, so that none of the eight copies made from it for training purposes would reveal the facts.

The *Athenia* incident became the first event in a war-within-a-war: a war of statement and counterstatement, charge and countercharge, action and reprisal. Contrary to Allied belief, the German Navy did begin waging war under the strict prize law of the 1936 London Submarine Agreement. That Agreement required submarines to behave in all respects like surface warships when stopping, searching, and sinking merchantmen, even if the merchantmen were armed with guns for self-defence. Only in the event of resistance could a submarine dispense with the rules assuring safety for passengers and crew and stating that lifeboats were not a refuge unless the proximity of land or another ship made them so.

Theoretically such rules might have worked for a time had the British believed in German willingness to comply with them; but the rules quickly broke down under the pressure of war. Theoretically, under the Agreement, the British would not even have had to arm their merchantmen. They could have continued sending lone, unarmed ships across the Atlantic, provided that they were willing to run the risk of having them stopped, searched, and – after the removal of passengers and crews – sunk.

The British, however, naturally distrusted the Germans, especially in view of the sinking of the *Athenia*; moreover, the risks of such a policy were unacceptably high. They had planned, long before the outbreak of war, to arm their merchant ships and to order them to use their radios, not only to summon aid for the crews but to call for British naval units to attack the submarines. The presence of guns on the British ships forced the submarine commanders to decide whether such guns were intended to be used offensively or defensively – that is, before or after hostile actions by the submarines. That was a distinction impossible to draw from the rolling, pitching conning tower of a vulnerable submarine. The British considered the use of radio to be an essential defensive move; but the submarine commanders considered radio silence to be the essence of security. They deemed merchantmen using radios to be belligerents serving British Naval Intelligence – as indeed they were.

After Hitler's 'no passenger liners' order, only warships, merchant ships under surface or aerial convoy, and ships offering any form of resistance were subject to sinking without regard to crew safety. Because Hitler still hoped to come to some political agreement with France and Britain after the conclusion of the Polish campaign, he restrained his submarines from attacking French ships – though, curiously, showing no such forbearance towards British ships. French ships were not even to be stopped, although they used their radios to draw destroyers to submarines checking their identities. Working under such regulations, the eight or nine submarines which Dönitz expected to have on patrol at one time were not expected to be able to inflict serious damage on Allied shipping.

Within two days of the outbreak of war, it became apparent that the Agreement was not going to work. On September 5th, Lieutenant-Commander Herbert Schultze in *U48* tried to stop the merchantman *Royal Sceptre* with a shot across the bows – only to have her call for help and try to run. He stopped her with fire from his 3.5-inch gun, and most of the crew abandoned ship; but the radio operator continued to send the SSS (submarine) call. Fearful of hitting the lifeboats with shellfire, Schultze sank her with a torpedo. The radio operator continued to send his SSS to the last, and went down with his ship. Soon afterwards Schultze stopped the British ship *Browning* and ordered her to aid the *Royal Sceptre* survivors – to the amazement of the *Browning*'s crew, which had taken to the boats at Schultze's first shot.

Time after time in the first weeks of the war, British ships sent the SSS call. In one case Schultze himself sent an SSS: '... to Mr Churchill. Have sunk British SS *Firby* ... Please pick up crew.'* This was not mere bravado (for it endangered his submarine), but a sincere attempt to honour the spirit of the prize law.

The British, however, had no intention of abandoning resistance. One merchantman retaliated with a deck gun; another tried to ram. Still, German commanders tried to comply with the intent of the Agreement. Lieutenant-Commander Heinrich Liebe rescued survivors from a tanker's oil fires, even though she had used her radio. He issued them his own crew's life jackets until he could put them aboard a neutral ship. Other submarine officers tended wounded victims, righted capsized lifeboats, and provided food, water, and charts to survivors.

In the face of the submarines' experiences and the British announcement that all their merchantmen would soon be armed, Raeder was able to persuade Hitler to

* Wolfgang Frank, *The Sea Wolves*, p 29.

remove some of the restrictions on the submarines. Step by step, in late September and early October, the proposed changes were approved: all merchantmen using radios could be attacked without warning; French ships lost their special immunity; prize law was not to apply in the North Sea – and, subsequently, in a large area west of the British Isles; darkened ships off the British and French coasts became targets. Neutrals were warned against acts that might appear belligerent, but search of neutrals was discontinued around the British Isles because of the danger from British forces. Passenger ships under hostile flags were still exempt from attack.

The need for more submarines was discussed continually. Almost every conference with Hitler included mention of submarine building. Raeder even induced Hitler to visit Wilhelmshaven to see the submarines and their successful crews. It was suggested that sumbarines be bought abroad; but Hitler refused to broach the question to Russia since it might indicate weakness to the Russians, and Italy and Japan declined to sell. Russian and Japanese bases for submarine operations were offered, however, and accepted. The Russian base was never used by German submarines, but a Japanese one was eventually put into operation. Repair and supply ships to serve as floating bases in distant waters were also considered.

Working under the legal restrictions of the early weeks of the war, the submarines could not use their full tactical capabilities. Night attacks – the most efficient for submarines – caused only 3 per cent of Allied losses. The British also were handicapped. Aware of the weakness of their escort forces, they attempted to provide extra protection for many ships scattered to the west of the British Isles – and in so doing gave the German submariners several unexpected opportunities in the first weeks of the war.

* * *

The first opportunity came on September 14th, to *U39* – and her commander reacted promptly. Three torpedoes sped towards the aircraft carrier *Ark Royal.* All three exploded. *U39*'s crew was jubilant for a moment, then settled to the grim task of dodging the trio of destroyers that closed in for repeated depth-charge attacks. Soon *U39* was damaged and was forced to blow her ballast to surface. Surrounded by enemies, her crew abandoned ship. Not until their submarine had sunk and they were aboard a British destroyer did they realize that the *Ark Royal* was sailing serenely on. All three torpedoes had missed astern and had exploded in the turbulence of the carrier's wake. *U39* was the first German submarine lost in action in the war.

Three days later, Lieutenant-Commander Otto Schuhart was holding a 10,000-ton passenger ship in sight through his periscope. Then a carrier-type aircraft appeared beyond the liner, which turned away so Schuhart could neither identify her nor get in a shot. His next look for the liner, some time later, revealed an aircraft carrier, well down on the horizon but heading towards him. Abandoning his search for the liner, Schuhart stalked the new target. Neither the escorting destroyers nor the aircraft sighted the momentarily exposed periscope or the dark shadow in the sea as Schuhart manoeuvred to get into position for a shot; but the carrier was zigzagging, and two hours went by as the ships approached each other without an advantage being gained. Finally, however, the carrier zigged sharply, exposing her broadside, and Schuhart fired three torpedoes, guessing at most of the vital firing information because he was looking directly into the sun. Then down deep went *U29,* with everyone aboard listening intently for the sound of a successful strike. Two explosions echoed through the boat. They were followed by the sounds of secondary explosions, as the carrier's own explosives or boilers blew up.

While Schuhart's crew endured (and survived) the inevitable depth charging, the neutral liner *Veendam,* a witness to the engagement, rushed in to help the destroyers and a freighter save 682 men from the oil-covered water; but 518 men, including her captain, died as the *Courageous* quickly capsized to port, floated keel up for a moment, then sank. Only fifteen minutes had elapsed from the time the torpedoes struck to the carrier's disappearance beneath the waves.

Finding the two carriers had been fortuitous; but the next operation was the realization of a twenty-five-year-old dream: to singe the King of England's beard by striking at his naval might at its main base of Scapa Flow, as Drake had burned the Armada ships in Cadiz Bay. Hard-driving Lieutenant-Commander Günther Prien was chosen for the attack. (A similar attempt had cost two submarines in World War I.)

Scapa Flow is a vast basin lying between islands. All channels between the islands were blocked by sunken hulks except the entrance channel, and that was barred by movable nets. The Germans reconnoitred the Flow by air and, accidentally, with a submarine that had been drawn close to several of the entrances by powerful currents. One channel seemed insufficiently blocked; and it was that channel that Prien's surfaced *U47* stood into on the night of Friday, October 13th. The tide was pushing her towards the narrowest point, where block ships and a rocky shore threatened. Quick, confident manoeuvres under full power guided the craft through the dangerous gap, working her free when she grounded momentarily – and *U47* was in. A dazzling display of Northern Lights had aided Prien's entry, but it ended before he cautiously began his survey of the harbour. He soon realized that the bulk of the Home Fleet had gone to sea that day, but he fired three torpedoes at what appeared to be two battleships. Only one hit was observed, seemingly on the farthest target – although actually on the bow of what was the only ship present – so he turned to fire from his stern tube, again with no result.

Still on the surface of Britain's greatest naval harbour,

Prien cruised away from his target in order to reload two of his torpedo tubes. The harbour was strangely quiet despite the explosion, for the British believed it had been internal. Then Prien moved in for a three-torpedo attack on the ship. That time they all struck. First, columns of water rose next to the battleship; then columns of fire burst upwards as her ammunition flared. Prien turned his craft and headed towards the gap between some block ships and a jetty. By superb manoeuvring, the submarine left the scene of the Imperial Navy's greatest humiliation, having paid at least part of the twenty-year-old debt.

U47 reached home safely, while the British admitted the loss of the *Royal Oak*, with a toll of 833 dead. In Germany, Prien was the hero of the hour. Raeder and Dönitz met his submarine at the dock and the crew was flown to Berlin, where Prien received the Knight's Cross of the Iron Cross from a delighted Hitler, who fully appreciated the exploit's value for morale. The Navy rose sharply in Hitler's esteem.

On October 16th, 1939, two days after receiving the news of Prien's attack, Hitler agreed that henceforward all enemy merchant ships could be torpedoed without warning and that, after announcement had been made, passenger ships in convoy could be destroyed. The moves were announced in reprisal for British orders and actions that had made merchantmen dangerous to the submarines. A month later all German restrictions on attacking enemy passenger ships were removed, as it was clear that they were armed. No announcement was made of that subsequent order.

With all enemy shipping subject to attack without warning, the next step was to restrict neutral shipping going to the British Isles. The Pan American Republics' neutrality zone, which extended 300 miles into the Atlantic, and the American combat zone declaration, which prohibited Americans from entering a larger danger area in the eastern Atlantic, made the German task easier. The neutrality zone was respected by the Germans, while the

American restriction cleared the combat zone of the most important and sensitive neutral. Other neutrals were then warned to stay away from dangerous areas around the British Isles.

On December 1st, 1939, the first 'mine danger zone', involving shallow waters along the British coast, was declared. Within that area German submarines were to sink with torpedoes all ships except those of benevolent neutrals. The sinkings would be blamed on mines. In effect that order established unrestricted submarine warfare in limited areas. Pressure for extension of the danger zone, by declaring a 'siege of England', was brought by Raeder throughout December; but Hitler wished to move slowly. Some countries, however, that had been selling or chartering ships to the British were to be subject to reprisals. On December 30th the decision was made to allow attacks without warning on ships of such countries, beginning with Greek ships. The rate of the attacks was to be gradually increased, and the new policy was to be stated in general terms when other offensives were announced. A 'no rescue of survivors' order was issued to submarines late in 1939 because of the hazard of the submarines operating close to British air and naval bases. It did not apply to more distant submarines. The submarine had established its own operating rules, based on the balance of expected advantages versus expected liabilities for each side and on mutual distrust – as new weapons systems have created new rules of war throughout history.

Encouraged by Prien's success and by the British Fleet's use of insecure secondary bases while Scapa Flow was being strengthened, Dönitz continued to deploy a few submarines for torpedo and mine attacks on British Fleet units, even though this meant a corresponding reduction in the war on commercial traffic. Many opportunities made by that deployment were missed, however, because of faulty torpedoes. The worst experience was that of *U56*, which daringly worked its way through a large destroyer screen to launch three torpedoes at the battleship *Nelson*.

All three were heard to strike – but none exploded.* A few weeks later the battleship *Barham* was damaged by a torpedo fired by *U30*. A German Fleet that had not expected to accomplish much by attrition of heavy enemy naval forces was performing remarkably well. That was just the beginning.

At the outbreak of war, two of the *Deutschlands* – the *Deutschland* herself and the *Graf Spee* – were already at sea. In their forays and in those of raiders, large and small, to follow them, the techniques of commerce disruption were to be developed to new highs. Radio interception and decoding systems, which gave the Germans a very good picture of Allied moves, enabled them to send frequent intelligence summaries to the raiders. All routes, meeting points, and the like, had code names; therefore a raider commander had to listen to headquarters radio and respond with a single-letter acknowledgement indicating his choice among the alternatives. Radio also was used for deception, with the *Deutschlands*, battleships, cruisers, auxiliary cruisers, and submarines imitating each other and sometimes imitating enemy ships. Sometimes captured Allied ship radios were used. Disguising the auxiliary cruisers became quite an art – even the *Graf Spee* disguised herself with an extra turret and stack. Tactically, the German heavy ships had a range-finding radar with a range of eighteen and a half miles, in addition to excellent optical instruments.

Although only a minimal military service force existed that was suitable for high-seas use, a remarkable substitute was ready: the Secret Naval Supply Service. Organized long before the war, the Service functioned only in neutral ports. It consisted of employees of steamship lines who had received codes and instructions from the communications officers of visiting warships before the war. Money, per-

* Strangely, the incident is not mentioned in the British official history. S. W. Roskill, *The War at Sea*, Vol 1, p 82. The date was October 30th. Compare with Karl Dönitz, *Memoirs*, p 71.

sonnel, and correspondence were handled under the cover of private business. The task of the organization was to equip German merchant vessels, load them with critical supplies, and get them to sea to meet raiders in designated areas. With care such voyages could be made to appear, to local officials in the neutral ports, as regular commercial trips. The organization also equipped blockade runners, which brought valuable cargoes to Europe and, in a few cases, supplied submarines with fuel. The Supply Service functioned well until 1941, late into the period of surface raiders.

In Germany supply ships were outfitted at the beginning of the war to supplement the few specially built tanker-supply ships. Those armed naval auxiliaries were sent out with the major surface warships. The *Graf Spee* and the *Deutschland,* for instance, had one tanker-supply ship each, which waited in unfrequented locations near the operations area. The only real difficulty was the problem of transferring supplies. The system of high-line transfer between ships sailing parallel had not yet been developed. Small boats or rafts were used for general cargo, and stern-to-bow hose transfers for fuel. Those methods were slow and exposed the ships to attack while they were stationary and encumbered; but since such operations took place in isolated areas, there was seldom interference. Captured vessels, such as tankers and refrigerator ships, provided additional supplies.

At the beginning of the war only the *Deutschland* and *Graf Spee* were ready for high-seas cruises, and they were already on station. The two small battleships *Scharnhorst* and *Gneisenau,* the *Scheer,* and the two heavy cruisers were being overhauled or were finishing training and shakedown. The two large battleships were unfinished and would take almost two years to complete.

The *Deutschland* and the *Graf Spee* were waiting for orders to commence operations. The *Deutschland*'s area of operations was in the North Atlantic, while the *Graf Spee*'s was in the South Atlantic and Indian Oceans. The ships were ordered to wait before beginning operations because Hitler expected to be able to conclude a settlement with England and France once the Polish campaign was over and he did not want to provoke those powers.

On September 23rd, 1939, the restrictions were lifted. *Deutschland* cruised until mid-November, when she successfully broke through the British cordon of auxiliary cruisers in the Denmark Strait, between Iceland and Greenland, and returned home. Her score was only three ships, of which she sank two. The third, the American freighter *City of Flint,* she manned with a German crew and attempted to route to Germany via Murmansk and the route through Norwegian territorial waters that passed between many of the Norwegian islands and the mainland. The *City of Flint*'s capture caused a furore in the United States and other neutral nations, which the British tried unsuccessfully to capitalize on by intercepting her on the run south. The Norwegians interned her prize crew, however, and released the ship to her own crew.

Hitler had been worried about losing the *Deutschland* because her name had considerable propaganda value, but Raeder had been able to persuade him that she was safer at sea until the long nights of November could shield her return. She was then renamed the *Lützow,* after the flagship of the battle cruiser squadron at Jutland, so that no ship with the name *Deutschland* could be lost. The *Graf Spee,* still in the South Atlantic, was not scheduled to return until after the new year had begun.

Hitler's desire to recall the *Deutschland* illustrates one of the major command problems facing Raeder: Hitler's fears, and the interference with operations that resulted from them. The Führer worried about the big ships to the point that he could not sleep when one was out. He told Raeder: 'On land, I am a hero. At sea, I am a coward.'* In early 1941, for instance, when the *Scheer* was in the Indian Ocean, Hitler badgered every naval officer he met with questions about her activities. No major ship went to sea

* David Woodward, *The Tirpitz,* p 135.

without his permission; and as time went on he involved himself more and more frequently with tactical details, even giving orders for submarine dispositions that conflicted with Raeder's and Dönitz's opinions. His extreme caution and fear of losses were apparently caused by the prestige value such losses had for the British and by a peculiar psychological quirk that prevented him from accepting the idea that his enormous and powerful ships might be sunk. He could not visualize them as expendable under any circumstances; so his restraining orders hindered operations to a great extent, sometimes preventing decisive action. At the same time, apparently not realizing the inherent contradiction in his views, he maintained that warships should fight warships, not merchantmen, and he questioned the courage of officers who refused battle.

The small battleships *Scharnhorst* and *Gneisenau* acted at first as a fleet-in-being in the North Sea, to pin down heavy British units while the raiders were at sea. From October 8th–10th, 1939, the *Gneisenau* and the light cruiser *Köln*, escorted by nine destroyers, sortied to intercept the British Fleet light units and merchantmen off southern Norway. Despite the cooperation of 148 aircraft, no contact was made by surface ships, and no hits were made by aircraft on either side.

The two small battleships had been named after the pair of armoured cruisers that had led the German Asiatic Squadron in 1914. Travelling across the Pacific, that cruiser force had destroyed a smaller British squadron in the Battle of Coronel off the Chilean coast, and had been destroyed in turn by a British naval force while attempting to bombard the Falkland Islands in the South Atlantic.

The new *Scharnhorst* and *Gneisenau*, under the command of Vice-Admiral Wilhelm Marschall, sailed on November 21st to put more pressure on the British Fleet dispositions. Their main purpose was to force the Allies to keep numerous fleet units in the North Atlantic. The ship which was to benefit from the diversion was the *Graf Spee* – which had been named after the admiral killed in the Falklands battle, Rear-Admiral Graf Maximilian von Spee, and which was raiding merchant shipping in the same South Atlantic region. Admiral Raeder, who controlled the operations of all the ships, had been the historian of World War I's cruiser warfare in distant oceans and was well aware of the value of dispersed forces, which made it necessary for his enemies to spread far larger forces thinly over vast areas; his own preference, however, was for the massed strength of the battle line, whose development Hitler's diplomacy had prevented.

The *Scharnhorst* and *Gneisenau* sailed far to the north and then west, rolling heavily in enormous seas. By the evening of November 23rd they were still undetected as they moved into the Iceland–Faeroes Passage. The *Scharnhorst*'s lookouts sighted a large ship, which answered the summons to heave-to with gunfire, used her radio to call for help, then tried to lay a smoke screen to cover an attempt to flee. The *Scharnhorst* sustained one hit, but her 11-inch guns quickly crippled her adversary. The ship, a British auxiliary cruiser, was burning brightly in the early dark when the *Gneisenau*'s guns joined in the attack. Fourteen minutes after the first shot the British ship had stopped, and crewmen began blinking signals for help with their flashlights. The *Scharnhorst* and *Gneisenau* then spent nearly two hours rescuing survivors from the 16,700-ton auxiliary cruiser *Rawalpindi* – the only time in World War II that German heavy ships could do so after battle.

With the *Rawalpindi* burning beaconlike in the surrounding darkness, the uncertainty about the situation, and finally a shadow sighted dead astern (which turned out to be the British light cruiser *Newcastle*), the battleships were forced to leave the scene of the sinking. They quickly lost the British ship by a high-speed run and a smoke screen. Deciding that any further move to the west would needlessly expose his ships to the alerted British Home Fleet, Marschall took his ships north-east to evade the British scouts. He waited nearly two days in far-northern latitudes until the weather closed down again and he had received enough intelligence of British dispositions from Berlin. Then he headed south through seas that flooded the forward turrets and bridges, doing far more damage than the *Rawalpindi*'s sole shell hit. The storm screened his ships from the massive British search effort, however, and they arrived home unseen by the enemy.

Raeder felt that the cautious conduct of the cruise had achieved its general goal of diverting British forces, but he disagreed with Marschall's tactical decisions not to engage the *Newcastle*, not to renew the breakthrough attempt, and not to return immediately to Germany having once decided against the breakthrough into the Atlantic. Marschall insisted on the doctrine that unescorted heavy ships should not attack torpedo-carrying light ships in low-visibility conditions. He felt Raeder's other criticisms to be unwarranted attacks on the freedom of action of a commander at sea, who was in the best position to judge the situation. In fact Marschall's rapid withdrawal after the contact with the *Newcastle* did save him from a confrontation with the far superior Home Fleet.

The *Graf Spee*, meanwhile, continued her successful cruise in the South Atlantic. Her aircraft had enabled her to avoid a British heavy cruiser early in September, and she had sighted and avoided still another ship on the same day. Freed of restrictions by Hitler's order of September 23rd, she sank her first ship off the bulge of Brazil just one week later. Since her victim sent off a radio message before going down, the *Graf Spee* then shifted her search to the British trade route that curves around the Cape of Good Hope, swings wide past the Gulf of Guinea, and passes Freetown on the bulge of Africa. On that route four ships were captured and sunk in October. During that month the raider's supply ship, the *Altmark*, had a narrow escape from the *Ark Royal*'s aircraft: the *Altmark*'s signalmen convinced the pilots that she was an American.

At the suggestion of the Naval Operations Staff, Captain

Hans Langsdorff took the *Graf Spee* wide around the Cape into the Indian Ocean to create a diversion, which succeeded when he sank a small tanker off the south-eastern coast of Africa in mid-November. Coming back to the Cape-to-Freetown route, the *Graf Spee* took two more prizes in early December; both of those sent RRR messages (meaning 'attacked by surface raider'). Realizing that the radio messages nullified the effect of the *Graf Spee*'s Indian Ocean sortie, Langsdorff ordered his light weapons to hit the bridge of the second victim when she persisted in transmitting. Three men were wounded – the first casualties of the campaign. Dodging possible pursuit, the *Graf Spee* then met the *Altmark* farther out in the Atlantic to refuel, resupply, and transfer prisoners, as she had been doing approximately every two weeks.

Langsdorff very much wanted one big victory before returning to Germany in January 1940. He hoped to intercept a convoy off the estuary of the River Plate, a point where rich trade routes converged. A convoy attack would probably involve a battle with one or more escort ships, but Langsdorff believed that the need for avoiding damage was no longer so pressing as the cruise neared its end. He seemed to have little fear of enemy warships, but considered the greatest threat to be a fast cruiser that would shadow him and call in a concentration of heavy ships. To meet that threat he decided on the peculiar tactic of closing rapidly with the enemy. His theory was that he could thereby put the opposing ships out of action before they worked up sufficient speed to dodge out of range and then begin pursuing his own ship – whose moderately fast speed of 28.5 knots had been reduced to about 25 knots by tropical growths on the hull. The tactic sacrificed one of the *Graf Spee*'s biggest advantages: her accurate 11-inch guns, which outranged cruiser guns. The advantage, however, had to be balanced against the fact that long-range battle would use up too much irreplaceable ammunition.

Langsdorff's raid started well, with another ship captured and sunk on December 7th. The victim did not have time to call for help. That raised the raider's total to nine ships, totalling 50,089 tons – none of which had been kept as a prize. Langsdorff prided himself that there had been no loss of life and that the prisoners had been well treated. His ship was in excellent condition, and morale was high. The only disadvantage was a cracked engine block in his spotter plane, which would keep it out of action for several days.

First light on December 13th revealed nothing to the *Graf Spee*'s lookouts. By four minutes before sunrise, the visibility had increased to twenty miles, and the light swell and moderate breeze promised another beautiful day. At that moment a lookout sighted two tiny masts almost dead ahead and moving at right angles to the *Graf Spee*'s course. Quickly four more masts were spotted. The main range finder on the foretop turned its stereoptic and electronic eyes on the masts and measured a distance of seventeen miles. Battle stations were called, speed increased, and battle ensigns hoisted.

Within minutes the heavy cruiser *Exeter* was identified; her two consorts were assumed to be destroyers. Langsdorff thought that they must be screening a convoy that lay beyond them, below the horizon. The *Graf Spee* sped towards the enemy ships, which grew more distinct as the range closed. No more masts appeared on the horizon, however, and the truth soon became painfully apparent. Langsdorff, expecting the British to do what he wanted them to do, had taken his ship towards not a convoy but a hunting group: the ships he had taken for destroyers were in fact light cruisers, each with eight 6-inch guns. Commodore Henry Harwood of the British hunting group had made the same decision as Langsdorff about the value of the River Plate traffic, and had concentrated his small force there at the price of leaving the Rio de Janeiro and Falkland Islands areas exposed.

Langsdorff did not try to break off but turned to port, to substitute a parallel fight for his planned quick rush. The pair of light cruisers sped ahead on a nearly parallel but slowly closing course, while the *Exeter* turned to a reverse course and closed in more rapidly. The *Graf Spee*'s main guns opened the battle at ten and a half miles, followed by the *Exeter*'s 8-inch guns when the range had dropped about another mile. The German gunnery was excellent, straddling the *Exeter* on the third salvo and hitting her four minutes later. The *Exeter* also straddled the *Graf Spee* with her third salvo, and the *Ajax* and *Achilles* quickly joined in at what was extremely long range for their guns. Langsdorff was at first undecided about his gunnery policy, shifting his forward triple 11-inch turret's fire to the light cruisers, then back to the *Exeter*, during the first phase of the battle. That reduced the *Graf Spee*'s fire effectiveness somewhat; but the *Exeter* was soon hit on her second 8-inch turret by a 670-pound shell. The turret was wrecked and the bridge was torn by steel splinters that killed or wounded all but three men, destroyed the wheelhouse and communications equipment, and sent the ship out of control. Captain F. S. Bell managed to re-establish a command station aft and, using a boat's compass and a chain of sailors to relay messages to the aft steering position, brought his ship back into action.

The *Exeter* then fired her starboard torpedoes; but the *Graf Spee* reversed course and laid a smoke screen, both to forestall a possible light-cruiser torpedo attack by leaving them astern and to sail parallel to the *Exeter*. The *Graf Spee*'s reversal avoided the *Exeter*'s starboard torpedoes, so the *Exeter* turned to fire her port torpedoes, then turned parallel to her adversary again, suffering repeated 11-inch hits. Flooding in forward compartments put her three feet down by the bows; she listed seven degrees to starboard; and her forward 8-inch turret was knocked out. Fires flared in various parts of the ship, but her aft twin 8-inch turret continued to fire in local control, using the turret range finder and sights rather than information from the fire-control director.

Meanwhile the two light cruisers had circled astern of

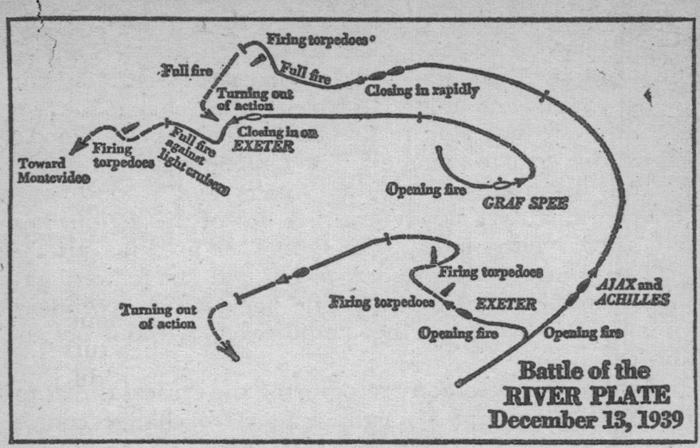

the *Graf Spee* and were trying to close the range from the opposite side. The *Ajax* had been straddled early in the battle. Both ships 'chased salvoes' – sailed towards close shell splashes and away from distant ones to confuse the German gunners – successfully for about fifteen minutes, until the *Achilles* was damaged by a shell that exploded in the water and threw fragments into the ship. That near miss caused casualties throughout her upper works, particularly in the fire-control director and the bridge. With dead men at some of the fire-control instruments, the *Achilles*' director was incorrectly pointed – but the turret crews continued to receive directions automatically from the director. Since no one ordered the gun crews to fire in local control, the *Achilles*' fire became very inaccurate until the dead men could be replaced. Meanwhile the *Ajax*'s spotter aeroplane confused the splashes from the *Ajax*'s shells with those from the *Achilles*, causing the *Ajax* to adjust her fire on the wrong basis; and her salvoes also drifted off target. Langsdorff, however, was too busy with the *Exeter* to take advantage of the light cruisers' distress.

After the two light cruisers solved their gunnery problems, Harwood ordered them to shorten range at maximum speed. That was a hazardous move, since it cut British firepower temporarily; during their change the two cruisers were not able to fire their aft guns. Harwood's gamble nevertheless paid off. The *Graf Spee* turned sharply away from the two light cruisers and towards the *Exeter*, which was slowly drawing out of the action, her last turret having failed. The *Graf Spee* fired her aft 11-inch guns at the *Ajax* and *Achilles*, and her forward 11-inchers at the *Exeter*. Meanwhile her 5.9-inch secondary guns fired on whatever they could reach, without noticeable effect.

Harwood, immediately recognizing the critical threat to the *Exeter*, ordered his light cruisers to change course enough to allow all sixteen 6-inch guns to bear on the enemy. At the very short range of five and a half miles they deluged the *Graf Spee* with 112-pound shells, forcing Langsdorff to bear up, away from the *Exeter*, and concentrate all his fire on the *Ajax* and *Achilles*. The *Ajax* then fired four torpedoes, but the *Graf Spee* sighted and avoided them. Finally the *Ajax* paid the price for her short range when an 11-inch shell tore into her and knocked out both aft turrets. The *Graf Spee* also fired torpedoes, which were spotted by the *Ajax*'s plane and avoided. As the range went down to four miles, the *Graf Spee* brought even her 4.1-inch anti-aircraft guns into action against the light cruisers. Shells geysered all around the thin-skinned cruisers, and only excellent manoeuvring and considerable luck saved them from crippling damage. The tremendous volume of fire forced Harwood to order his ships out of action under a smoke screen. The battle had lasted just under an hour and a half.

The *Graf Spee* had been hit twenty times, mainly by 6-inch shells. Many of the hits were insignificant. Two shells, for example, had merely bounced off the heavy armour of the aft 11 inch turret; and others had failed to explode. The effective hits, however, had reduced parts of the upper works to a shambles, killing thirty-six men and wounding fifty-eight – including Captain Langsdorff, who was twice nicked by splinters and once knocked out briefly by a blast. The galleys were wrecked; many secondary guns were out of action because of ammunition hoist damage; a 5.9-inch gun was disabled; much other equipment was damaged; and there were many holes in the deck and sides, including a six-foot-square hole above the waterline and smaller ones at and below the waterline.

The light cruisers dropped behind the *Graf Spee*, intending to trail her until darkness, when they would be able to close with less danger to themselves. The crippled *Exeter* slowly made off towards the Falklands, with fifty-three dead and many wounded. The Captain of the harried *Graf Spee* had crucial decisions to make. His first inspection convinced him that his ship was not seaworthy enough to attempt a breakthrough to Germany. From that point on, his thoughts and actions appear to have been concerned almost exclusively with his ship and crew; he failed to analyse his tactical and strategic situations. Langsdorff turned his ship towards Montevideo, rejecting Buenos Aires because the mud in the shallow channel of the Plate beyond Montevideo might clog the water ducts that cooled the engines. Since Uruguay was neutral, he expected his ship to be interned.

Through the remainder of the day and on into the evening the three ships moved steadily towards the Plate. The *Graf Spee* fired occasional Parthian shots at whichever enemy came too close; and once, in the evening, she accompanied gunfire with a smoke screen. Langsdorff did not attempt, however, to outrun the cruisers or change course. In the midst of the pursuit, the British merchantman *Shakespeare* blundered into the *Graf Spee*'s path. Her crew stared into the muzzles of 11-inch guns, but for some inexplicable reason they failed to abandon ship on demand. Langsdorff had intended to sink her and had radioed the cruisers to pick up her crew; but he dismissed the idea when the crew remained on board. He did not wish to create an incident when his own ship and crew would soon be dependent on the good will of a neutral nation.

The British also had problems. In mid-afternoon a ship was sighted that was thought at first to be a German heavy cruiser, manoeuvring to trap Harwood's force; but it turned out to be just a merchantman with a streamlined funnel. The chase continued. Harwood had to consider the possibility that the *Graf Spee* would turn out to sea or that she would enter one of the Plate channels and then try to come out through another one after dark. If she did that, she might be able to evade the cruisers or to run the limited-endurance ships out of fuel in a high-speed chase. She might even search for the crippled *Exeter*. Harwood was greatly relieved when the *Graf Spee* dropped anchor in Montevideo at midnight. His cruisers then took up position outside the port to wait for reinforcements and a chance to fill their fuel tanks.

Time became the crucial factor for Langsdorff. He had to stay in port long enough to repair at least the galleys and side plating; yet he could not afford to give the British time enough to bring reinforcements into position. His request for repair time and facilities opened a diplomatic battle over the rights of belligerent warships. Langsdorff asked the Uruguayan Government for two weeks, claiming that the unseaworthy condition of his ship justified it. The British officially demanded that the *Graf Spee* be either limited to twenty-four hours for repairs or interned for the duration of the war. At the same time the British tried to hold Langsdorff in port by ordering their merchantmen to put to sea at the rate of one a day. Since international law provided that a merchant ship leaving a neutral port had to be given a twenty-four-hour head start over an enemy warship, the British hoped that this tactic would give them time to bring more naval vessels to the area. Faced with the opposing demands, the Uruguayan authorities compromised by allowing the *Graf Spee* three days, starting the evening after her arrival when an inspection had been completed.

Langsdorff soon began to receive reports of British heavy units off the Plate estuary. On December 15 – the second day of his stay – a report from Buenos Aires said that an observer in a private plane had seen four cruisers off the estuary. Langsdorff's own gunnery officer claimed to have seen the battle cruiser *Renown*, the aircraft carrier *Ark Royal*, and several destroyers through the *Graf Spee*'s director sights. The latter report served to strengthen persistent rumours (inspired by the British) that reinforcements were close at hand.

That same day Langsdorff had the melancholy duty of leading his men to the funeral of their fallen comrades. The ceremony was attended by the *Graf Spee*'s former British prisoners and many sympathetic Uruguayans. At its end all the Germans gave the Nazi salute – except one. Captain Langsdorff gave his dead the old naval salute, in full view of the world's Press photographers.

With two days to go before the Uruguayan deadline, Langsdorff asked the Naval Operations Staff for advice. He reported British heavy ships off the port and said he intended to try to make his way to Buenos Aires, despite the risk of mud in his engine cooling system. If that should prove impossible, he wanted to know whether he ought to scuttle his ship or allow it to be interned. Although Raeder and his staff did not believe that the British reinforcements had yet arrived, they did not send Langsdorff their own intelligence survey, believing that the *Graf Spee*'s captain, as the man on the scene, could make the best evaluation of the situation. They did approve Langsdorff's plan to head for Buenos Aires, but rejected the internment alternative.

The next day the Germans at Montevideo could not charter a plane to check the British dispositions. At 6.15 PM the British destroyed Langsdorff's freedom of action by sailing another merchant ship. Instead of having all night and day available to make a surprise dash, he would have to sail between 6.15 the next evening and 8.00 – the end of his legal stay – and the British would be fully alerted. That evening he held a council with his officers, and a later one with embassy officials. A fighting exit from the bay was rejected because of its shallow waters. If the *Graf Spee* engaged the British and settled slightly as a result of combat damage, she would become grounded – helpless to fight or even to blow herself up, because her ammunition supply would be much reduced by combat. Retreat to Buenos Aires was also dismissed. Even if she could be taken up the shallow channel, the long run back to sea would make her eventual escape attempt even more difficult; and time was on the British side.

Early the next afternoon it was learned definitely that the *Ark Royal* and the *Renown* had arrived in Rio de Janeiro. Even that did not alter the situation in Langsdorff's view. It was still the refuelled cruisers off the Plate, whatever their number, that held the initiative. He believed they would either fight in the Plate estuary or would simply shadow the *Graf Spee* until the fast British heavy ships arrived.

At 6.15 PM on December 17th the *Graf Spee* left Montevideo Harbour with battle flags flying. She was followed by the German merchantman *Tacoma*. The crowds on the shore and radio listeners all over the world waited tensely as three British cruisers moved in. Beyond the three-mile limit the two German ships were joined by several small ships from Argentina. The *Graf Spee* moved on again, then stopped again. Just at sunset, the distant watchers saw a flash of flame from the dark hull, followed by more explosions and eruptions of flame. Fire spread to engulf the entire ship.

Sir Henry Harwood, KCB, newly knighted and promoted to Rear-Admiral, led the *Ajax*, the *Achilles*, and his only reinforcement – the heavy cruiser *Cumberland* – past the flaming wreck. Captain Langsdorff took his crew to Buenos Aires in the small ships. He called the men together and addressed them one last time, ending the meeting with the old naval salute and leaving with his senior officers. Late that night he unrolled the ensign of the Imperial Navy, under which he had served at Jutland, and shot himself.

Langsdorff had fought a fine campaign but a poor battle. The commerce raiding had been conducted with great skill, but the decisions to fight with warships and, once engaged, to allow the British ships to close the range and the *Exeter* then to escape were all errors. His concerns for his ship and crew were very human but also very shortsighted, leading him to allow British pursuit while he sailed into 'the trap of Montevideo', as he called it in his last letter.*

The *Graf Spee*'s loss is a classic illustration of the problem of a raider in distant waters. In normal circumstances a dockyard would have been able to replenish her ammunition and to repair her relatively minor damage quite quickly. In distant waters, however, the battle damage that threatened her watertight integrity in bad weather; a lack of positive information about the opposing forces; and insufficient ammunition to both fight and scuttle, if a fight in the shallow Plate estuary were unsuccessful, resulted in her self-destruction after a tactical victory.

The loss of the *Graf Spee* aggravated the difficulties Raeder was having with Hitler over tactics. Before the Battle of the Plate, Raeder had already considered not sending the *Deutschlands* to sea again, unless Italy entered the war to draw off Allied forces. Hitler did not appreciate the factors involved in the *Deutschlands*' operations and felt that they should fight decisive battles with enemy warships rather than disrupt commerce. The glory of battle victories was his desire. Raeder, on the other hand, believed that the *Graf Spee* should not have fought at all.

The raider strategy certainly was successful in the sense that it forced the British to spread their naval forces and divert their merchant shipping. In addition to reports of ship attacks bravely sent out by radio operators under fire, numerous false reports about heavy raiders, submarines,

* Dudley Pope, *Graf Spee*, p 236.

and armed merchantmen had to be checked out by the British and French. Convoy protection was impossible except in a few areas, and there were too few ships to cover the many focal areas. To aggravate the problem, the raiders were normally more powerful than the individual patrol vessels. Early in October the British Admiralty had grouped four battleships and battle cruisers, thirteen light and heavy cruisers, and five carriers into nine hunting groups to chase the raiders; it also sent four battleships and battle cruisers, two light cruisers, and a carrier to the main North Atlantic convoy route between Halifax, Nova Scotia, and the British Isles. For other areas diversive routing was necessary. That was an immense accomplishment for two cruiser-size raiders.

After Germany had defeated Poland, the Western Front settled down to the 'Phony War' – a winter of monotonous waiting along the opposing Siegfried and Maginot Lines. No phony war existed at sea, however, where merchant-ship sinkings were extremely high in proportion to the tiny number of German submarines at sea. Even when they were forced to submerge in the presence of British escorts, the submarines discovered that Asdic was not so dangerous as the British had expected. Although Asdic provided the ranges and bearings of submerged submarines, it did not provide depth data; and submarine commanders accidentally discovered, to their delight, that they could take their boats to 400 feet to avoid the depth-charge patterns, or could manoeuvre beyond the half- to three-quarter-mile range of the search device. Since the submarines generally operated independently close to the British coasts, controlled operations in which submarines were massed against convoys were rarely practicable, because the submarines were too scattered to form groups rapidly. The first such attack – an experiment to see if the controlled-operations system would function advantageously – occurred on October 17th, 1939, using three submarines. Together they sank three merchantmen. That action, and a few other such operations, showed the system to be efficient if enough submarines could be made available to locate the convoys.

Tactical control at sea was found to be unnecessary, and often undesirable, because it kept one submarine on the surface well away from the convoy, where it could use its radio without interference from British escorts but where its commander could get no better picture of the situation than had Dönitz's staff on land. In addition, excessive use of radios by the submarines gave the British valuable information about submarine dispositions. When the command was forced to dive, all control was lost – a disability that shore headquarters did not suffer. By the beginning of 1940, Dönitz had taken over the entire direction of submarine attacks: furnishing information, altering dispositions, and assigning beacon submarines. Once in contact with a convoy, each commander was on his own. A slight tendency to over-control operations was reduced as the Submarine Staff's relationships with the commanders at sea became more confident through experience.

Raeder's conferences with Hitler had one continuous theme: the submarine fleet must be increased. Although each sinking added new evidence for Raeder's case, Hitler, worried about the Ruhr, wanted the land question settled before giving high priority to submarines. He still felt that a decision on land would drive Britain out of the conflict. Materials were very short, and in March of 1940 the monthly construction target was temporarily reduced from thirty to twenty-five submarines.

The submarine building programme was a casualty of Hitler's tendency to make compromises between programmes, preventing any one of them from being developed to its full potential. First there was the Polish campaign, and then the Western Front, to face; but the latter was supported so half-heartedly in 1939 that even tank production remained at ridiculously low figures compared with Germany's industrial capacity. Limited German resources were only part of the problem; for mobilization of existing resources and curtailment of non-essential civilian production were not pressed vigorously early in the war. Had the German High Command planned an all-out war with Great Britain, there would have been submarines built, figuratively, on every meadow next to every stream deep enough to float one – as the Americans had built privateers from green timber on the shore of virtually every wooded cove along the Atlantic seaboard, to challenge Britain's merchant marine in the long-ago days of 1812.

The early months of 1940 were quiet ones for heavy surface ships. The interest of both the British and the German Naval Staffs was centred on a sequel to the *Graf Spee*'s cruise. In February 1940 her supply ship, the *Altmark*, with 299 British prisoners on board, arrived in Norwegian waters after slipping through the Iceland-Faeroes patrol line. She was sailing in neutral waters well south of Bergen, when British destroyers and a cruiser were sighted. Two destroyers moved in to board; but the *Altmark*'s captain refused to stop and, with the aid of the Norwegians, was able to take her into a nearby fiord and anchor there. The British destroyer *Cossack* followed her in – only to be told by the Norwegians that the *Altmark* was unarmed and entitled to use neutral waters. The *Cossack* withdrew to ask for instructions.

That night the *Cossack* reappeared. Captain Philip Vian demanded of the Norwegians that the *Altmark* be jointly escorted back to Bergen for another inspection. The Norwegians refused. Suddenly the *Cossack* turned towards the *Altmark*; the *Altmark* attempted to push the oncoming destroyer into the shore with her stern, but the British ship turned faster and ran alongside. A British boarding party then leaped for the German deck with all the spirit of Nelson's tars. In the brief battle that followed, seven German sailors were killed. Vian's men then released the 299 prisoners to the cry 'The Navy's here!' The action made Vian a hero and gave an enormous boost to the popularity of Winston Churchill, First Lord of the Admiralty, who had ordered Vian to board the German vessel. Vian's discovery that the *Altmark* was armed with machine guns blunted Goebbels' propaganda about British violations of neutral waters and vitiated the Norwegian position, casting doubts on the extent to which the Norwegians would defend their neutrality against either side.

One brief moment of excitement did not, however, alter Britain's situation. The British Navy had to keep watch over a long blockade line with limited forces. In February 1940 the German battleships *Scharnhorst* and *Gneisenau*, the heavy cruiser *Hipper*, and an escort of destroyers sortied towards the Bergen area but found nothing, because the British had been alerted by one of their bombers. In turn British Fleet units failed to intercept the German force. The surface-force activity kept the British pinned down, for they had to have ships both at sea and ready at their bases to counter German moves – dispositions that put a great strain on their resources. British aircraft were not good enough at that time to take over many long-range search and attack duties.

Despite directives and requests, the German Air Force did little to aid in the naval war. Occasional attacks on British shipping and bases brought few successes and provoked comment from the Air Force that its cooperation was of little value and would be undertaken when the Air Force thought it necessary. Göring cut naval aircraft allocations throughout the autumn of 1939, and even naval aerial observation was curtailed by lack of modern aircraft. Attacks off southern England were given up because of high losses; and Air Force reconnaissance, intended to replace such activity by the Navy, proved so inefficient as to be practically useless. Despite obvious deficiencies, Göring and Hitler ordered all long-term research work on weapons, search devices, and other war-related projects halted in the spring of 1940, on the assumption that they could not be completed in time to affect the war.

The attitude of Raeder regarding aircraft carriers was never firmly set. Initially, in October 1939, he felt that a carrier was too vulnerable and not useful enough in the

North Sea, where land-based aircraft could operate. Later he considered that a carrier might operate with cruisers in the Atlantic. The lead time from orders to production was always great, and lack of aircraft a problem. The project languished.

The problem of lead time also affected the armed merchant cruisers. They were not prepared until after the war had begun, and few began operations during the first year. Small, inconspicuous ships were used for that purpose. Germany had approximately 250 ships of between 5,000 and 10,000 tons; but few were suitable for the conversion because of cruising range, speed, or engineering deficiencies. When the war started and conversion began, relatively little planning had been done, and much of the work was directed by the captains themselves. The merchant raiders' great assets were their ability to change their appearance and (of less importance) their firepower, which usually consisted of six 5.9-inch guns, torpedo tubes, light guns, and reconnaissance aircraft. They, like the *Deutschlands*, could be dangerous to the ships sent to hunt them down. The problem of getting them to sea was not a great one at first; but the use of Russian and Japanese bases was discussed, and arrangements were made to send raiders through the North-East Passage. None of the preparations came into effect until just before the Norway operation in the spring of 1940.

Offensive minelaying by German destroyers had to be broken off in March 1940 because of the shorter nights, but for once the Air Force took over effectively. More than a thousand aerial mines were laid from April through June in conjunction with the Army's spring offensive, and shipping was bombed effectively for the first time. British and French losses mounted rapidly.

From March 1940 on, the Norway operation absorbed almost all the forces of the Navy. That situation was accepted by Hitler and the OKW, and the Navy's part in the spring offensive on the Western Front was limited to submarine and motor torpedo boat action in support of the land forces. Belgium and Holland were considered of little value for naval bases because of their proximity to the British Isles and because the English Channel was blocked. As more and more neutrals became involved in the war, an indirect advantage to the Navy was expected to be the elimination of most of the problems of controlling contraband and neutral shipping that had plagued the submarine commanders and others trying to maintain pressure against British-neutral commerce. The acquisition of French Atlantic bases, it was recognized, could change the entire strategic picture; but no serious thought was given to that seemingly remote possibility. The highest Army officers said that capture of the Dutch coast would be a long, costly operation, and that the French coast might be won in two years of stubborn conflict.

Chapter 3

NORWAY

The daring stroke
April 1940–June 1940

From the lessons of the Great War came a concern on Germany's part for her northern sea flank, which led to one of the most audacious actions ever undertaken by a numerically inferior sea power.

On October 10th, 1939, Raeder first mentioned the desirability of Trondheim as a base at one of his meetings with Hitler. Those meetings occurred at irregular intervals (usually two weeks to a month apart) and supplemented the reports of the permanent naval representatives at Hitler's headquarters. In addition to Raeder, Hitler, and Hitler's naval adjutant, those present included OKW leaders and sometimes others who might be concerned with the problems to be discussed.

Long before the subject of Trondheim was first mentioned to Hitler, the German Navy had a very clear idea of Norway's strategic potential. A barrier of British mines, similar to that of World War I, was likely to be laid across the North Sea and extended again into Norwegian neutral waters – with or without Norwegian aid. That would endanger submarine egress, block surface-warship sorties and merchant-ship movement along the Norwegian coast, and seriously curtail the iron-ore shipments that came from Sweden to Narvik by rail and then down the Norwegian coast in winter. A British move into northern Norway would threaten the Baltic Sea and northern Germany, endangering shipping and submarine training, and laying open all of northern Germany to aerial assault. A second front could thus be opened, perhaps giving Britain a decisive advantage in the war.

A base in Norway, in addition to shoring up Germany's defences, offered other advantages to a Navy that had little prospect of obtaining French bases. From Norway the German Navy and Air Force could menace Britain's communications – and Great Britain herself. It also would be possible to deprive Great Britain of the ore and timber she received from all of Scandinavia.

Reliable intelligence from numerous neutral (including Norwegian) sources indicated British interest in Norway; but the risks of German action in the face of the British Fleet were very great. German occupation of Norway, it was believed, would present a major problem of defence later on. At that early stage of the war Hitler wanted merely to study the problem.

The Russian attack on Finland of November 30th, 1939, changed the situation markedly. After the denunciation of the invasion by the League of Nations, the Allies began sending supplies to Finland via Norway. As the south-eastern portion of Finland was closed off by Germany and Russia, the only access the Allies had for the large-scale aid that they contemplated was through northern Norway and Sweden. Since such an operation would violate the rights of those neutral nations anyway, it seemed likely to German military planners that the Allies would take advantage of the occasion to seize the sources of Germany's iron ore at the same time. Both sides realized the possibilities, but neither could move until spring.

In early December, immediately after the beginning of the Russo-Finnish War, point was given to the Navy's ideas by the visit to Germany of the leader of Norway's small Nazi-type party. Vidkun Quisling and his associate, Viljam Hagelin, first made contact with the Nazi racial theorist Alfred Rosenberg, who put them in touch with Raeder. Their idea was that an uprising could be instigated in Norway, using as a pretext the action of the legislature in lengthening its own term. They felt that German-trained Norwegians, with some German aid, could carry it off. They also stressed the likelihood of British moves into Norway, with the acquiescence of the bulk of the Norwegian people, who were at the time afraid of Russia. While Raeder agreed to arrange a meeting with Hitler, he discouraged the idea of a German move in mid-January because no operation could be launched that quickly.

In a conference with Hitler on December 12th, 1939, Raeder went over in detail the advantages and disadvantages of an attack on Norway. While warning Hitler that Quisling's motives were hard to evaluate, he suggested that the OKW be asked to make two plans: one for an operation in support of a Quisling uprising and one for a direct military occupation. Hitler, after conferring three times with Quisling, ordered the OKW to begin planning on the basis suggested by Raeder. The Navy worked on its share of the operations study while Captain Theodor Krancke, the naval representative, worked on the overall plan at OKW headquarters.

In his next conference with Hitler, on December 30th, Raeder stressed the likelihood of a British move and the probable lack of Norwegian resistance to a German blow. Later in the same conference he mentioned the preponderance of British surface forces in the North Sea area and the Navy's preparations to send submarines, the *Lützow* (formerly the *Deutschland*), and auxiliary cruisers to the Atlantic. Those factors were to influence the form the Norway operation would take.

January and the first half of February 1940 saw the development of the plans and the accumulation of information on the Norwegian area in relation to the war. Iron ore needs were studied, and the likelihood of British intervention was assessed. The chartering to England of 90 per cent of the Norwegian tankers was noted. By January 13th, when the Navy received a draft of the preliminary OKW study, Raeder was convinced that the British intended to occupy Norway soon. However, some members of the Naval Operations Staff felt that it was too risky an operation for the British to attempt in the face of German air and sea power, especially since the Germans could counter it by moving into Denmark, Sweden, and southern Norway. The British, it was argued, would also be risking war with Russia. The Naval Operations Staff members later changed their minds about Britain's intentions; the tactical prognosis of Britain's ability to sustain a Norwegian campaign was remarkably accurate, however.

Raeder's next conference with Hitler, while not directly on the subject of Norway, dealt with planning of high-seas operations and with an assessment of the damage already sustained by the British Fleet – both important indirect considerations in drawing the final, detailed Norway plans ordered the next day – January 27th. Hitler was becoming more convinced of the inevitability of a Norwegian campaign, despite the hesitancy engendered by his lack of familiarity with such a combined land-sea-air operation. The *Altmark* affair of February 16th was taken as a clear warning that Norwegian neutrality was not respected by the British, and that the Norwegians would not defend it either.

On February 21st a commander for the projected operation was selected. In a conference held two days later, Raeder expressed his opinion to Hitler that Norwegian neutrality was still the most desirable situation. While Norway was not to be allowed to fall into British hands, the problem of defending the Norwegian coast and coastal traffic once they were in German hands was a cogent reason for holding back until the operation became vital.

The Norway Directive, issued by Hitler on March 1st, 1940, adopted the Navy's reasoning about the necessity for a German invasion because British moves were imminent. Under the command of Army General Nikolaus von Falkenhorst, the operation was planned as a surprise move of small forces, transported by air and sea and protected by the Air Force and Navy. The command structure for the operation was, as usual in the Nazi period, too complex, too fragmented, and too scattered. To those familiar with the highly knit, unified commands in such operations as the Allied invasion of Normandy, the three German Services often appear to have fought three separate wars on all command levels, justifying the grimly humorous saying that World War II was fought with the Prussian Army, the Imperial Navy, and the Nazi Air Force.* For the Norway operation there was no fully integrated inter-service staff, although Colonel-General Alfred Jodl's Operation Staff at OKW had general control. Naval Groups East and West had control ships, with Raeder's Naval Operations Staff keeping close touch and ready to intervene. Air Force Headquarters in Berlin had control of the aeroplanes. General Falkenhorst, provided with a special three-Service staff, controlled the land forces and had tactical control of aircraft in the combat zone. Only excellent personal cooperation at the middle and lower command levels gave the operation a chance of success.

The Air Force was to send paratroops to southern Norway to take the airfields at Oslo and Stavanger, which were to be used for bringing in additional troops by air transport. Fighter and bomber air cover was set up to attack the British and intimidate the Norwegians. Cruisers and varied smaller ships were to land troops at four locations in southern Norway from Oslo to Bergen, the plan being to go past the forts directly into the harbours.

The most daring parts of the plan were the proposed attacks on Narvik and Trondheim, in northern Norway, by troops from a cruiser and fourteen destroyers, sup-

* Hitler's often-expressed version was, 'I have a reactionary Army, a Christian Navy, and a National Socialist Air Force.' ('Imperial' was sometimes substituted for 'Christian', which apparently was a reference to the stiffly correct and religious Raeder.) Alfred Jodl, in *Trial of the Major War Criminals*, Vol. XV, p 294; quoted in Walter Ansel, *Hitler Confronts England*, p 14.

ported by the two small battleships. It was intended also that the *Lützow* would distract the British Fleet by breaking out into the Atlantic to attack commerce. The northern landing forces were to disembark and the ships to leave that same day, with reinforcements coming overland later. The supply ships for those forces were to start for Norway some days before the warships so as to arrive at about the same time. They were to proceed under the guise of regular commercial ships in the coastal trade. Submarines were to act as lookouts and to interfere with British countermoves once the troop-ships entered the fiords. Reinforcements were to go only to Oslo on the first, third, and fifth days; they were to advance overland from there to clear the country of opposition.

Because of its dependence on storms and low visibility, and in order to forestall the British, the operation was given precedence on March 3rd over the attack on the Low Countries. The next day orders went out to complete preparations so that after March 10th the operation could be carried out on four days' notice; and on March 5th Jodl met with the three commanders-in-chief for final discussions. This, oddly, was the first time Göring had been consulted about the plan, although Air Force men had long been involved in the preparations.

By the time of Raeder's next conference with Hitler on March 9th, the operation was in the stage of final detail study. The difficulties of the breakthrough from the northern ports after the landings had been executed were discussed, and Raeder stressed the need for maximum air cover for the returning warships. Air Force agreement to aerial mining of Scapa Flow was also requested. Raeder suggested that the Russians might be allowed to take Tromsö in northern Norway; but Hitler disapproved, and the decision was made to take the town later by sending German soldiers overland.

British plans also were developing rapidly. On March 10th Chamberlain publicly assured Finland of aid. Two days later, however, Finland made peace with Russia –

the only decision that could be taken in the face of a hopeless military situation. There was some hope in the German Naval Staff that peace might avert a British move on Norway; but intelligence reports and British actions against German shipping in Norwegian coastal waters indicated otherwise.

On March 26th Raeder again presented the case for carrying out the invasion quickly, pointing out that even if the British did not act immediately, they would probably harass the ore traffic, perhaps creating an incident as a pretext for invading Norway themselves. Weather and preparedness were in Germany's favour, and Hitler agreed that it was time to strike; but he set no date. Three days later more details were discussed; but again the date was not set, because the extremely severe winter had created lingering ice problems in the Baltic entrances. The Great Belt, a key waterway among the Danish islands, did not open until the first week in April. At that time Hitler said he wanted to change the plan. He wanted naval forces left in Narvik and Trondheim to support the Army; but Raeder was able to dissuade him in regard to Narvik by pointing out that the naval force would inevitably meet with, and be destroyed by, the superior British Fleet. The Trondheim support problem was left open. An argument with the Air Force, which had failed to mine Scapa Flow to hinder British moves, also clouded the meeting.

On April 2nd the invasion date was finally set for the 9th. The next day vessels of the supply group began moving along the Norwegian coast in the guise of normal shipping. Foreign Minister Joachim von Ribbentrop was first informed of the coming action at that time.

From that point on, the offensive moves of each side created a reaction on the other – for both had the same operation in train, with the Germans only a day ahead of the British. The British were further hampered by concern for a show of legality. They were hoping for unopposed landings, while the Germans had abandoned hope of much help from the Quisling group and were executing an operation based on ruthless use of surprise.

On the evening of April 6th the heavy covering forces and the invasion forces destined for northern Norway left port. They were the two small battleships, the heavy cruiser *Hipper*, and fourteen destroyers. Ten destroyers were to land 2,000 men at Narvik; the cruiser, escorted by four destroyers, was to land 1,700 men at Trondheim. The battleships were temporarily under the command of Vice-Admiral Günther Lütjens while Marschall was on sick leave. They were to act as cover and then cruise north to decoy British heavy forces away from the Norwegian coast. Although the *Lützow* was to have been a member of the group, her engines were giving trouble, so she was placed in one of the southern landing groups. An auxiliary cruiser, the *Orion*, sailed with the purpose of creating confusion in the North Atlantic.

The other groups sailed later for the southern Norwegian (and a few Danish) ports. They comprised the *Lützow*, the heavy cruiser *Blücher*, light cruisers, and many smaller craft.

The German main forces were sighted and unsuccessfully attacked by air on the day after they sortied. They appeared to have lost the vital element of surprise – although the purpose of the sortie might, they hoped, still elude the British, who were always worried about German warships breaking out in the Atlantic convoy lanes.

Early the next morning (April 8th, one day before the invasion) the British destroyer *Glowworm*, a detached member of a force engaged in mining Norwegian waters, found, reported, and engaged a German destroyer of the *Hipper* detachment off Trondheim in violent weather. The *Hipper*, with her 8-inch guns, was soon brought into the close-range fray, and tried to ram the *Glowworm*. Seeing his ship battered and fearing annihilation to be imminent, Lieutenant-Commander Gerard B. Roope earned his Victoria Cross by ramming his little vessel into the *Hipper*, buckling and gashing 120 feet of her side plating and letting in 528 tons of water. As the *Glowworm* fell away, she blew up. The *Hipper* group proceeded towards Trondheim – the *Hipper* operating with a four-degree list to starboard but with all vital equipment functioning.

The British announced the completion of mining of Norwegian waters early that same morning. They pulled out a destroyer force that had guarded the minelaying off Narvik in order to help search for the *Scharnhorst–Gneisenau* group, which appeared to be headed for the Atlantic. A few hours later the German troopship *Rio de Janeiro* was sunk off the southern Norwegian coast by the Polish submarine *Orzel*, which had escaped the German attack of the previous September and was operating from the British Isles. Some of the German troops told their Norwegian rescuers that they were on the way to Bergen to protect it against Allied invasion; but, incredibly, the Norwegians failed to call an alert, and the British missed the significance of the information.

Early the next day, the 9th, the *Scharnhorst* and *Gneisenau* were alone in a stormy sea well off Narvik. Suddenly, in a moment of cleared visibility, the battle cruiser *Renown* appeared, and began to fire her 15-inch guns at a nine-mile range during the fitful breaks between snow squalls. A few minutes later the Germans replied with their 11-inch main batteries. A ten-minute duel ensued before the Germans worked up to full speed and slowly outran their older pursuer, in weather so wild that none of the nine British destroyers accompanying the *Renown* could catch up with the battle. Lütjens had determined to follow his orders to lead British forces north-west, away from the Norwegian coast, rather than fight a ship that mounted such formidable guns. As it was, before losing the *Renown* in the mists astern, the *Gneisenau* received three 15-inch shell hits. One of them smashed her main fire-control system and another disabled her forward 11-inch gun turret, while the German ships landed only two unimportant hits on the *Renown*. As the battleship's role of drawing off British capital ships was being fulfilled, however, the damage to the *Gneisenau* was a modest price to pay for that success.

Commodore Paul Friedrich Bonte's ten destroyers had sailed through Vest Fiord unopposed during darkness. At dawn they sank two Norwegian coast-defence ships, which would not surrender after a formal parley. The destroyers landed their troops at the town of Narvik itself. Bonte was anxious to get away; but one tanker had been sunk and only one had arrived, so refuelling was very slow.

At Trondheim the damaged *Hipper* and her four destroyers confused most of the Norwegian coast-defence battery crews by Morse-code signalling in English. Only the innermost battery opened fire, but the *Hipper* soon silenced it. The town offered no resistance, and the batteries were taken from behind by the German troops and were manned against a British counter-attack.

At Bergen the shore batteries damaged the gunnery training ship *Bremse* and the light cruiser *Königsberg*, but the city was quickly taken. Egersund was taken without difficulty from the sea, and Stavanger by airborne forces – after a Norwegian destroyer had sunk a supply ship and been sunk in turn by German dive bombers, operating from an airfield that had been captured by the paratroops. Surprise was impossible at Kristiansand because of fog, which delayed the German approach; but the naval forces succeeded in passing the batteries at the third attempt after the Air Force had smashed the gun positions.

Oslo's defences were the most formidable, and they dealt the heaviest blows. At Oslo Fiord's narrowest point, well below the city, the alert gunners hit the heavy cruiser *Blücher* repeatedly. Then two torpedoes from a shore battery sank her. She was the only heavy ship sunk that day (thus repeating the history of her predecessor, the armoured cruiser *Blücher*, which had been the only ship sunk in the Battle of Dogger Bank in 1915). The other ships landed their troops farther down on the fiord, to work their way behind the fortifications while the Air Force struck the batteries and the paratroops took the airfield. The delay allowed the escape of the King and Government and the removal of the gold reserves.

Within hours the occupation was clearly a brilliant success – despite the loss, mainly to the numerous British submarines, of most of the tankers and supply ships needed in the northern ports to supply the destroyers for the run south. Denmark was overrun the same morning with naval help, and protective minefields were laid in the western approaches to the Skagerrak.

The most difficult task for the Navy was still to come. The ships had to be brought back to Germany from the west-coast ports before they could be bottled up and destroyed by an aroused British Navy. Some ships made the move that night. However, the British submarine *Truant* caught the light cruiser *Karlsruhe* on her way south from Kristiansand; the *Truant*'s torpedoes so damaged the cruiser that she had to be sunk by her escorts. The light cruiser *Königsberg* could not repair her damage quickly enough, and British dive bombers found her still alongside a Bergen pier the next day. They hit her with three bombs – and gave her the dubious distinction of being the first major warship in history to be sunk by hostile aircraft. The German Air Force retaliated by sinking the British light cruiser *Curlew* later in the campaign.

The approach to Narvik, Ofot Fiord, is a long, narrow waterway between steep banks, leading far inland from Vest Fiord. Smaller fiords, generally hidden behind rocky peninsulas, join the main fiord at irregular intervals. The town lies along the shore of one of the small fiords near the eastern end of Ofot Fiord. Five of the German destroyers trapped at the town by fuel shortage were surprised by a dashing dawn gun-and-torpedo attack by three British destroyers under Captain B. A. W. Warburton-Lee. In a few chaotic minutes Commodore Bonte was killed, two of his destroyers sunk, and the other three damaged. The British pulled out into the main fiord but returned with two more destroyers to sink six merchantmen; they then withdrew towards the open sea.

Captain Warburton-Lee's daring attack had earned him a Victoria Cross, which he would never see. At his moment of victory three German destroyers surprised the British by appearing suddenly from a side fiord, while two more pulled out of another side fiord ahead of the retreating British. The brief, fierce running fight killed Captain Warburton-Lee and sank two of his destroyers. The other three fled, one of them badly damaged; but the Germans did not pursue. On their way out of the fiord the British sighted and fired on a German cargo ship, which blew up when hit. She had been carrying most of the landing force's ammunition.

Later the same day the *Köln* left Bergen, the *Hipper* and a destroyer left Trondheim, the *Lützow* left Oslo, and the battleships began their run home from far to the north-west – their mission of decoying British Fleet units away from the Norwegian coast successfully completed. All avoided the British Home Fleet in the prevailing foul weather, but the *Hipper* escaped contact by a very narrow margin. She joined the battleships a day and a half later, early on the 12th. The *Köln* appeared later in the day for the last hours of the run to Germany. Only the *Lützow*, on the shortest, safest route, was unlucky. The submarine *Spearfish*, operating with great daring at the entrance to the Kattegat, damaged her so badly with torpedoes that she had to be towed home and put into a dockyard for a year. The smaller warships returned to Germany later in small groups, with few losses.

The fuel shortage held the eight remaining destroyers in Narvik. They had to wait three days for the Second Battle of Narvik to begin. When it did, their only support came from the submarines that Dönitz had deployed along the Norwegian coast. On April 13th the British battleship *Warspite*, screened by nine destroyers and preceded by her reconnaissance plane, moved up Vest Fiord towards the town. A German submarine, moving in at periscope depth to attack the battleship, ran on a rock, broke surface, and barely escaped being the victim instead of the attacker. The plane's observer reported a destroyer in an ambush position behind a small promontory, then moved farther up the fiord to sight and bomb another submarine in a side fiord, sinking it.

The British destroyers, after sinking the outlying ambush ship, moved in to engage the six operational German destroyers. The unequal battle was made a quick rout by the *Warspite*'s 15-inch covering fire. Only one German destroyer was sunk in the main fiord; the others were relentlessly pursued up various side fiords to destruction. By evening, none remained of the ten destroyers that had landed the Narvik occupation force only four days before. The ships' 2,100 survivors joined the 2,000 Alpine troops in the town and prepared to contest the expected British counter-attack, despite their severe ammunition shortage and the absence of their motor transport, which had been aboard a supply ship captured by a British destroyer. The British loss in the battle was two badly damaged destroyers.

Raeder discussed the situation with Hitler while the Second Battle of Narvik was in progress. The use of several auxiliary cruisers for commerce war was expected to compensate partly for the absence of the *Lützow* from the Atlantic. It was expected that operations by those vessels would distract the British and prevent them from counter-attacking with their full force. The assignment of submarines to supply Narvik and attack the British was also discussed.

Thirty submarines – all those available, including the training flotilla – were in use either off Norway or off the British bases. Dönitz was shifting them from place to place as the situation changed. It had been hoped that such a concentration of submarines would have significant results, but the submarines were having their troubles. Twice they had failed to intervene against, or even report, the British forces moving towards Narvik. Although poor weather had played a part in those failures, they re-emphasized the fact that a submarine's low, rolling conning tower is an unreliable observation platform. As the British counter-attack developed, the submarines did find many targets.

Two ace commanders, each already the holder of the Knight's Cross of the Iron Cross, were in excellent positions. Lieutenant-Commander Herbert Schultze found a heavy cruiser about midday on April 11th, fired a spread of three torpedoes, and heard one explode in the open sea far beyond its target. The others also had missed. That evening another heavy cruiser came into his sights. Another salvo of three torpedoes ran for the target; all exploded prematurely. That was the worst of a string of similar reports reaching a worried Dönitz. He ordered the submarine commanders to switch from magnetic to contact detonators for most targets. A few days later Schultze caught the *Warspite* force leaving Vest Fiord after destroying the German force at Narvik. Two destroyers and the battleship itself were saved when the torpedoes failed again.

One day later it was the turn of Günther Prien, whose *U47* carried the 'Snorting Bull' of Scapa Flow, painted on her conning tower, to commemorate the sinking of the *Royal Oak*. Prien found a group of British ships anchored in overlapping rows in a channel north-west of Narvik. They were disembarking troops for an attack on the German forces in the town. Prien made a careful submerged attack after dark, choosing two cruisers and two transports as targets for his first four torpedoes. He fired into the quiet anchorage. Nothing happened! Prien pulled out, and his crew reloaded the tubes. Back they came, on the surface, for another four-torpedo spread. That time there was an explosion: one torpedo had turned and hit the rocky fiord bank. The furious Prien turned *U47* for the run out to sea – but she ran aground, with British escort vessels charging down the channel behind. By pulling full astern with both engines, blowing the forward ballast, and rocking the boat by marching men back and forth from port to starboard on the after deck, she finally worked free. Despite British depth-charge attacks. Prien managed to escape down the fiord to the sea.

Desperately Dönitz withdrew the submarines from the fiords and called a conference with the Inspector of the Torpedo Department. On April 17th he put the submarines back on magnetic torpedo firing, except in confined waters, and called in all those that were operating off the southern Norwegian coast. Two days later Prien found the *Warspite* and fired two torpedoes at her. The only result was an explosion at the end of one torpedo's run that brought a swarm of destroyers in for very severe depth-charge counter-attacks. The next day he sighted a convoy in a favourable position, but refused to risk his boat and crew in another attack. Back at headquarters Prien told Dönitz that he 'could hardly be expected to fight with a dummy rifle'.*

The grim score for the Norway campaign eventually reached four submarines lost against one British transport sunk. Fourteen attacks on cruisers, ten on destroyers, and fifteen on transports were failures. The battleship *Warspite* escaped four attacks. The completion of six supply runs to Trondheim was probably the most important contribution of the submarines to a campaign on which they could have had major impact if their weapons had been reliable.

Starting on April 14th, the British and their Allies began to land forces on both sides of Trondheim and near Narvik. They captured the latter and drove the German troops inland. German air attacks hampered the British land forces and harassed their supporting Fleet units, sinking a light cruiser, several destroyers, and other craft and damaging ships up to heavy-cruiser size. German

* Karl Dönitz, *Memoirs*, p 89.

supply and reinforcement through Oslo were quickly established, and the build-up of forces in south-eastern Norway for movement north was never seriously threatened by the Allies. British submarines sank a variety of German ships, mainly in the early days of the campaign, while losing two of their number in the first week. A third, the 2,150-ton minelayer-submarine *Seal,* was disabled in the Kattegat by German mines. She surfaced with difficulty and was captured by German submarine chasers because she had not been fitted with scuttling charges.

The British moves had caused Hitler some anxious moments, and Raeder some troubles. On April 22nd a variety of projects was discussed: submarines were to supply the troops in northern Norway; a sortie of the heavy ships to interfere with British reinforcements was mentioned; and Raeder pressed for aerial mining of Scapa Flow. Göring, however, had forestalled him by telling Hitler that his pilots were too inexperienced to carry out the operation.

On the 26th most submarines were released for commerce war after their early withdrawal from Norway because of torpedo failures. Passive defence of Norway using such devices as mines, shore guns, and anti-submarine nets was discussed consequent to an unsuccessful French surface raid into the Skagerrak. The problem of defending Norway was to worry Hitler for the rest of the war. Hitler was also thinking of using some large transports to take troops to Trondheim; but Raeder was able to dissuade him from such a dangerous course.

During that period the auxiliary cruisers *Atlantis* and *Orion* were making their presence felt for the first time. By sending a radio message in which one posed as a British merchantman under attack by a *Deutschland*-class raider, by minelaying, and by destroying ships, those first two merchantman raiders hoped to draw off some British forces.

In mid-May repairs to the damaged *Hipper* and the

Gneisenau were close enough to completion to permit their use in early June. An operation for the relief of the Narvik area troops by bombardment of the nearby British base at Harstad was planned, to be followed by a sweep even farther north to threaten British communications with Narvik and thereby relieve the pressure on German communications in southern Norway. A convoy was to be sent to the front north of Trondheim at the same time under cover of the sortie.

Meanwhile, unknown to the German High Command, the German Army columns moving north from the Oslo area with German Air Force support had decided the land war. The threat of German attacks through Sweden from the Baltic, the need for Allied troops on the Western Front, and the demand for ships to face a more belligerent Italy hastened the British withdrawal, on May 3rd from the Trondheim area and on June 8th from Narvik, which they had wrecked.

The German naval force, consisting of the two battleships *Scharnhorst* and *Gneisenau,* the heavy cruiser *Hipper,* four destroyers, and a supply ship, sortied on June 4th under the command of the newly promoted Admiral Wilhelm Marschall. After sailing north for four days, it found itself in the midst of the British evacuation of Narvik. On the 7th, aerial reconnaissance had told Marschall about five groups of ships. The next morning, when the German force approached the latitude of Narvik, a tanker in ballast and her trawler escort were sighted and quickly sunk. A short time later an empty troop transport and a hospital ship were found. The hospital ship was not molested and, in turn, did not use its radio; but the 20,000-ton transport was sunk. At that point Group West intervened with an order to leave the convoys to the *Hipper* and the destroyers, while the battleships were to attack the naval forces, shipping, and depots in the Harstad area near Narvik. Marschall ignored the order because aerial reconnaissance had not provided the information necessary for him to locate the supply depots and because the only firm information he had was that no valuable shipping was in the port. He did send the cruiser and the destroyers to Trondheim to refuel. That move made them available for his second task – to attack the British naval units that were harassing the German Army route near the coast.

Marschall kept the *Scharnhorst* and *Gneisenau* well out at sea, looking for the targets (particularly aircraft carriers) that his shipboard radio intercept service had indicated were sailing there. Only three hours after he had split his force on that eventful June 8th, smoke was sighted on the horizon. It was a rare, brilliantly clear day with almost unlimited visibility, so it was only minutes later that the aircraft carrier *Glorious* and two destroyers were identified. Racing in to the attack, the *Scharnhorst* opened fire at the extraordinarily long range of fourteen miles. The carrier had no planes aloft, for reasons that will never be known, and German gunnery hit the flight deck early, flipping large sections of it up, 'like the lid of a box', in Marschall's words. The destroyers *Ardent* and *Acasta* went to full speed to charge at their massive foes and protect the helpless carrier. They laid a smoke screen and fired torpedoes and 4·7-inch guns at extreme range, but their gallant assault could be nothing but a death ride. The *Glorious* was set afire, with her own fuel and ammunition adding to the holocaust. As she stopped, her crew abandoned ship. The *Ardent* was overwhelmed by 11-inch shells and sank quickly. Then the *Glorious* capsized and sank. The *Acasta* fired her last torpedoes. Their tracks could not be seen, and the run of one of them was misjudged by the *Scharnhorst*'s captain. He turned his ship to an evading course for three minutes, then – too soon – back towards the enemy. As the British destroyer was crushed under the two battleships' massive shells, the *Scharnhorst* was hit near her after turret, sustaining heavy damage. Admiral Marschall, who had led the German surface ships to their most successful day since the Battle of Coronel in 1914, turned his force towards

Trondheim in the early evening, leaving the survivors in the water.

The *Acasta*'s torpedo may have saved a lightly escorted convoy with 14,000 troops that was a hundred miles north of the German force and right in its path. The torpedo also eliminated any German thoughts of rescuing survivors, because it was believed to have come from a submarine. So effective was German radio jamming and so unlucky were the survivors that none of them were sighted for two and a half days, when only forty-six were found and rescued. Only the cruiser *Devonshire* had heard a badly garbled message from the *Glorious*; and she dared not repeat it, as she had the King of Norway aboard and was only a hundred miles from the battle scene.

The Royal Air Force attacked the ships at Trondheim three days later, without result. The Home Fleet, scattered in response to false alarms in the Iceland-Faeroes area and the imperative demands of the Dunkirk evacuation, did not strike back until five days later. The *Ark Royal*'s bombers pressed home an attack against the ships at Trondheim against stiff fighter opposition and the ships' anti-aircraft fire. Only one dud bomb hit the *Scharnhorst*, for which the British paid with eight downed aircraft. On June 20th the *Gneisenau* and the *Hipper* feinted towards Iceland to cover the damaged *Scharnhorst*'s move south; but the submarine *Clyde* cut the sortie short with a single torpedo hit on the *Gneisenau*, and the ships returned to Trondheim. Eventually all of them reached Germany, where most of the Navy's heavy ships underwent major repairs. That ended the Norwegian campaign – but not its repercussions.

The Naval Operations Staff criticized Admiral Marschall's refusal to adhere to the plan for the sortie. Marschall argued with Raeder about a sea commander's freedom of action and what he considered Group West's interference with operations. Those arguments led to a breakdown in Marschall's health and to his request for extended sick leave. Two years later he was appointed

Commander of Group West, which he considered a vindication of his earlier ideas.

Marschall was the second Commander of the Fleet to resign in little over half a year. His predecessor, Admiral Hermann Boehm, had also differed with Raeder over the role of the group commands and over the use of heavy ships to cover the destroyers' offensive minelaying sorties in the first two months of the war. He also was later placed in a position of great responsibility as Naval Commander in Norway. The next Commander of the Fleet after Marschall – Vice-Admiral Günther Lütjens – was to feel constrained to follow orders as literally as possible. That eventually helped to bring about the German Navy's greatest tragedy.

While the Norwegian campaign was still in progress, Dönitz demanded an investigation of the torpedo failures, which eventually led to several courts martial. The mechanical defects were eliminated one by one, but not until February 1942 was the cause of the depth-regulator failure discovered, and a reliable magnetic detonator was not supplied until December of that year. The improved contact detonators closed the gap until then; but since hits on ships' sides were not as destructive as below-the-keel explosions, more torpedoes were needed to sink ships. As a result many ships were only damaged, and many submarines were forced to break off patrols early when they ran out of torpedoes.

The value of Norway as a base against Great Britain was not so great as had been anticipated because of the unexpected conquest of France, with its far-better-placed Biscay ports and Channel-coast airfields; but access to the Atlantic and the French bases would have been far more difficult without the Norwegian bases. The Norwegian bases lacked proper facilities, and military activities there were monitored closely by the British-Norwegian espionage net. The route through the Iceland Passages was dangerous for surface ships – although shorter and less dangerous than the old one between Norway and the Shetlands and then through the Iceland Passages. Iceland itself was occupied by the British.

The Russian attitude was one of benevolent neutrality. As soon as they heard of the Norway move, they expressed their appreciation to the Germans for clearing their flank against the Allies. They were to see the new German bases in quite a different light one year later.

The iron-ore traffic was temporarily interrupted but later restored. Economically, the gains at least balanced the losses: access to Swedish ore was saved and the British-Scandinavian trade was stopped.

The Allied naval losses – one aircraft carrier, two cruisers, nine destroyers, six submarines, and smaller ships, as well as damage to four cruisers, eight destroyers, and some others – were serious but not in any sense crippling. Had German torpedoes been effective, many more British ships would have been sunk or damaged.

The German naval losses were heavy, but that had been expected. One heavy cruiser, two light cruisers, ten modern destroyers, four submarines, and some smaller ships were lost; and the two battleships, one *Deutschland*, one heavy cruiser, and several other ships were damaged at the campaign's end. The delay in getting the heavy units back into action was serious, especially as it freed British naval forces to reinforce the Mediterranean fleets; but the only losses that affected the war against England on the high seas were those of the new heavy cruiser *Blücher* (a ship of rather moderate range anyway) and the four submarines. The others were valuable ships but were too short-ranged to operate in the Atlantic, so they could not have affected the strategic situation significantly.

The one German failure was in the political sphere. The Norwegian King and Government escaped, and while the Germans forced the surrender of the various Norwegian Army units in the field, they were never able to get the support of the people for the régime.

All in all, however, the Norwegian campaign was a brilliant military success.

Chapter 4

SEA LION

The hesitant victors
June 1940–September 1940

THE *'Sitzkrieg'* was blasted into history's scrap heap on May 10, 1940. German armour poured westwards through Luxembourg and the Ardennes Forest to end the Phony War by driving a fifty-mile-wide wedge between the French Army at the Maginot Line and the British Army to the north. Within days the Maginot Line became a mocking monument to French defeatism; and the shattered bravado of the song, *We will hang out our washing on the Siegfried Line,* haunted British columns falling back towards the trap of the havenless coast, their march accompanied by the shrieking hell of the Stuka dive bomber and their ears attuned to the wraithlike rumble of the Panzers ahead of them to the south. The German Army thrust covered more than 200 miles in eleven days to strike the coast. Then the Germans turned north to annihilate the British Army.

The Dunkirk evacuation of May 27th to June 5th was primarily a German Air Force problem because of the Navy's involvement in Norway, although the motor torpedo boats sank several destroyers and other craft. German small submarines, operating in constricted waters full of British escort vessels, accomplished little, though they were at that time permitted to sink any ship in shallow waters without regard to prize law. Mines could be blamed if any diplomatic repercussions followed. The Allied evacuation was an excellent example of how a determined use of sea power could carry through an operation despite an opposing Air Force. Admittedly conditions for aerial interference were not ideal; yet British and French willingness to accept losses made the operation possible.

The Dutch Fleet had retreated to England, as expected, and remained loyal to the Queen in exile. The Dutch bases were soon put to limited use by German light forces.

The French Fleet retreated first from its Channel bases and then from its Atlantic ones, with French North Africa being the ultimate destination of most of its units. No warships were left to the Germans. Motorized German naval commandos followed the Army to secure as many ships as possible, but those commando forces were too small for independent action. The totally unexpected speed of the advance apparently prevented the planning of any surprise operation to take some ships before the French could move or destroy them. How much value the Army leaders would have placed on such operations is questionable, as inter-service cooperation was usually poor. During the French retreat the most valuable of the last-minute refugees, the incomplete battleship *Jean Bart*, escaped just hours before the Germans arrived in St-Nazaire, although, because her anti-aircraft guns were inoperable, she would have been easy to stop with bombers.

Hitler had won his greatest victory and had given the Navy its greatest opportunity to wage a high-seas war against Germany's sole surviving opponent; but first a complex series of alternatives had to be considered and a strategy had to be fought out – not in the broad Atlantic but among the wills of such diverse personalities as Raeder, Hitler, Göring, and Colonel-General Franz Halder, Chief of the Army General Staff.

As early as November 1939 Raeder had anticipated a demand for an invasion of England should the Army's planned offensive reach the Channel. He had ordered the Naval Operations Staff to investigate that seemingly academic problem. The study had been sent to the Army and Air Force Staffs once it had been determined that the operation had a chance of success; but the Air Force was very negative and the Army requirements were too large. Neither Hitler nor the OKW was informed of those tentative moves, for the rapid defeat of France seemed quite unlikely. Neither at that time nor at any other did anyone in authority seem to have been wholeheartedly in favour of Operation Sea Lion – the projected invasion of England – yet the potential consequences of its success impelled its development.

In late May of 1940, when the German Army had reached the Channel, Hitler had not yet thought seriously about the next step in the war against Britain. In a conference on May 21st, 1940, when Raeder first brought up the Naval Operations Staff study, Hitler showed little interest. Raeder had done his duty in pointing out the new strategic possibilities; with that rebuff he initiated little additional planning.

The imminent collapse of France produced no marked change in the situation. The size of the Army was cut by one-fifth, and no Service other than the Navy was thinking seriously about Sea Lion. The Navy's earmarking of shipping, collection of information, and other similar staff activities were by no means full-scale preparations; they were preliminary preparations for a possible directive only. The French request for armistice negotiations, followed by Churchill's 'finest hour' speech, still made no apparent impression on Hitler. Raeder explained the continuing naval preparations for Sea Lion on June 20th, but Hitler added nothing to the discussion. Raeder stressed the need for aerial supremacy, but there was no mention of prior consultation with the Air Force Staff. The Army Staff considered the operation almost impossible and had done nothing. As a final indication of his interests at the time, Hitler toured the Western Front with World War I comrades; visited Paris, where he ordered a victory parade prepared; and then spent the last week of June and the first week of July in the Black Forest, far from his command organizations. On July 6th he made a triumphal entry into Berlin – but quickly returned to his mountain retreat, where he did very little towards the further prosecution of the war. He seemed, in fact, to regard it as over.

In that first week of July the Army and the OKW began to take some notice of the possibilities of Sea Lion. Weeks had already been wasted when Army-Navy Staff talks on technical problems began on July 1st. The talks anticipated by one day the OKW order to all Services to investigate the feasibility of Sea Lion. The directive assumed that aerial supremacy would be essential, and allotted basic tasks on that assumption. The Army was asked to investigate only coastal artillery support for the crossing and to gather intelligence on British powers of resistance. The Air Force task was to estimate the chance of obtaining aerial supremacy, the degree of that supremacy, and the value of airborne landings. The Navy, the weakest of the three Services, was to survey landing sites and British coastal defences, estimate the number of its available ships, and select the best sea routes for a wide-front assault by twenty-five to forty highly mechanized divisions. Even at first glance it seemed a very difficult assignment, for at the time Germany had practically none of the heavy warships that were essential to support the myriad transports and small craft comprising the invasion shipping.

On July 3rd the British emphasized their determination to fight on by their attack on the French Fleet units that had fled to the French North African port of Oran. The British obviously were preparing for a long war by destroying any naval forces that might be drawn into Hitler's orbit. The attack was carried out despite French pledges that the ships would never be handed over to Germany. The British decision to attack a former ally provided a grim warning that Sea Lion was no longer an academic problem.

Within a week of the OKW directive the Navy was warning the other Services of some limits to the operational possibilities. Defining Sea Lion as basically a transport problem, the Naval Operations Staff stated that the Dover area was the only one suitable for large-scale landings because of the absolute necessity for protection from air and naval attack. The Army and Air Force were asked to state their operational intentions, but the geographical limits were emphasized. Already disquieting problems were being found, ranging from a lack of intelligence to a distrust of the value of firing heavy guns over the Channel.

Göring, speaking to the Army's Halder on July 11th, was confident that he could destroy the Royal Air Force in a month or less; but Raeder, who was faced with the most difficult part of the project, was much less optimistic when he talked to Hitler on the same day. He advocated intensification of submarine and air activity under a proposed 'siege of Britain' announcement by Hitler. He also suggested bringing the full impact of the war home to the British people by cutting off their imports and disrupting the life of the nation through air attacks on such cities as Liverpool and London and by mining of the Thames. Those moves, he thought, might force the British to come to terms. Sea Lion he termed a last resort, and one he could not recommend. Its absolute requisites were complete air superiority and a mine-free naval passage flanked by heavy minefields. The preparations for it involved a heavy drain on the German economy, especially on its inland waterways transport. Hitler seemed to agree with Raeder, mentioned his pet heavy guns, and went on to other topics. He still seemed unconvinced of the value of Sea Lion.

Hitler discussed the British problem with the Army leaders two days later, remarking on Britain's stubborn unwillingness to make peace and asking for opinions. Based on Army recommendations, the OKW order of July 15th directed that preparations be made for execution of Sea Lion at any time after August 15th. Directive 16, of July 16th, caught the Navy by surprise and faced it with unexpected problems of timing and scale. Clearly showing the impress of Army ideas, Directive 16 was still based on a contingency: elimination of Britain as a base against Germany by invasion was to be accomplished only 'if necessary'. Sea Lion was to be a surprise operation on a broad front from Ramsgate to Lyme Bay (200 miles), with the Air Force to act as artillery and the Navy as engineers. The destruction of the RAF was assumed, so that mine clearance and mine-barrier laying could be accomplished, while heavy guns would cover the operations. The Italians were to tie down much of the British Fleet in the Mediterranean, and Home Fleet units in the North Sea were to be bombed and torpedoed. Other questions mentioned were preliminary seizure of the Isle of Wight or the coast of Cornwall and the use of paratroops as assault-wave or later-wave troops. The preliminary-invasion idea was not heard of again, but the scope of the operation worried Raeder, especially as the Army had suddenly begun to favour the move, looking upon it as a large-scale river crossing.

Three days later – the same day Hitler made an extremely vague 'peace offer' to the British in a speech to the Reichstag – Raeder sent the OKW a memorandum discussing all the problems of the operation from the Navy viewpoint. The issues posed in the memorandum were to be threshed out in varying terms until the autumn. First Raeder examined the physical problems. Damaged and limited-capacity harbours and waterways, unpredictable weather, rapid currents, and extreme tides created great hazards for landing craft committed to open beaches. Next, British defensive capabilities were assessed. Not all the British mines could be eliminated; and German mines probably could not stop a fully committed British Fleet, which could isolate the first troop wave despite the German naval forces. The ability of the Air Force to clear the air of RAF interference and to damage the British defences severely without seaborne heavy-artillery support was also questioned.

Despite those great difficulties Raeder asserted that no final conclusion could be reached until the transport problem was fully evaluated. Further comments of the Naval Staff at that time credited the British with a high degree of preparation for breaking up a landing by using their air, sea, and mobile land forces, which could not be surprised.

Despite the new optimism of the Army and the OKW, who were already planning the operations to take place on English soil, Hitler remained unconvinced of Sea Lion's value. His attitude in a conference on July 21st with Raeder, Commander-in-Chief of the Army Field-Marshal Walter von Brauchitsch, and Chief of the Air Force General Staff General Hans Jeschonnek was that Britain had no hope of alliances elsewhere and that an end to the war, while desirable, was not necessary. Hitler described Sea Lion as a daring operation against a determined enemy and mentioned the problems stressed by Raeder, but he maintained the necessity of using forty divisions despite the problems, if the invasion was ordered. Because of the bad autumn weather in the Channel, he set a deadline of September 1st for completion of general preparations, and of September 15th for completion of the aerial battle and placement of minefields and artillery. Several questions regarding naval preparedness and deadlines were asked; but Hitler's statement that inability to complete preparations by September 1st would call for the consideration of other plans closed the interview.

Throughout the period of planning for Sea Lion, Hitler's strange love-hate attitude towards Great Britain was evident. He did not understand sea power and feared its strength. For that reason, and because he felt the British were a people kindred to the Germans, he wished to form an alliance with them. Yet at the same time he was

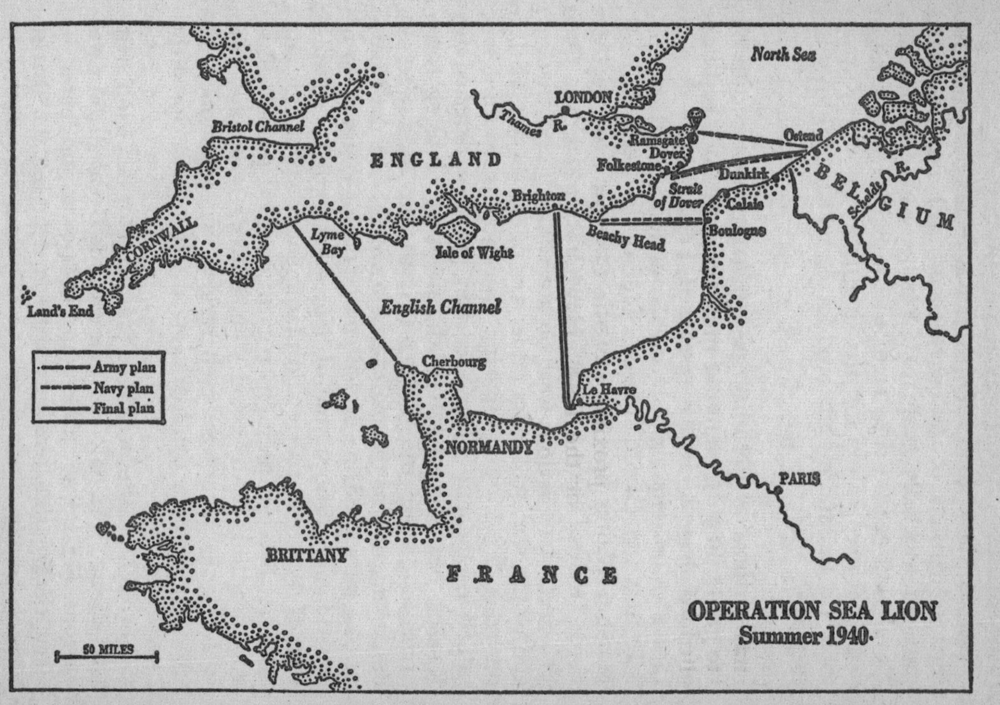

OPERATION SEA LION
Summer 1940

tempted by the prospect of another smashing triumph – especially if it could be gained with little risk.

During the remainder of July and early August various problems were defined in more concrete terms. The Army's minimum first-wave requirement of 100,000 men, and the shipping for them, was calculated. The size of the other waves was still not decided.

Since Dunkirk the Air Force had done little against England. Frequent small-scale raids had helped the flyers become accustomed to night flying and had tested a new navigational device that used intersecting radio beams to guide them to targets at night; but the raids had done little damage, and the British had been given time to build up the RAF. Only attacks on coastal convoys had brought the RAF to serious battle – at a disadvantage because of the proximity of the German bases and the lack of time for the RAF aircraft to concentrate. Even the coastal operations were on a small scale, and losses to both sides were not very heavy. On July 24th the Air Force had 3,500 aircraft available in three air fleets. Fighters in large numbers began to range over south-eastern England, expecting the RAF to challenge them in battles that would soon destroy it by attrition. The British failed to feed in their fighters, however, and the short-range German aircraft could not seek them out. When the bombers were sent out with the fighters some battles did take place, but the results were not at all satisfactory to the German Air Force.

During the next weeks, naval preparations continued, based on Directive 16 but with a requirement of thirteen divisions (260,000 men) rather than forty. The wide-front landings requested by the Army and the narrow-front capability of the Navy were not yet reconciled, nor were the Army's request for two to three days' landing time and the Navy's ten-day capability. Raeder believed that if Sea Lion were granted top priority and if aerial superiority could be achieved during the build-up, the basic requirements might be met by the end of August.

The advancing preparations did not mean that Raeder approved the operation, though. He had been cautious throughout; and on July 31st, in a conference with Hitler, he came out with his most vigorous statement of the naval viewpoint. Setting the earliest date as September 15th, he reviewed all the problems again, emphasizing the exposed position of the transports and the necessity for a narrow front. Then he recommended that the invasion be delayed eight months – until May 1941! Hitler still insisted that an attempt be made to prepare the operation for September 15th, setting the final decision aside to await the results of a week's heavy aerial assault on Britain, which had been ordered on July 30th to begin August 5th. He followed up the conference with a comprehensive directive emphasizing the September 15th target date but also directing that preparations were to continue beyond that date if postponement was necessary, so long as those preparations did not hurt the economy.

The decisive aerial battle opened rather quietly, with several nights of leaflet dropping. The leaflets were English translations of Hitler's 'peace offer' speech, and the fact that they were dropped shows that he still had some hope that the British would give in. British actions in attacking minesweepers and invasion shipping did not seem to influence Hitler's thinking. On the other hand, an offer by the King of Sweden to act as mediator, which met with no reaction in England, made no apparent impression on Hitler either.

The 'Day of the Eagles', delayed because of weather, finally came on August 15th. That day 1,790 aircraft were committed to the attacks on Britain. For the following two weeks Göring's 'Eagle Assault' hit a wide variety of targets, with forces totalling 2,669 aircraft. Coastal towns and shipping, industrial centres (with emphasis on aircraft factories), advanced fighter bases, and radar stations were attacked. Results were uncertain, and objectives varied from day to day, reflecting a basic confusion of purpose. The all-out assault on August 15th cost the Germans seventy-six aircraft and did relatively little damage, as the RAF broke up four out of five major attacks. The British fighters were very effective against the bombers, so that in the next few days the proportion of bombers to fighters in the German force was decreased to less than one in four. The vulnerable Stuka dive bombers were withdrawn from battle. The Germans had temporarily lost tactical flexibility in the need to protect their own bombers rather than attack British fighters.

Meanwhile a crucial battle was being fought on the strategic level. The key meeting took place on August 7th between Chiefs of Staff of the Army and Navy, Colonel General Halder and Vice-Admiral Otto Schniewind, respectively. The Navy's representative re-emphasized the advantages of crossing the Channel on a narrow front, and stated that concentration of minesweepers, defensive minefields, aircraft, coastal guns, and invasion shipping was absolutely essential. Halder likened the proposed concentration to feeding his troops into a sausage machine; for in the good defensive land around Dover his armour would have practically no opportunity for surprise, deployment, or manoeuvre. Field-Marshal Brauchitsch, the Army Commander-in-Chief, supplemented Halder's stand with a memorandum – which found support at OKW, where Jodl still hoped that the Air Force could hold the British in check.

Raeder asked for a decision in a conference with Hitler on August 13th. The Führer replied that a decision would be forthcoming after he had conferred with Army leaders and assessed the results of the aerial bombardment. Hitler again agreed with Raeder in calling Sea Lion a last resort – which, if it failed, would furnish the British a great victory.

Within the next week a compromise was finally worked out. While satisfying no one, it at last recognized the limitations of the available shipping. The Lyme Bay landings were cancelled; the Brighton landing to the east was reduced to a diversion, utilizing between 4,000 and 5,000 troops; and the Ramsgate landing was to be of similar size, made by paratroops. The main crossing was to be a modified narrow assault of six infantry divisions within six days, followed by six more divisions within ten days. The troops were to be carried mostly in barges – 1,722 of them, towed by 471 tugs – while 1,161 motorboats and 155 small transports of 3,000 to 5,000 tons were also to be employed. The ships were to be covered primarily by the Air Force, with additional support coming from thirteen coastal guns of 11-inch to 15-inch calibre; 6,800 mines; and twenty-seven coastal craft mounting 3-inch and 1.5-inch guns. As a diversion, four large, empty transports and four large warships were to feint towards the north-eastern coast of Britain, while the *Hipper* and the *Scheer* were to move to the Iceland-Faeroes area and perhaps into the Atlantic.

The effort was enormous; yet it was a confession of terrible weakness. The first troop waves were issued tiny, unarmoured river assault boats, which were fitted for launching from minesweepers and similar small craft. The large river barges were energetically collected from all over western Europe, modified with low bow ramps, floored with concrete, and sent by river and canal to the invasion ports extending from Boulogne to Ostend. Special landing craft that were being developed by each of the three Services (despite nominal naval priority) were too far from mass production to be considered for use at that time. The river barges were essential for the transport of submersible tanks, horses, equipment, and many of the men. The plan was for them to be towed across the channel in pairs by tugs, at an estimated speed of five knots. So many were involved that some of the barge groups were expected to be twelve miles long – without allowance for straggling, tides, currents, wind, or enemy action. After assembly off the German-held ports, their passage time would be, it was estimated, up to fifteen hours. Upon approaching the beaches the barges would be deployed into line and lashed into pairs of one powered and one unpowered barge. Then would begin the ponderous movement towards the shore for beaching.

The Army and Navy units in the ports cooperated enthusiastically, but practice had to be very limited – in an operation where skill and teamwork were critical. The small transports were far handier than the barges, but the unloading time was estimated at thirty-six hours. The left-flank move, from Le Havre to Brighton, was to be made by 300 small craft moving at seven knots – a situation best characterized by the German idea of *Himmelfahrtskommando* ('Heaven-bound command').

Waiting for that enormous collection of German craft were, according to the reasonably accurate German estimates, three or four light cruisers and twenty destroyers, ready to plunge in from each flank. Those British vessels would be supported quickly by more destroyers, light and heavy cruisers, battle cruisers, battleships, aircraft carriers, and hundreds of torpedo boats and other small craft. It was all strongly reminiscent of 1588, when Justin of Nassau kept his fleet safely tucked away in the mouth of the Scheldt, ready to pounce upon the Spanish the moment they embarked for England. As the Spanish commander, the Duke of Parma, had refused the bait, so Raeder saw commitment of the troops as an appalling prospect, no matter how much effect his submarines, mines, and light surface craft might have. Raeder, unlike Parma, could not ignore his sovereign's orders. He continued to counsel caution, however.

Still, preparations for the invasion continued in mid-August. A blockade announcement was issued, delimiting a large submarine operational area around the British Isles. Dover was shelled by heavy batteries across the Channel for the first time. The English-language German radio, which masqueraded as a British undercover operation, attempted to spread defeatism and dummy parachute harnesses were dropped on England for the same end. Despite all this, Hitler was secretly hedging. Attack plans against Russia were in preparation without Raeder's knowledge; and Hitler told some newly appointed field-marshals that he was opposed to gambling on Britain because he expected her to be defeated without invasion, but that an invasion would be undertaken if conditions were favourable. Hitler's exact attitude at any given time is hard to establish with certainty, but it appears that he was ready to welcome any alternative to invasion.

The last week in August saw preparations in full stride, with even the Air Force settling on a single, possibly decisive objective. Beginning on August 24th, Göring's flyers attacked the 'brains' of Fighter Command – the sector stations that provided the British with the means of correlating information from radar and other intelligence sources so as to send orders and information to their fighters. The stations enabled the RAF to concentrate aircraft to defeat the mass German attacks. With some stations out of operation, and with British aircraft drawn into battle under unfavourable conditions, resulting in losses almost equalling the Germans', the RAF was facing a potentially fatal attrition.

At month's end, major German shipping movements towards the Channel began according to plan. The ships in transit as well as in the harbours were attacked by British air and sea forces, while damage to inland waterways delayed them somewhat. Eventually about 10 per cent were sunk or damaged.

The Army's final orders were also issued at that time, amid growing discouragement within the Army High Command at the prospect of attacking a narrow defensive line with insufficient forces and few reinforcements. The compromises with naval necessity had largely changed the Army's mind. On September 3rd, an OKW directive set September 21st as the earliest potential invasion date, with orders for the execution of the move necessary ten days in advance.

With the deadline for decision so near, Hitler made a public speech in which he promised to wipe out all major

English cities in retaliation for two small RAF raids on Berlin. He also declared that, if the English wondered about his invasion plans, the answer was, 'He is coming.' In fact, however, Hitler knew that his Air Force could either support an invasion or attack the cities – but not both; and he had already made his choice.

London received its first mass attack, by 625 bombers, on September 7th, beginning an epic defence by the British that would rouse the admiration of the world. The beginning of the Blitz also marked the end of Sea Lion. The London raid had originally been planned as a one-day preamble to Sea Lion – an attempt to unbalance the British command structure through terror warfare; in the event, however, it became Sea Lion's substitute.

As early as the day before the Blitz began, Raeder had told his staff that Hitler expected to defeat the British without a landing. The Navy continued to prepare for the invasion date, going so far as to begin laying the defensive flank minefields and sweeping the British ones. However, notations as to the use of shipping in the event of a cancellation and comments on the air war suggest that Raeder, too, had hopes of British capitulation. Or perhaps he was simply thankful that an alternative had been presented to the patently hazardous Sea Lion.

Pessimistic reports continued to come in during the next few days. The weather was abnormally bad for flying, and it was apparent that the German Air Force had not gained control of the skies over south-eastern England.

On September 11th Hitler postponed the final decision for three days. Then, on the 13th, he told a group of generals that since the situation was favourable for Germany, the risk of Sea Lion was unnecessary. That made Raeder's memorandum prepared for the September 14th meeting with Hitler virtually unnecessary. In it Raeder re-emphasized the risks and advocated the continuation of the air attacks and the invasion preparations – the latter to keep pressure on the British. During the meeting Hitler agreed with Raeder. The methods for keeping continuous pressure on the British were reviewed, and the decision was again postponed, that time to the 17th.

After severe losses to the Air Force on September 15th Hitler decided to postpone the operation indefinitely. The conference of September 17th, 1940, marked the conclusion of serious consideration of the invasion of Britain.

The break-up of the preparations commenced two days later with a thinning out of the invasion shipping, to cut its losses from British action. Although some of the transport vessels were diverted to other purposes, they were not dispersed entirely. In mid-October dispersal was approved, but it was accomplished as unobtrusively as possible. Planning towards a possible resumption of the invasion operation in the spring of 1941 was continued.

Sea Lion was dead. Despite nominal preparations that did not end officially until February 1942, everyone in authority knew that it was over. All the destruction of the Blitz of London then became merely a product of an unworkable air-power theory and of the distorted idea that adversity would force the British civilians to give in.

Certainly Sea Lion did not reflect Raeder's ideas on sea power. The operation could be accomplished neither by surprise nor by the clash of two sea powers. The Norway operation could not be repeated, nor was the German Navy strong enough to clear the way by defeating the British Fleet. To the landsman Hitler, the psychological consequences of possible failure, rather than physical facts, were probably the biggest deterrent.

Sea Lion was an idea so obvious that it had to be considered. Once explored, it was then called off to prevent the slaughter of the troops during the crossing. Germany's invasion song *We are sailing against England* thus joined Britain's song of the Siegfried Line as a bitter memento of 1940's lost hopes.

Chapter 5

GRAND STRATEGY

The Mediterranean
June 1940–November 1942

THE British withdrawal at Dunkirk and the imminent collapse of France led Mussolini to take his unready country into the war, on June 10th, 1940, in hopes of sharing the spoils. The German armour shifted southwards from the Channel, drove deep into France, took Paris, and forced the French to sign an armistice on June 25th – in the same railway car at Compiègne in which the Germans had been humbled in 1918.

The French armistice completely transformed the naval war. From a situation in which the German and Italian Fleets were limited to defence of small segments of confined seas by far-superior enemy forces, the two Fleets suddenly found themselves in a remarkably improved position. While still inferior in numbers, they could challenge the British with the hope of at least local successes from much better-placed bases closer to the British lifelines. Conversely, the British lost the use of valuable bases, which lengthened their distances between havens and prohibited strikes from bases close to their enemies' home ports. The change was particularly important in the cases of French and French North African bases formerly used by British convoys and Fleet units; and of French Atlantic ports, newly available for German ship and submarine use.

In the coming naval struggle, the big questions were to be the disposition of the French North and West African colonies and, to a lesser extent, that of the French Fleet. Those problems were essentially political ones, and their resolution had to be found in the intricate and delicate relationships among the leaders of France, Germany, and Italy – with British action periodically upsetting the plans of one or all. A week before the armistice Raeder had sent Hitler a proposal for increasing German naval strength by moderate requisitions from the French Fleet; but Hitler had immediately rejected the idea, believing that the suggestion would simply drive the French Fleet into British ports. Basically Raeder believed in a more subtle approach to the problem, and the idea of requisitioning French ships was not broached again. Raeder and the Naval Staff hoped that it would be possible to come to some working agreement with the French Navy after the armistice if political concessions were made to the Vichy Régime. Hitler's attitude was that the war was practically over, and he was concerned that concessions to France would be resented by Mussolini; so he neither demanded French support nor granted a generous peace.

Mussolini had taken a reluctant nation into an apparently decided war by attacking France on June 10th. With better strategic sense than Hitler was displaying at the time, he asked the Germans for Tunisia, some Algerian ports, and Corsica; but since he had made no attempts to take them in his fifteen-day war, Hitler gave him nothing at the armistice. The French Fleet, together with its Mediterranean and West African bases, was neutralized, and Hitler pledged that Germany would make no claims on the ships, either then or in the future. The pledge eased the relationship between the German and French Navies and made German use of the French skilled-labour force in the French Atlantic dockyards much easier to arrange.

The French Navy's Commander-in-Chief, Admiral Jean François Darlan, had issued rigid orders that no unit of his Fleet was to be allowed to fall into the hands of any foreign power. Hitler's official solicitude for French honour was probably a reflection of his inability to seize the ships and of his failure to grasp the strategic potential of French cooperation. The idea of a country surrendering its fleet was unthinkable to Raeder, who had agreed with the Imperial Navy's scuttling in 1919 and who, twenty years later, had ordered the *Graf Spee*'s captain to scuttle in preference to internment.

Somewhat offsetting the German failure to benefit to the greatest extent from the French armistice was Italy's belligerence. At first the Italian Fleet, which had not expected war before 1942 at the earliest, was on a strategic defensive despite Mussolini's pronouncements. The Italian High Command began the war without operational plans or grand strategy, and Mussolini declared to his advisors that he would fight a 'parallel war, not with or for Germany, but only for Italy at the side of Germany'.* The naval leaders told Mussolini that they could gain nothing against the British and French and could expect to lose the Fleet and the Air Force. In fact the main task of the Italian Navy turned out to be convoy work to Libya, an area that pre-war naval plans had expected to be self-sufficient. In addition, the Navy carried out attacks on British convoys and Malta.

By the time of the French armistice several engagements between French and Italian naval and aerial forces had taken place, but they had not changed the situation significantly. With the armistice broader strategic plans could be made, including an attack on the British-held island of Malta; but the Italian High Command did not agree with the Italian Navy's plan to take the island. A short war was expected, and the Italian Air Force promised to neutralize the weakly defended base. Italian East Africa was written off should the war be long, for it had no communications.

So matters stood in late June 1940. The Italians wanted no German aid for fear of German domination, and no

* Friedrich Ruge, *Der Seekrieg*, p 132.

GREENLAND
Denmark Strait
Reyk
Boundaries, Summer 1940
Limits of first phase, Mediterranean campaign
Possible later moves
Capital ship dispositions, July 1, 1940
(All Home Fleet ships are show
off Scapa Flow, although they
were constantly on the move.)
Battleship or battle cruise
Aircraft carrier
British
French
Germa
Italian
CANADA
Halifax
UNITED STATES
Azores Is.
Cape Hatteras
North Atlantic Ocean
Gulf of Mexico
GERMAN NAVAL STRATEGY
Summer 1940
German
Italian
Caribbean Sea
Aruba
Curaçao
Martinique
Trinidad
Cape V
PANAMA CANAL

North Cape
Barents Sea
Alten Fiord
Tromsø
Harstad
Narvik
Murmansk
Vest Fiord
ARCTIC CIRCLE
White Sea
ICELAND
Faeroe Is.
Trondheim
SWEDEN
FINLAND
Shetland Is.
Bergen
Oslo
Leningrad
Stavanger
ESTONIA
Baltic Sea
LATVIA
UNION OF
SOVIET SOCIALIST
REPUBLICS
North Sea
Danzig
LITHUANIA
ENGLAND
Berlin
IRELAND
London
GERMAN EUROPE
English Channel
Stalingrad
Brest
SWITZERLAND
St. Nazaire
ROMANIA
Ploesti
Bay of Biscay
UNOCCUPIED FRANCE
Black Sea
Balkans
Caspian Sea
PORTUGAL
ITALY
Istanbul
ALBANIA
SPAIN
Naples
Taranto
TURKEY
Sicily
Cape Matapan
Gibraltar
MOROCCO
Algiers
Tunis
SYRIA
Crete
LEBANON
Casablanca
Oran
TUNISIA
Malta
Mediterranean Sea
IRAQ
IRAN
FRENCH MOROCCO
Benghazi
PALESTINE
Alexandria
Tripoli
Tobruk
El Alamein
JORDAN
ALGERIA
Persian Gulf
SUEZ CANAL
EGYPT
LIBYA
SAUDI ARABIA
Red Sea
FRENCH WEST AFRICA
ANGLO-EGYPTIAN SUDAN
Dakar
ITALIAN EAST AFRICA

real cooperation existed between the two powers. Italy was plagued with its own organizational fragmentation – which followed German lines fairly closely, though not intentionally. For Italy's numerous Mediterranean problems the OKW had little sympathy, understanding, or interest, and Hitler usually considered the Italian theatre of war unimportant despite Navy pleadings. Each side sent high-ranking accredited observers to the other's headquarters, but those had little influence.

The prospects for cooperation were obviously not good; yet the Italians had six battleships available or being refitted, nineteen cruisers (with more being built), and numerous destroyers. Although deficient in night fighting, torpedo work, radar, underwater sound ranging, and anti-aircraft armament, and with almost non-existent Air Force cooperation, the ships were fast and could shoot well. The position of Italy in the mid-Mediterranean forced the British to split their Mediterranean fleet and offered unusual opportunities to the Italians. They had to be considered in any German plans.

In that new strategic world Raeder and the Naval Operations Staff very quickly developed their second great plan: the Mediterranean Plan. (The first was the Z-Plan.) They saw that the two key points in the British Mediterranean power structure – Gibraltar and Suez – were vulnerable. By capturing those two bases Germany would force the British out of the Mediterranean, free the Italian Fleet for use in the Atlantic and Indian Oceans, and hasten victory over Britain by making possible the maximum deployment of force against British oceanic communications.

The assault on the Mediterranean would involve German troop movements through France, Spain, and probably French North and West Africa. Once Gibraltar was taken and the French and Spanish leaders became committed to working with Hitler, bases in Spain and French West Africa, such as Dakar, would become available to the German and Italian surface and submarine forces. Those forces would seriously threaten the British South Atlantic and Indian Ocean commerce. Already German naval power was reaching into the Atlantic, as a result of the acquisition of ports on the Bay of Biscay. Those ports provided bases for German surface and submarine units and an Italian submarine group; but they were close to British home ports and thus subject to surveillance and, later, to interdiction.

The projected southern bases were out of effective British reach – a fact particularly important for surface ships, which were vulnerable to air attacks when in port. Another advantage would accrue to the Germans: the acquisition of more repair yards would free German shipyards to concentrate on new construction, especially of submarines. The Atlantic phase of the Plan, then, would open numerous naval opportunities with few risks. Secure occupation of the Canaries was even considered feasible, through German aerial and maritime reinforcement of their Spanish garrisons once Spain was committed to joining the war. Those islands would furnish an excellent location, together with continental European and African bases, for air bases to cooperate with surface raiders and submarines against British commerce.

Meanwhile, in the eastern Mediterranean, according to the Plan, the Suez Canal would be seized and troop movements through Palestine and French-mandated Syria would be expedited. Those actions would place Turkey and the Dardanelles, as well as the Balkans, out of reach of British help – and therefore under German power. Italian East Afria would be saved, its ports made available for Italian Fleet units, and the British–India trade threatened from a new direction. Farther eastwards still, the vital British oil supplies of the Middle East would be open to easy conquest. Russia's sensitive Georgian oil frontier and her long Black Sea coast could be threatened at will, while her northern flank lay exposed along the Baltic and White Seas.

To the German naval strategists the appeal of a Mediterranean campaign lay not only in its objectives but in its economy of force. In the west, political concessions such as African colonial adjustments, supplemented by small Army and Air Force units and brief Navy participation, would be required; but the most important campaign – the attack on British commerce in the Atlantic – could be continued with hardly a break. Commerce-raiding cruises by German heavy surface ships would in fact aid Mediterranean moves by distracting the Gibraltar and Home Fleet and by preventing reinforcement of the Alexandria Fleet. In the east, no German naval forces would be involved but only a small number of armoured divisions and air groups cooperating with the Italian Navy, Air Force, and Army.

The German Navy's Mediterranean Plan was predicated on the solution of some complex international political problems; but with the threat of the overwhelming strength available in the German Army and Air Force, it is difficult to conceive how such men as Spain's Fascist dictator, Generalissimo Francisco Franco, or France's Admiral Darlan could have held out long against German pressure. So favourable was Germany's position that Hitler needed the cooperation of only one of the two leaders. He could have played them off against each other. The occupation of Gibraltar, Spanish Morocco, and the Canaries would have flanked French North and West Africa while the western Mediterranean was sealed. As an alternative, occupation of the French territories and seizure of Malta would have threatened Gibraltar and flanked Spanish Morocco while the central Mediterranean was sealed. In any case, from the German Navy's viewpoint the political problems were Hitler's to solve, not Raeder's. Russia, the timid giant, was to be offered concessions in the region of Iran, Afghanistan, and north-western India as the Germans took the Dardanelles.

Defence of that vast new area would be based on the Mediterranean – with the unassailable Sahara, to the south, fringed by a few heavily fortified ports on the rugged and inhospitable western African shore. To the north an 'Atlantic Wall' would be buttressed by mobile forces operating on interior lines in western Europe. Mussolini's 'Mare Nostrum' would become an Axis military and commercial highway, and the lower North Atlantic a baseless and dangerous wasteland for the British.

With Joseph Stalin's unwillingness to fight except defensively and with all the resources of western Europe concentrated against the British Isles and their supply lines, the chances for forcing British capitulation would have been quite good, especially if Hitler's demands had been moderate. It is doubtful if even Churchill could have led the British through long-sustained warfare if British supplies had dropped to the starvation level. The United States of 1940–1, no matter what political decisions were taken, was incapable of rapidly mobilizing sufficient forces to alter the British condition decisively.

Hitler ordered practical preparation for carrying out the plan as early as July 1940, but to what extent he supported it is not clear. He never clearly opposed it; but even as he gave the orders, his energies and ambitions were being drawn in other directions. Already he had his eyes on Russia. He was also considering some highly impractical schemes, such as the seizure of Iceland – a notion that shows how poor was his understanding of naval capabilities.

While the Germans hesitated in regard to the Mediterranean, the British acted. The French Fleet was too dangerous, in their eyes, to be allowed to remain at large despite the armistice terms and French pledges. On July 3rd, 1940, all French ships in British home ports were seized by the British and added to their Navy. The French force at Alexandria was neutralized by a gentleman's agreement between the admirals there – but only after the French had awakened on July 4th to stare into the uncovered muzzles of the British Fleet's guns. The Oran group of two old battleships and two new battle cruisers, six large destroyers, and a seaplane tender was faced with a British ultimatum backed by two battleships, a battle cruiser, an aircraft carrier, two cruisers, and eleven destroyers. The French were given the choice of joining the British fleet and continuing the war against Germany; leaving for the USA, a British port, or the West Indies; scuttling; or fighting the British. Just six hours was permitted for a decision because of the danger that French forces from nearby ports might intervene or that the ships at Oran might raise steam and make a run for the open sea.

The diplomacy on both sides was poor; the ultimatum was rejected and the French cleared for action. The British then reluctantly conducted a military execution. The old battleship *Bretagne* was set afire before she could get under way, and eleven minutes after the first shot she capsized and sank, with 977 dead. The new *Dunkerque* was crippled by four 15-inch shells and forced to anchor minutes after getting under way. The old *Provence* was beached to prevent her from sinking. Of the heavy ships only the fast, new *Strasbourg* cleared the harbour, accompanied by five destroyers and pursued unsuccessfully by the British. The sixth destroyer had her stern blown off when her own depth charges were set off by a British shell.

Three days later the British returned to score an aerial torpedo hit on an escort ship lying alongside the *Dunkerque*. The explosion of the small vessel's depth charges damaged the battle cruiser severely. Two days after that, the incomplete battleship *Richelieu* was torpedoed at Dakar by carrier aircraft. The *Strasbourg*, meanwhile, had entered the harbour at Toulon, which was in that area of France not controlled by Germany and called the Free Zone. The battle cruiser soon became the centre of a concentration of cruisers and destroyers from various North African ports. Later the temporarily repaired *Dunkerque* joined them.

The Germans promptly permitted the French Fleet to remain on a war footing rather than disarm. That moment of French demoralization and confusion might have offered an opportunity for dramatic German political moves, especially if they were directed towards the shaken and enraged commanders of the French Fleet; but nothing was done. Hitler, secure in his mountain retreat and waiting for the British to come to terms, failed to take the long-range view, as usual. The British, on the other hand, had clearly demonstrated their traditional interest in the Mediterranean and their determination to remain there even at the expense of the Home Fleet. As in the days of Pitt and Nelson, they had displayed their willingness to take risks, sure that the resiliency of their sea power would enable them to shift forces enough to make up for losses wherever they occurred. Despite deficiencies in equipment and bases, the British were ready to take the initiative and to fill gaps with forces from outside the Mediterranean if necessary.

While Italian and British Fleet units fought several engagements, which did not change the balance of power, the German High Command moved to consolidate the Mediterranean from several directions. On July 15th Vichy was asked for use of French North African bases, but refused to grant them. Hitler did not press the French. The Germans offered aid to the Italians for a drive on Suez, but Mussolini felt that accepting the two proffered Panzer divisions would result in German control of 'his' war. The move to Gibraltar through Spain also was being planned.

In August the Italians reached their peak strength of five operational battleships, two of them new ships that were among the finest in the world. The British also built up their forces, increasing the Alexandria Fleet to four battleships and two aircraft carriers plus smaller units. Both sides prepared for a showdown in the Mediterranean.

Early in September German plans for Gibraltar, Suez, and the Canaries were again discussed by Raeder and Hitler. The decision to allow French ships to go to West Africa to defend against Free French and British attacks added urgency to the planning. On the 23rd the expected blow was struck at Dakar; but the French beat it off in a three-day battle, losing two submarines and a large destroyer in exchange for damage to several British ships and the destruction of four carrier aircraft.

One day later Raeder made his strongest presentation of the advantages of concentrating on the British, particularly in the Mediterranean, rather than on Russia. He insisted on moves towards Gibraltar; the Canaries, with Air Force aid; and Suez, by the Italians with German aid. He pictured the Mediterranean as the pivot of the British Empire, and Italy as Britain's main target, although the Italians were unaware of it. Stressing the need for haste because of likely American intervention, he showed the advantages of having the Mediterranean in German hands for moves on Turkey and the Indian Ocean, as well as for securing supplies for southern Europe. Raeder urged efforts to obtain the use of French North and West Africa lest the British take advantage of their possibilities. Hitler seemed to agree. He was already doubtful of Franco's aid, but would seek it and that of France in exchange for colonial advantages granted to those powers. He was also interested in the Portuguese Cape Verde and Azores Islands, but Raeder tried to dissuade him on that point.

By mid-October, with Sea Lion out of the way, Mediterranean planning was moving forward well; and German naval units were ready to reinforce the Spanish garrison of the Canaries prior to Air Force descent on the islands and Spanish entry into the war. On October 23rd came the first sharp setback to the Plan, however: Franco, who had seemed cooperative, hedged in a meeting with Hitler and refused to commit Spain until the Germans had demonstrated a clear superiority over the British by the capture of Suez or the invasion of Britain. As in his dealings with the French. Hitler accepted Franco's refusal even though he could have forced compliance.

Five days later the Italians invaded Greece, against the advice of Italian naval leaders and without informing their ally. That led to an enormous dispersion of Italian resources and to a fatal weakening of the forces designated for the conquest of Egypt. In addition, the Greeks granted bases on Crete, in mainland Greece, and in the Aegean Sea to the British, which supplemented Malta and threatened the stretched Italian convoy routes. In effect a Balkan front was opened, which decreased the chances of defeating the British and which would have been entirely unnecessary had Suez been taken.

The Italians were still unwilling to accept German armoured divisions early in November, but the Air Force had started a group of more than 400 aircraft *en route*. According to the OKW's Jodl, in a conference with the Navy's Schniewind, the British in Greece had become a threat to the Rumanian oil fields, which were crucial to Germany's war economy. A move to cut the British off by seizing Suez, through Turkey and Palestine via French Syria, was considered too difficult. Hitler's determination to take Gibraltar as a combined operation of the German Army, Air Force, and Navy with Spanish aid, and his interest in the Canaries and Cape Verdes were stressed by Jodl. He also assured Schniewind that France would cooperate and asked if Portugal might not be of use to the Navy.

While the OKW tried to reassure the Navy, another blow fell. Shortly after sunset on November 11th, 1940, the British aircraft carrier *Illustrious* launched a tiny force of twenty aircraft, eleven of them slow biplanes carrying 18-inch aerial torpedoes and the rest carrying bombs and flares, against the Italian battle line in Taranto Harbour. Diving into the midst of the defence from several directions, dodging barrage balloons and antiaircraft fire, the planes lined up on the capital ships, which were silhouetted by parachute flares. Six torpedoes found their targets – an incredibly high percentage of hits – and did very heavy damage. The single torpedo that hit the old *Cavour* sank her in shallow water, putting her out of the war permanently. The old *Duilio*, also hit by a single torpedo, required six months to repair, while the new *Littorio* survived three hits and was safely moved away from an unexploded torpedo with magnetic detonator that was embedded in the mud under her keel. She was out of action for over three months. The remainder of the battleships withdrew to Naples, clearing the east central Mediterranean of Italian heavy ships. That massive tactical and strategic victory was gained at the price of two downed British aircraft. One airman was killed and three were captured.

On November 14th Raeder and Hitler went over the situation in about the same terms as had Schniewind and Jodl at their conference; but the real threat to the whole Mediterranean operation was clearly stated in Raeder's warning not to attack Russia—a country Hitler had been thinking of attacking for some time. Raeder also had considerable difficulty in dealing with Hitler's tendency to divert strength towards hazardous objectives. At that time such an objective was the Portuguese Azores, which Hitler wanted for air bases against the British and, eventually, against the United States. Raeder pointed out the problems of taking and holding the islands and indicated the political problems involved in their seizure from a neutral. Hitler thought the British would take them, with Portugal neutral or not. Raeder preferred a neutral Portugal, and called the other islands, the Cape Verdes and Madeiras, useless to either side. Raeder returned to the topic of Gibraltar at his next meeting with Hitler on December 3rd; but Hitler then was interested in the nearly impossible project of acquiring Irish bases for aircraft.

Meanwhile the British were planning to take the initiative in Africa. On December 9th Major General Richard O'Connor began an operation with 36,000 men—which was to end on February 7th, 1941, with the annihilation of the 200,000-man Italian Army and the capture of all of eastern Libya.

Then the final blows to Raeder's strategic scheme were dealt by Hitler himself. On December 11th an OKW directive cancelled the Spain-Gibraltar-Canaries operation because 'political conditions' had changed. On December 18th, Führer Directive 21 (code-named 'Barbarossa') ordered preparations for an assault on Russia before the end of the war with Britain. Russia was to be overwhelmed in a rapid campaign, during which the Navy was to continue operations against Britain with some Air Force aid. Raeder protested against the Russian offensive for the last time on December 27th. He reiterated all the strategic ideas of the past months; but Hitler stated that Russia had to be eliminated quickly. Directive 21 really ended any hopes for fighting and winning a single-front war in the Mediterranean and on the Atlantic sea lanes. In the next months the Southern Front was to be treated as a holding operation, to keep Italy in the war and leave the opportunity open to develop its potential after the Russian campaign was over in late 1941. The Mediterranean Plan could not be merely shelved, however. Once postponed, it was useless, for the Russian campaign so altered the balance of power that Germany never regained the opportunity to set the Mediterranean Plan in motion.

During the summer and autumn of 1940 German naval planners considered the possibility of extending the sea war to the Orient. Again Hitler acted cautiously, as did the Japanese. While a military alliance was tentatively offered by the Japanese in June 1940, it was not until September that a ten-year defensive alliance was signed. It was obviously aimed at the United States, not at Great Britain. Raeder kept insisting that German strategy demanded a Japanese attack on Singapore, to pin down British military strength in the Far East while also threatening the entire British commerce in the Indian Ocean. Hitler seemed to appreciate the concept. The Russo-Japanese Non-Aggression Pact of April 1941 seemed to Hitler to provide just the opportunity for Japan to strike at Singapore; but a month later the Japanese situation had to be described as 'confused'.

Really it was always so, for neither side trusted the other with basic secrets, neither informed the other of major operations, and both fought for their individual special purposes – to which others might contribute incidentally. The great dream of a German-Japanese pincer on the Indian Ocean existed only in the minds of German planners.

The Naval Operations Staff Indian Ocean strategy could have been implemented by Germany to a far greater extent than it at first appears. The Mediterranean Plan, with its Middle Eastern oil lands corollary, could have drawn the Japanese westwards, bypassing the Philippines by coercing the Dutch Loyalist Government in the Indies and the Vichy French Government in Indochina to provide the bases and economic resources that the Japanese needed in order to reach the Singapore gateway to the Indian Ocean. In 1940 and early 1941 the Japanese were still uncommitted as to their next moves, while President Roosevelt faced formidable 'America First' sentiment, which made American intervention unlikely. None of that stirred Hitler's imagination.

The spring of 1941 saw the opening of the Balkan campaign, which resulted from Italy's failure in Greece and which was a preliminary to the Russian campaign. The German Army was to take the entire Balkan Peninsula, including mainland Greece. Hitler regarded the campaign as just a holding operation, to keep Italy in the war and preserve the flank of the Eastern Front against British interference. He even believed that he could afford to lose North Africa without serious consequences – although German armoured units, under Lieutenant-General Erwin Rommel, were finally committed to the desert in February.

Raeder, however, saw Rommel's planned North African offensive and the German campaign in Greece as opportunities to fulfil at least partially his Mediterranean hopes. Therefore he encouraged the taking of all Greece;

Italian naval action to interdict British supplies to Greece; support of a rebellion in Iraq; and an operation to take Malta. Raeder personally pressed his views on the Italian Commander-in-Chief of the Navy, Admiral Arturo Riccardi, in February, encouraging offensive use of the Italian Fleet despite Italian misgivings. Further pressure, exerted at still higher levels, finally resulted in orders by the Italian Supreme Command for the Italian Navy to support the German land moves by cutting the British Alexandria–Greece supply line.

The most important Italian action was a sortie towards Crete by the battleship *Vittorio Veneto,* supported by eight cruisers and thirteen destroyers, from March 26th to the 30th. Massive air cover and aerial reconnaissance had been assured to the force commander. That included direct cooperation by the German Air Fleet X for the first time. The Italian force lost the element of surprise on the afternoon of the second day, when it was sighted by a British long-range aircraft. The next day, although not covered by a single friendly land-based plane, two of the Italian ships launched small spotter planes, which soon brought them into contact with a British cruiser-destroyer group off southern Crete. An indecisive long-range engagement was broken off when British carrier-based torpedo planes attacked the *Vittorio Veneto* unsuccessfully. No British convoys had been located, and at least part of the British Alexandria Fleet was obviously near; so the sortie was terminated.

All afternoon the Italian retreat was harassed by British aerial torpedo and bomb attacks, while the skies remained empty of the promised overwhelming German and Italian air support. In mid-afternoon a dive-bomber attack attracted the *Vittorio Veneto*'s gunners long enough for three torpedo planes to slip in to close range. One torpedo smashed her port propellers, and 4,000 tons of water sluiced into the battleship, stopping her more than 400 miles from a haven. Efficient damage control enabled the Italians to restart the starboard engines and eventually to bring the battleship's speed to over 20 knots. Her accompanying cruisers and destroyers formed a tight defensive formation around her.

After sunset ten British torpedo planes flew into the blinding searchlights, smoke screens, and massive anti-aircraft fire to deliver a twenty-minute attack that stopped the heavy cruiser *Pola* dead in the water. The battleship with its escort continued towards port, but two heavy cruisers and four destroyers turned back to aid the crippled cruiser. As the would-be rescuers reached the *Pola,* British destroyers caught them in their searchlights; and three British battleships tore the cruisers *Zara* and *Fiume* apart with three minutes of 15-inch shellfire at a range of one and a half miles. The British destroyers, aided by the battleships' secondary batteries, sank two of the Italian destroyers in a brief mêlée. The *Pola* was sunk before sunrise by the British destroyers, which removed the crewmen who had remained aboard. The entire operation cost the British one aeroplane and its crew, as against 3,000 dead Italian sailors.

The bloody end of the Battle of Cape Matapan confirmed the Italians in their reluctance to move offensively to the east. In the broad view, however, it was not the German insistence on action that was faulty, but the typical incredibly fragmented command structure, which made coordination nearly impossible. Four independent commands were involved: the Italian Navy, the Italian Air Force, the German Air Fleet X, and the Air Force of the Italian Governor of the Dodecanese Islands. No one – not even Mussolini or Hitler – could give orders to all four!

Despite his discouragements Raeder kept trying to point out the value of North Africa to Hitler, as well as the danger that the British, possibly with the aid of the French Fleet, would put the Italians on the defensive. Hitler, however, continued to show little interest in the Mediterranean.

More encouraging were Hitler's negotiations in May

with Admiral Darlan to open Syria, Lebanon, Tunisia, and Dakar to limited German use. In the long run nothing came of the talks. Considering the complex Vichy French politics, it is likely that the negotiations were never meant to achieve anything. In early June the British forestalled German moves by seizing Syria and Lebanon – a move that the French could not oppose effectively short of going to war against the British, which they did not want to do.

Meanwhile the Afrika Korps dramatically changed the desert war.* Striking on March 31st, Rommel pushed the main British Army eastwards out of Libya. Only the encircled bastion of Tobruk held out, its back to the sea. The British had lost the advantages of their earlier victory when they were stripped of many fine units that were sent to Greece. Only a fuel shortage and the menace of Tobruk, which did not break despite persistent German assaults, kept Rommel from dashing deep into Egypt.

The German Army in Europe, meanwhile, swept through the entire Balkan Peninsula, including the Greek mainland, in three weeks. The remaining British troops retreated to Crete and Alexandria after losing 12,000 men in the defence of Greece. The ships suffered severely from air attacks during the evacuation. The German Air Force proposed the capture of Crete for establishing an air base against the British and to deny them use of the island for attacks on the Rumanian oil fields and the Aegean area. The OKW Operations Staff, agreeing with the Navy, declared that Malta was more important than Crete; but Hitler's thoughts were bent eastwards, and he was especially sensitive to any threat to the Ploesti oil fields. He decided on Crete.

The airborne assault, begun on May 20th, became a viciously fought twelve-day battle of preponderantly light armed forces. The British had lost most of their heavy weapons in Greece, and the Germans could not bring up

* This was an Italian-German force, but the German divisions and the personality of their commander were so dominant that it is referred to as if all-German.

seaborne reinforcements through the tenacious British naval defence. Two small German convoys were turned back with losses, but the British Alexandria Fleet lost heavily to the German Air Force in the defence and later evacuation of the island. By the conclusion of the brief campaign, the British had lost three cruisers and six destroyers sunk, and two battleships, an aircraft carrier, six cruisers, and seven destroyers damaged, as well as many transports sunk or abandoned. The lesson of Dunkirk – that naval forces could operate under massed hostile air power only at great cost – was re-emphasized in Cretan waters. In exchange the German Air Force's élite parachute and glider troops were so mauled that Crete was their last employment as an independent striking force.

The German Air Force's Pyrrhic victory gave the Axis a flanking position on the Alexandria–Malta route, but Italian naval operations to destroy large parts of the retreating British forces at sea were never mounted, because of pressing commitments in the Sicilian Channel and because of lack of German aerial cooperation. The Italian Fleet also failed to stop a vital convoy sent by the British through the Mediterranean with supplies to stabilize the Egyptian Front. Ironically the hard-won position on Crete was to give the Germans practically no offensive advantages because the supply system through Greece was inadequate, and aviation gasoline and aircraft were consequently scarce. Even the relative nearness of Ploesti was no help: the oil had to be shipped to Italy for refining and then back to the island. By 1941 Italy was gripped by a severe fuel and tanker shortage, so Crete remained an isolated base.

Over all the plans and operations of the early months of 1941 hung the spectre of the supreme gamble of modern military history – the impending war with Russia. In late May all major operations in the eastern Mediterranean, including the drive to Suez, were postponed until after the end of the Russian campaign; its successful conclusion was anticipated in the autumn of the same year! With those orders all the promising moves broke down. Air Fleet X, which had been shifted to support the Balkan campaign, was not returned to Sicily at its conclusion. The Mediterranean conflict degenerated into a series of vicious battles – employing every weapon from battleships to mine-carrying swimmers – which exacted heavy losses from each side. The Italians tried to reinforce North Africa; the British in Malta tried to cut the Afrika Korps' lifeline; and the British in Alexandria and Gibraltar tried to keep Malta reinforced – in what proved to be the most dangerous convoy run of all time.

Every convoy to Malta for the next year and a half had to run the gauntlet from the moment it left Gibraltar until its ships reached port. Submarines lay in wait along the route; aircraft attacked from Sardinia and Sicily; torpedo boats struck during the night passage of the Sicilian Channel; minefields threatened in the Sicilian Channel and off Malta; and Italian Fleet units up to battleship size could and sometimes did intervene. The rare convoys from Alexandria to Malta were similarly assaulted.

The results to the British were often catastrophic. On one occasion two supply ships, one of them damaged, reached Malta – out of sixteen dispatched. Five were sunk, and nine turned back. Six British warships were lost, compared with one Italian; sixteen British warships and three merchantmen were damaged compared with two Italian.

Again and again the pattern was repeated: of three ships leaving Alexandria two were sunk, and the other damaged so that she had to turn back; one damaged ship reached Malta out of four, while nine warships were damaged. When the British ships reached Malta they were often destroyed by bombing before they could unload. In return, when Malta was not thoroughly neutralized, because German aircraft were called away to other theatres of war, a similar Allied punishment was inflicted on Italian convoys to North Africa.

To complicate the situation the Italians were greatly hampered by a worsening fuel shortage, which cut their monthly supplies in half by the summer of 1941. As Eastern Front demands increased, German shipments did not supply enough fuel to maintain even the 50-per-cent figure for Italy. Rommel, starved for supplies and aircraft by the demands of the Russian Front and by British attacks on his supply line, and faced with increasing British strength, was forced back.

There was one more try to get England to come to terms before the two-front war began. Deputy Führer Rudolf Hess parachuted into Britain on May 10th; but that was a vain hope of Hess himself. Hitler tried to convince the higher commanders of the three Services and the OKW of the need for the Russian operation in a speech on June 14th, but Raeder retained his scepticism. He felt sure that Russia would not attack Germany, and he reasoned that the loss of German use of Russian raw materials, Arctic bases, and northern sea routes, as well as the Russian threat to Baltic shipping and naval training areas, would all reduce the effectiveness of the German Navy in its assault on British supply lines. He still considered the commerce war the critical one; and he desired peace treaties with France and Norway and cooperation with Russia as the best ways to secure German freedom of action. There was no point in again pressing Hitler on the folly of the two-front war, so Raeder followed orders. The Navy, also, wanted Leningrad as a seaport and facility for naval construction.

The naval part in the Russian operation was quite small, as the Navy's principal enemy was still to be Britain and as Russia's naval capabilities were judged, correctly, to be very limited. Light forces were sufficient to contain the Russian Baltic Fleet until minefields in the Gulf of Finland blocked them permanently. Seaborne supply for the Army was not used to speed the advance. In the Arctic an Army move towards Murmansk received light naval support but did not get very far. Later, light forces in the

Black Sea supported the Army.

Perhaps all-out Navy cooperation could have affected the Russian campaign of 1941, but it is doubtful that it could have decisively altered it, as Leningrad was the only major objective near the sea and the critical battles were fought in central Russia. Everywhere the Russian Navy operated for its Army's benefit; but it was not at all aggressive and had little more than nuisance value throughout the war. Hitler once had fears about the Russian Baltic Fleet and ordered a deployment in September 1941 to prevent its breaking out to Sweden; but nothing happened. It was the last time the Baltic situation called for attention of major Fleet units until late in 1944.

Hitler's 'rapid campaign of annihilation' began on June 22nd, 1941, and rolled to victory after victory across the Russian plains. Russian troops surrendered by the hundreds of thousands. City after city and region after region fell to the invaders. Leningrad was besieged and German troops marched to the edge of Moscow – the first invaders to do so since Napoleon's Grande Armée in 1812. Then the campaign froze to a halt in the first days of December; and with that halt all hope died of an early return to German concentration on Britain and the Mediterranean.

Those summer months had seen the Axis Mediterranean position grow steadily worse, as the Russian Front absorbed the energies of the German war machine. Most critical of all was the lack of German aircraft to pound down Malta and keep that island bastion from launching its ships and planes against the Italian convoy route to Africa. The situation became so desperate that six German submarines were dispatched into the Mediterranean at the end of September by Hitler's order. Four more were drawn into the struggle in early November; and in December all the Atlantic submarines were divided between the region west of Gibraltar and the Meditarranean itself.

The sudden redeployment of the submarines was a fundamental change of strategy. From a view of the Mediterranean campaign as a supplement to the North Atlantic commerce war, Raeder seemed to shift to a concept of the Mediterranean campaign as an end in itself. A basic error of strategy was committed the moment submarines were deployed in support of the Mediterranean campaign instead of being supported by it. Victory in the Atlantic would have guaranteed victory in all western and southern Europe; victory in the Mediterranean would have been limited to that very important but self-contained region.

Committing the first submarines wrought a startling change in German Mediterranean prospects. Lieutenant-Commander Friedrich Guggenberger's *U81* had slipped past Gibraltar on the surface and was spending Friday, November 13th – its first day east of the Straits – dodging aircraft and destroyers, when Dönitz ordered her captain to search for a British force headed towards Gibraltar from the east. Early in the afternoon a number of aircraft, then a battleship, and finally two aircraft carriers appeared, the whole force screened by six destroyers and headed straight for *U81*. Guggenberger raised his periscope for the briefest of sights, trying to gauge the speed, range, and bearing of his targets while keeping the destroyers in view. The heavy ships turned sharply on a zigzag; a destroyer on collision course turned suddenly away; and Guggenberger loosed a full four-torpedo salvo. Down went the submarine in a crash dive of 360 feet, while the dull shocks of two explosions were caught by intent crewmen. Three hours and 130 depth charges later, *U81* escaped the British destroyers.

Actually, only one torpedo had hit the carrier *Ark Royal*, but she listed heavily and had to be towed towards Gibraltar. Hours later a fire broke out – and she sank early the next morning, only twenty-five miles from safety. Named after the British flagship in the Spanish Armada campaign, the *Ark Royal* had been the most famous and most active carrier in the British Navy. She had been attacked, unsuccessfully, by a submarine in the first month of the war; and German propaganda had 'sunk' her innumerable times since then. Her end introduced another grim period for the British in the Mediterranean.

On the pleasant afternoon of November 25th, with the surface ruffled just enough to hide his periscope, Lieutenant Hans Diedrich Freiherr von Tiesenhausen steered *U331* straight into the Alexandria Fleet from ahead, closing so fast that the battleship column almost ran past before the submarine could fire. Four torpedoes rushed at the second battleship; but their release upset the submarine's stability, and her conning tower broke surface in the midst of the British formation – seemingly just under the ram bow of the third battleship. For forty-five seconds she wallowed on the surface, then dove uncontrolled to 820 feet – a depth that should have crushed her – before she could be brought to equilibrium and slowly raised to a less hazardous depth. She then ran a successful evasion of the British destroyers. Far above, the *Barham*, an honoured veteran of Jutland, had been hit by three torpedoes, which set off secondary explosions. Within five minutes a magazine exploded, tearing the ship apart and killing 862 men.

Three weeks later the Alexandria Fleet lost the light cruiser *Galatea* to *U557*'s torpedoes. Then it was the Italians' turn. On the night of December 18th a submarine surfaced off Alexandria Harbour to launch three slow electric torpedoes, each of which carried two men seated astride it like horsemen on metal saddles. The men rode with just their heads above water to guide their 'pigs' through the harbour defences. Then they dove under their targets. One crew dropped its 500-pound warhead under the battleship *Valiant*; another fastened its charge to the battleship *Queen Elizabeth*; and the third attacked a naval tanker, hoping her fuel oil would catch fire when the explosive shattered her tanks.

All six crewmen were captured – two of them so quickly that they spent two hours in one of the lowest compartments of the *Valiant.* Then one of the Italian prisoners informed the British captain that his ship was about to blow up, although he would not say how. He was returned to the hold until the shock came; but both men escaped injury. Within minutes explosions also shook the other two ships. The Alexandria Fleet's battle line was wiped out (even though neither battleship sank), because both ships had to leave the Mediterranean by way of the Suez Canal for major dockyard work.

At the same time that the torpedo crews were planting their charges at Alexandria, Malta's destroyer-cruiser force ran into trouble. It had been destroying shipping destined for Rommel's forces with great success; but in one night it lost a cruiser and a destroyer and sustained damage to two more cruisers – all from a single minefield. It, too, was finished as a fighting force.

When Hitler had become convinced of the urgency of the Mediterranean crisis, he had responded by sending in aircraft as well as submarines. Air Fleet II began to operate from Sicily in January 1942, and soon had a devastating effect on Malta.

To cap the Axis change of fortune in the Mediterranean, the Japanese threat in the Pacific forced the British to divert the battleship *Prince of Wales* and the battle cruiser *Repulse* to Malayan waters. The sinking of the *Ark Royal,* and the grounding of the new carrier *Indomitable* during a practice cruise in the Caribbean in November, had deprived the British of their planned air cover. With the beginning of a new war at Pearl Harbor – which was as much a surprise to the Germans as to the Americans and British – the two capital ships, screened by four destroyers, tried to protect British possessions by sailing against Japanese invasion shipping off the eastern coast of the Malay Peninsula. Both ships were promptly sunk by Japanese land-based air assault. The British then committed five slow battleships and an aircraft carrier to the Indian Ocean. Although German cooperation with the Japanese remained limited to the maintenance of high-ranking liaison officers at each other's headquarters, Japanese operations had the desired effect on European strategy. A Japanese move on Madagascar, which was the hope of German naval strategists, never occurred, however; and after the cataclysmic Japanese defeat at Midway in June 1942 it was obvious that a joining of forces in the Middle East would not become possible.

Meanwhile Raeder was still hopeful of collaboration with Darlan in Middle Eastern affairs, although nothing came of several approaches to him.

In itself, however, the Mediterranean situation was again very favourable. Malta and the Alexandria Fleet were very weak, and supplies to Rommel's army moved across with little loss. On February 21st, 1942, Rommel began a drive towards Egypt that swept the British before it. Malta was to be taken as a joint German-Italian operation, as soon as Rommel advanced far enough to prevent British interference with the operation. For once, every group involved favoured the operation, and through February and March Malta was very effectively blockaded despite desperate British efforts, in which they suffered heavy losses, to supply the stronghold.

The plan was ruined by its own successes. The campaign against Malta was going so well that part of Air Fleet II was released to the Eastern Front, where Hitler's Stalingrad offensive was being prepared; and Rommel's drive carried him forward with such momentum that he persuaded Hitler to transfer the rest of the air support from Sicily to Egypt temporarily. With further successes, Hitler decided that the capture of Suez would isolate Malta. He feared to risk his airborne forces again after their losses in Crete, and he welcomed any alternative to the attack on Malta. He also dreamed that Rommel would continue beyond Suez, eventually linking with the Caucasus drive then in progress on the Eastern Front. Air Fleet II stayed divided between Africa and Russia.

In late June, with the danger to Malta from the air

reduced, the British reinforced the island with aircraft of all descriptions: twin-engined bombers, torpedo planes, single-engined bombers, fighters, radar-equipped night reconnaissance planes, and flare droppers. While the Army of Africa chased the mirage of the Pyramids across lengthening desert miles, Malta's aircraft cut into the convoys on which Rommel's hopes depended.

Rommel was halted on July 1st at El Alamein – only sixty miles from Alexandria. Mussolini, who had gone to Africa and had ordered a white horse flown in to him for his entry into Cairo, soon grew impatient at the delay and returned to Rome. The halt was expected to be temporary; but the longer Rommel had to wait the less opportunity he had, for the British build-up was more rapid than his own, while his long supply route across the Mediterranean and then along 1,000 miles of desert road and railway was particularly vulnerable. Throughout July and August Italian convoy battles once more became fierce. A crippling fuel shortage reduced the Italian capital ships to impotence as the British committed even Home Fleet ships to stem the tide. By October Italian losses reached 44 per cent of the cargo tonnage dispatched. In turn, the British suffered one of their worst tactical defeats when their one major effort of the summer to resupply Malta cost them an aircraft carrier, two cruisers, a destroyer, and nine merchantmen sunk, and three warships damaged. Only three undamaged and two damaged merchant ships arrived at Malta—but they kept the fortress alive. The Italians lost two submarines and two cruisers damaged.

As autumn came, the supply situation deteriorated steadily for the Army of Africa. Malta might verge on starvation, but it would starve out Rommel as well. Germany's last offensive chance in the Mediterranean burned itself out in the pyres of sinking Axis tankers and supply ships.

The autumn of the year 1942 saw the turning of the tide

Grand Admiral Erich Raeder. Commander-in-Chief of the Navy, 1928–43

Grand Admiral Karl Dönitz. Commander of Submarines, 1936–43; Commander-in-Chief of the Navy, 1943–5; the last Chief of State, 1945

Lieutenant-Commander Otto Kretschmer. The greatest ace of World War II sank one destroyer and 266,629 tons of merchant shipping before being captured when his submarine was sunk by the British escort *Walker*

U-47 and the *Scharnhorst*. After sinking the battleship *Royal Oak* at Scapa Flow, the Atlantic submarine *U-47* (foreground) is honoured by the battleship *Scharnhorst*. The *Scharnhorst* was considered a 'lucky ship' until her battle with the *Duke of York* and a cruiser–destroyer force off North Cape in December 1943

The *Graf Spee* scuttled. Faced with the alternatives of fighting with limited ammunition or internment of his ship and crew, Captain Hans Langsdorff blew up his ship. A few days later he shot himself

The *Ark Royal* sinking in the Mediterranean. This ship, whose aircraft had crippled the *Bismarck*, was hit by a torpedo from *U-81*. While being towed toward port she sank, only twenty-five miles from Gibraltar

The *Scheer*. The most successful of the *Deutschland*-class raiders, the *Scheer* made a 161-day cruise that is one of the classics of the war. She also served in Norwegian waters and in the Baltic. Lying alongside a dock at Kiel, she was sunk by aircraft in April 1945. Her capsized hull was buried when the dock was filled in

The *Gneisenau*. One of two 11-inch gun battleships, she and her sister ship, the *Scharnhorst*, operated together successfully for much of the war: against the British northern blockade line; in the Norwegian campaign; in the Atlantic commerce war; and finally up the Channel past the surprised British defences. She was taken out of action by a British bomber attack, while the *Scharnhorst* went on to participate in the attacks on the Murmansk Run

The RAF finds the *Bismarck*. This photograph clearly identified the *Bismarck* in Norwegian waters and warned the British Fleet that her sortie was imminent

A Type IX C submarine. *U-537* was a standard long-range submarine with six torpedo tubes, one 4-inch gun, and a variety of anti-aircraft guns. She met the unusual fate of being torpedoed in the Java Sea by an American submarine

The end of a submarine. Depth-charge and machine-gun-fire splashes are clearly visible. Long-range aircraft were very important in winning the Battle of the Atlantic

The *Prinz Eugen* rams the *Leipzig*. The light cruiser was cut through to the keel plate in this dramatic accident, and she served thereafter as a floating battery, never returning to ocean service. The lucky *Prinz Eugen* was soon back in action, furnishing fire support for Eastern Front troops

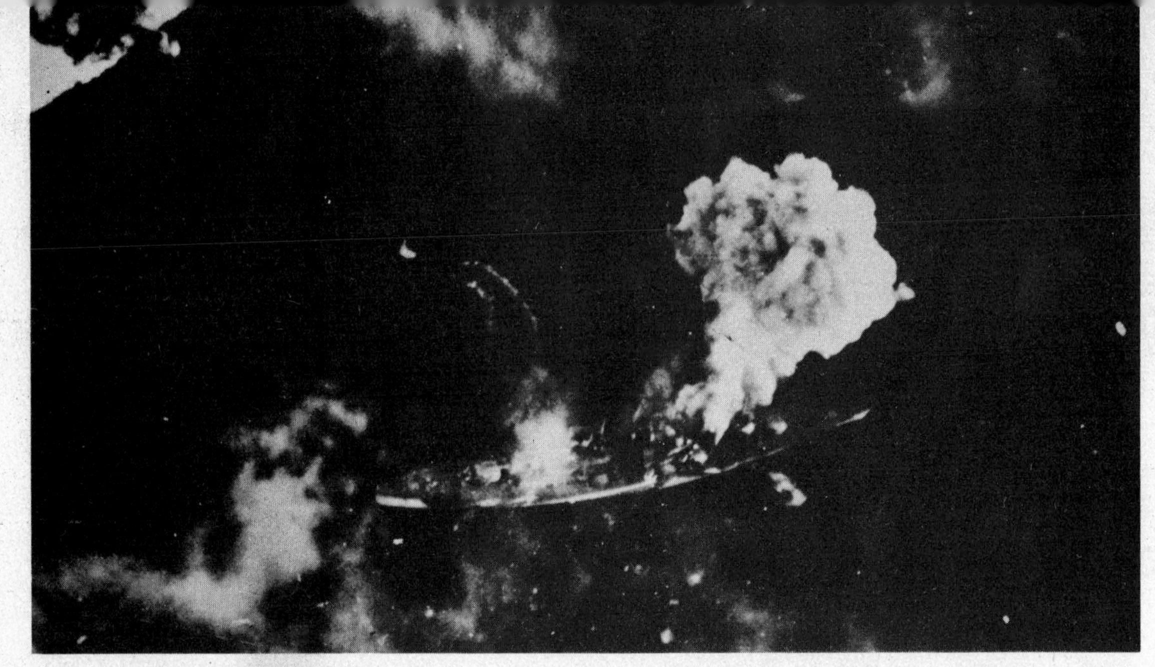

The *Tirpitz* under attack. Bombs from carrier aircraft produced the huge cloud of smoke forward of the bridge. Seven months later, heavy bombers destroyed her with six-ton bombs.

Camouflaged colossus. Security for the *Tirpitz* was all-important. She was the most dangerous ship in the world, and the most persistently hunted. Her mere existence influenced the balance of sea power in every ocean. This is a British reconnaissance photograph

The Fleet off Norway. The battleship *Tirpitz* is in the lead as she sorties with the *Hipper* and the *Scheer*

The Channel dash of 1942. A destroyer leads the *Scharnhorst*, *Gneisenau* and *Prinz Eugen* past Dunkirk in their daring daylight sortie. The heavy ships are screened by dozens of smaller ships and by an aircraft armada that is hidden in the overcast

The *Prinz Eugen*. A 'lucky ship', she survived the *Bismarck* sortie, the Channel dash of 1942, a torpedo hit, a collision, and Baltic Sea action – only to become an American atomic-bomb test target

against Germany. In October and November, after Rommel's belated August-September offensive had collapsed, the British Eastern Desert Army attacked and broke his forces at the Third Battle of Alamein. November saw the beginning of the holocaust of Stalingrad. At sea, the German Fleet had abandoned Atlantic sorties, and made its strategic retreat to northern waters, while the still-successful submarines faced ever-increasing defences. The German High Command awaited the next blow.

Although there had been worries over French North Africa for quite some time, no one was really sure where the Allies, with the mobility that sea power gave them, would strike, or when they would act. The Naval Operations Staff discounted French North Africa as a target because of the threat of the French Fleet, but it believed that a strike at Tripoli, to trap the Afrika Korps, was likely. The American and British landings of November 8th, 1942, to take Casablanca, Oran, and Algiers in French North Africa came as a surprise, then, both in place and in time. There was little German or Italian opposition, and the French, after extremely complex negotiations, stopped fighting three days later.

The German Government had asked for French permission to help defend French North Africa against Allied assault, but Hitler's representatives had been put off. The Germans soon forced Prime Minister Pierre Laval to give permission for their entrance into Tunisia, however, where their landings barely forestalled Allied moves. Tunisia became the strategic key to the German defence of the Mediterranean. If the Germans lost it, the Mediterranean would be freed for a short Allied convoy route to the Middle East and Russia through the Persian Gulf. The shipping saved by using the shorter route would be sufficient to enable the Allies to mount assaults anywhere in southern Europe. The Germans determined to hold on; so another vicious convoy battle developed in the Sicilian Channel. The Italians were overmatched by Allied sea power, which succeeded in sinking a higher and yet higher percentage of Axis shipments – finally reaching 41 per cent in March and April 1943. Italian sailors, carrying the goods in merchantmen and even on warships' decks, called the run the 'Death Route'.

As soon as the Allied forces were securely established in North African beachheads, Hitler decided to invade the Free Zone, to secure the French Mediterranean coast against invasion or, what was considered more likely, French duplicity. The armistice, however, remained in nominal effect. The Commander-in-Chief of the French Navy, Admiral Paul Auphan, requested of Raeder that the position of the French Fleet be respected: it remained loyal to Pétain and did not sail. Raeder replied that Toulon was to be defended by the French Navy without German interference, and hoped that the two Navies would in future cooperate on common tasks. The French replied, to that hope for collaboration, that they would defend their Fleet and base against anyone but would not engage in hostilities on either side.

Despite that agreement and the knowledge that taking the Fleet was practically impossible, Hitler ordered its seizure – at which point it was scuttled. Sea power in the Mediterranean had passed irrevocably to the Allies; for neither the decimated Italian Fleet nor the remaining German submarines could seriously hurt the huge Allied Fleets. Even a last attempt by Raeder to get Hitler to redress the balance by a land move through Spain to Gibraltar had no hope of success, for the forces were lacking.

From that time on, the German Navy could do little but advise the Army to hold, first, Tunisia to keep the Sicilian Channel blocked, and then Sicily to keep from exposing Italy and the Balkans. The Navy could guess, usually with some accuracy, at the next landing point; but the flexibility of Allied sea power forced the Germans to spread their defensive forces to cover all the possible invasion points, thus preventing them from concentrating enough troops to push the successive invasion forces into the sea. Another discussion of the value of flanking the Allied thrusts by moves through Spain and Portugal also foundered on lack of means, as did an idea for aerial assault on Gibraltar, Alexandria, and Suez.

A few more submarines were committed to the Mediterranean, despite the certainty of high losses against small gains. The sinking of the last of them in the autumn of 1944 was the last act in a theatre of war that had held such bright promise to the Germans in the victorious days of 1940–41.

Chapter 6

SURFACE FORCES

To all the seas of the earth June 1940–May 1941

The French defeat in June 1940 ushered in the German Navy's golden age, the time of great ships boldly forcing the Iceland Passages and German guns echoing across all the high seas of the earth. Whatever other plans might be in view, the dominant theme was that Britain must be fought upon the seas, her lifelines cut, her Empire and friends severed from her European island fortress.

With the fall of France, the German Navy, for the first time in its history, acquired bases on the Atlantic coast. Previously, German surface raiders had had to force the British blockade that stood across their routes to the Atlantic, then operate in seas devoid of havens while seeking to avoid a formidable array of roving Allied hunting groups. Once France was defeated and Italy had entered the conflict, a thin British picket line across the broad exits to the Atlantic from the Shetlands to Greenland, backed by the slow Home Fleet and slower convoy escorts, was all that remained to threaten the German marauders. Once on the seas, except for chance or maritime accident, the German ships were free.

One by one the raiders put to sea from German ports. Their supply and fuel ships sailed from France, and their prizes were sent there to add their cargoes to Germany's war potential. Destroyers and torpedo boats, too limited in fuel capacity to operate far at sea, provided escort across the Bay of Biscay, the most dangerous part of a deep-sea voyage.

Every German raider had three goals: to sink ships, empty or full, wherever they might be found, by guns, mines, torpedoes, or scuttling charges; to scatter British naval forces, wearing out the hulls and machinery and destroying the effectiveness of men; and to upset merchant-shipping schedules. So long as German heavy units kept the seas, British convoy schedules were disrupted, with the result that untold masses of supplies were not delivered to places where they were desperately needed. Lost shipping days could not be made up.

Warships and merchantmen were not the only forces affected: every British plane used over the oceans meant that one less was available for European operations. British grand strategy was directly affected. Whenever German heavy forces were in the Atlantic or in French ports, the British Gibraltar Fleet hung between them and the Italians: it could not act decisively in the Mediterranean for fear of being needed in the Atlantic. The Afrika Korps reached Tripoli at such a time in the 1940–41 winter.

The armed merchant cruisers were the first out. Drab ships, usually painted grey, brown, or black without even the relief of white striping for fear of being more visible at night, those vessels were well fitted to play the role of innocent merchantmen plodding along under whatever flag was most convenient at the moment. Raked bows might hint at a turn of speed above the ordinary, but no other external characteristic betrayed their differences from hundreds of merchantmen in British or neutral service. Behind hinged steel ports, however, were hidden six 5.9-inch guns and from two to six torpedo tubes. Falsework topside hid lighter guns, searchlights, range finders, and smoke generators. Some holds were fitted as prisons, others as crew quarters, mine rooms, aircraft hangars, ammunition magazines, auxiliary power rooms, refrigerators, dry-stores compartments, and extra fuel bunkers.

Galleys, bakeries, laundries, sick bays, and service facilities down to such details as shoemakers' and barbers' shops were provided for crews of up to 400 men who expected to live for over a year in ships which ranged from 3,287 to 8,736 tons.

The first of the armed merchant cruisers, the *Atlantis,* left Germany on the last day of March 1940, followed by five more raiders by early July and one more in December. The *Atlantis* made for the South Atlantic, and soon there were raiders in every ocean. The *Komet,* whose name seems suited to brilliant northern nights, reached the Pacific through the North-East Passage, courtesy of the Russo-German Pact. The icebreakers *Lenin* and *Stalin* opened parts of the long passage for the ship flying the Nazi flag, and Hitler's government paid Stalin's the equivalent of about $300,000 for the service. The others all broke out by the Denmark Strait, several of them barely escaping British submarines off Norway on the way.

The *Orion,* the second ship out, began the disguised raiders' successes with a sinking in the Atlantic and a false 'attacked by *Deutschland*-class raider' call to confuse the British during the Norway operation. Then she headed towards the Indian Ocean. The Naval Operations Staff directed the raiders skilfully from area to area, providing intelligence down to details of single enemy ship sailings and coordinating the movements of the raiders with those of supply ships, blockade runners, prizes, submarines, and heavy surface ships in intricate and constantly changing operations. They even sent out special repair parts on order. At one point they brought together five German ships at an Indian Ocean rendezvous: the raider *Atlantis,* the *Scheer,* one blockade runner, and two prizes. Another time there were six ships together, the largest German Navy concentration in distant waters since the Battle of the Falklands in 1914.

After the *Orion*'s first sinking, successes came quickly and continued for one and a half years. The raider captains began operations in the traditional manner: closing in on enemy merchantmen, firing shots across their bows, and sending boarding parties to remove the crews and take over the ships for scuttling or use as prizes. Very quickly that procedure became impossible. Ships turned away from any suspicious mastheads and often broadcast QQQ (disguised raider) or RRR calls. To some extent those calls were welcome as they furthered two of the raiders' purposes, the dispersion of British naval forces and the disruption of shipping. They were particularly welcome when the calls were in error, garbled, or partly jammed by the raider. One RRR, giving only a longitude, for instance, might force diversion of shipping in the entire eastern Indian Ocean. Sometimes the raiders used captured ship radios to cancel calls for help.

Merchant-ship suspicion forced more and more attacks to be made in darkness or poor visibility, and that often meant long chases. Even surprise night attacks did not result in easy captures. Intrepid captains and radio operators sent out RRR calls even when searchlights or starshells suddenly lit their ships and warning guns flashed from the darkness. Some ships tried to fight back with their old guns, conscious that a single lucky hit might disable a raider, but resistance was usually futile against a broadside of four 5.9-inch guns. Nonetheless, resistance led to another change in tactics. The raider captains began actions with broadsides aimed to cripple the enemy radios. Inevitably, casualties jumped sharply, and prizes were often so damaged that they had to be sunk.

Ironically, the man to first bear the burden of world opprobrium was one of the most gentlemanly captains, the *Atlantis*' Bernhard Rogge. On a brilliantly moonlit night in April 1941, Rogge sighted a blacked-out, zigzagging ship that he recognized as a British troop transport type. He feared that she might have been converted to an auxiliary cruiser like others of her type. Near dawn, the *Atlantis* closed in and opened fire, quickly obtaining six hits which smashed the radio room and hit the engine room and waterline. The ship stopped. Only then did her identity become apparent. She was the neutral Egyptian *Zamzam,* formerly a British troop transport but carrying 109 women and children in a passenger list of 202, of whom 140 were Americans. To make the situation even more awkward, 150 of the passengers were missionaries, and others belonged to the British-American Ambulance Corps. Most of the 107 crewmen were in the boats, while the passengers had been left to fend for themselves.

The *Atlantis* saved everyone from the sinking ship, the boats, and the water. There had been no deaths, an event ascribed to different causes by the Christian missionaries and the Moslem crewmen. Thankfully, Rogge transferred his unwelcome passengers to the supply ship *Dresden,* which took them towards France. The spectre of the *Lusitania* hung over the journey. The responsible naval officers worried about the effects on world opinion if the *Dresden* were sunk by the British. How much would German explanations about the *Zamzam*'s belligerent behaviour and contraband cargo (which included British-owned lubricating oil and steel) weigh against the loss of civilian lives?

Fortunately for all concerned, the *Dresden* arrived safely. One of the passengers, the editor of *Fortune,* wrote an article for *Life* magazine which, while somewhat inflammatory in tone, was factually correct. With the story went a photograph of the *Atlantis* taken by a *Life* photographer who had been on board the *Zamzam* and had managed to conceal the film from the German crews.

Another captain whose gunfire had international repercussions was Captain Helmuth von Ruckteschell of the *Widder* ('Ram') and later of the *Michel.* His tendency to shoot after enemy ships had stopped and his failure to pick up survivors from ships sunk hundreds of miles from shore led to his conviction for war crimes after the war and to a ten-year sentence. He died in prison, one of two German ship commanders to be convicted by their enemies.

Guns were the primary weapons of the raiders, but by no means the only ones. They carried under- and above-water torpedo tubes, but could rarely get into range to use torpedoes against merchantmen. They were often used to sink useless prizes quickly. Aeroplanes were invaluable on the limited occasions when they could be employed. None of the raiders had catapults, so take-offs were possible only from smooth water. The planes also broke down often. Most of the captains used their aircraft essentially as scouts, although some ordered them to snatch away the merchantmen's aerials with grapnels and to bomb and machine-gun their upper works. Captain Felix Krüder of the *Pinguin* made the most audacious use of an aeroplane in a night attack on a tanker in which the plane cut the aerials from between her masts, gunned her, and dropped a stop order in English on her deck. The ship stopped, and when the *Pinguin* came up she found the plane in the water, her crew watching the tanker, which had turned on her lights when ordered to do so. Krüder took three ships in that one night, the other two simply blundering into the *Pinguin*'s view.

Most of the raiders were equipped with a large number of mines. Those, laid in such widely scattered parts of the world as off the Cape of Good Hope and Auckland, New Zealand, had the usual dual effects of sinking and dislocating shipping. A number of prizes were fitted as auxiliary minelayers, among them a tanker which was chosen because no one was expected to think of a tanker as a minelayer.

Two raiders carried small motor torpedo boats capable of 40 knots. The *Michel*'s pair made four attacks, three of them successful. The method, designed to achieve surprise, was to launch the boat after dark so as to swing far ahead of a merchantman, then wait with engines stopped until the target was close enough for a torpedo run. The one failure was a daylight attack in which an alert ship's crew dodged the torpedoes and worked up enough speed to outrun the *Michel.*

A method of increasing the raiders' search capability was the formation of scouting lines including a raider or two, and one or more prizes or supply ships. The *Komet* also added to the raiders' nuisance value by borrowing from the surface raiders of World War I the idea of bombarding shore installations. She struck Nauru Island, north of the Solomon Islands. Her shells wrecked a phosphate pier, oil tanks, and other installations after her radio operator warned the island's radio operator to remain silent and to tell everyone to evacuate the target area so there would be no casualties. Another way to add to British defensive problems was to refuel and resupply submarines, extending their cruises and enabling them to operate in areas beyond their normal range. One raider even towed a submarine to increase its operating range. Some Italian submarines, escaping from Italian East Africa as the British closed in, were refuelled so they could complete their journey to France.

A few prizes were extremely valuable, so every effort was made to get them safely to France. By far the most important ones were two Norwegian whale-factory ships, their tanker, and eleven small whale-catchers, all taken in two days off the Antarctic coast by the aptly named *Pinguin.* Her radio operators had listened to the whale fleet's radio chatter, which led the raider through the ice floes to her quarry. That was the most successful of the many uses of intercepted radio messages. All but one catcher were dispatched to France, and only two catchers were intercepted on the way and scuttled. The three large ships brought 20,000 tons of eagerly awaited whale oil to the oil-short German economy. On another occasion, the *Thor*'s captain was rebuked for sinking a whale-factory ship he had captured with 17,662 tons of oil aboard. He thought the ship would have been too hard to run through the blockade.

Other prizes were valuable to the raiders themselves. The coal-burning refrigerator ship *Duquesa* carried 3,500 tons of frozen meat and fifteen million eggs when captured by the *Scheer*. She was sent to a South Atlantic rendezvous where she furnished supplies for a long list of grateful ships. When her coal ran out, she was towed by a supply ship, while her prize crew burned her own woodwork to keep the refrigerator plant running as long as possible. One of the raiders captured a loaded collier but sank it as useless, not knowing of the *Duquesa*'s plight, so the refrigerator ship was eventually sunk. Captured tankers extended many of the raiders' cruises, while prizes and supply ships served as prison ships.

Prisoners were a problem because of their numbers, yet to land them or send them to neutral ports was inadvisable because of their knowledge about the raiders, whose best weapon was anonymity. Feeding prisoners was an exasperating problem as they ranged from European dowagers on special diets to vegetarian Hindus and Moslem Malays. Some captains' galleys came to resemble League of Nations kitchens. No single decision was ever reached about prisoners, although as many as possible were retained in German hands. The worst problem was faced by Captain Otto Kähler of the very small *Thor*, who attacked a ship with 500 passengers and crew. A British warship radioed that she was on her way to help the sinking liner, so Kähler left the people to become problems for the British.

Supply was facilitated by the use of Japanese bases, first by supply ships and later by the raiders themselves. Up to the end of 1941, by which time the cruises of the first seven raiders had been completed, thirty-six supply ships and blockade runners and twenty-two prizes had been used to supply the raiders. Most of them were finally scuttled, sunk, or captured by the British, one of them being taken with the *Pinguin*'s war diary aboard. On the other hand, the Germans succeeded in capturing British secret papers on a number of prizes and in breaking the merchant marine code repeatedly, which gave them invaluable information about British ship movements.

The ships' abilities to change disguises and repair their own defects were remarkable. Masts, stacks, and superstructures were drastically altered, and small details such as having 'women' passengers on deck were assiduously developed for authenticity. Raiders were careened in mid-ocean by pumping fuel from port to starboard and vice versa so their crews could scrape, paint, and repair. Divers worked on underwater repairs, such as the replacement of a keel plate of the *Atlantis* which had been damaged when she had run aground. Several ships landed at uninhabited islands, usually in far southerly latitudes, but Rogge of the *Atlantis* gave most of his crew a brief shore leave on the coral-sand and coconut-palm atoll Vanavana, a South Pacific island that seemed right out of a romantic novel. His crew spent Christmas ashore on another island and capped the festivities with Christmas gifts for all hands, courtesy of captured ships' cargoes.

Maintaining morale was of great concern on those long voyages, and many methods for varying the routine were used. Special events, such as 'Crossing the Line', were observed with their traditional festivities, as were holidays, the day circumnavigation was completed, and the day a ship had spent a year at sea, that last record being achieved by over half the raiders. Motion pictures, amateur theatricals, and music helped to lighten the burdens of work, training, and tension. The *Kormoran* added a piano from a prize to its entertainment capability, while the *Stier* held a ship's fair, raising 3,000 marks for charity by a lottery and auctions. The *Kormoran* even had a small swimming pool. Some captains arranged for their men to go on shipboard 'leave' without duty except in emergencies.

Slowly, problems began to catch up with the raiders. Several of them with old steam turbines experienced repeated mechanical failures or ran out of fuel because of their high consumption rates. The diesel engines with which most of the raiders were equipped had far better fuel economy, but fuel worries troubled many captains. Some ships drifted for days or weeks waiting for the arrival of a tanker. Mechanical troubles, or the closing down of a boiler to save fuel, or the accumulation of growths on the hull slowed some of them until they could no longer catch the fastest and most valuable merchantmen.

The British moved actively and persistently against the raider menace, and only good luck saved several of them from destruction. The *Orion* was inspected by a patrol plane which failed to penetrate her disguise. On another occasion her seaplane sighted a British cruiser in time to permit evasive action by the raider. The *Atlantis* met a *Nelson*-class battleship and an aircraft carrier on a moonlit night, but slowly altered course and slipped away unseen. The *Thor* had the worst scrape when she was sighted and signalled to by the British light cruiser *Durban* off South Africa. She identified herself as a British ship, and the cruiser let her pass. The next day the auxiliary cruiser *Cheshire* did the same thing! The British had no sure method of checking ships' identities in the early war years, which helps to explain such errors.

The raiders had to face many hazards in addition to British warships and aircraft. The *Atlantis* was nearly rammed by a burning ship and nearly torpedoed when the jammed rudder on one of her own torpedoes caused it to circle and just miss her own bow. She was one of many which weathered hurricanes. One of the *Pinguin*'s victims hit her with a shell just above her mine room, but an excited gunner had forgotten to insert the fuse!

Eventually the raiders' luck had to end, and it fell to the 3,862-ton *Thor* to live up to her name by fighting when her disguise proved inadequate. On July 28th, 1940, the *Thor* found what appeared to be a large passenger ship off Brazil on a bright, clear morning with excellent visibility. The raider turned to investigate, then turned to run when the stranger swung towards the *Thor*. A chase began, the *Thor* starting with a ten-mile lead, which the 22,209-ton auxiliary cruiser *Alcantara* reduced steadily. Captain Kähler accepted the inevitable when the range went down to seven miles. The *Thor* raised her gun flaps, turned across the *Alcantara*'s bow, broke out a battle flag, and opened fire. The sun was behind the raider, which made the *Alcantara*'s gunnery very difficult, while the *Thor* fired rapid four-gun broadsides that hit early in the action. Steam poured out, and the British ship's speed dropped, although she hit the raider twice. Kähler turned his ship away under smoke, turned out of the smoke for a few more shots, and finally pulled out of the action under a smoke screen with three dead and four wounded aboard. Behind her, the *Alcantara* was dead in the water but still firing futilely. Leaving a damaged ship behind was hard for Kähler, but the possibility of receiving a crippling hit was too great to risk.

Four months later, the *Thor* met the *Alcantara*'s replacement when another British auxiliary cruiser suddenly emerged from a fog bank four miles away. Again Kähler tried a quick withdrawal, that time hoping to disappear into the mists with his retreat covered by a smoke screen, but again the auxiliary cruiser was too fast. Manoeuvring rapidly at ranges under four miles, the *Thor* fired two torpedoes and missed, but hit her opponent, the *Carnarvon Castle*, again and again with salvoes that sometimes were only six seconds apart. After an hour's action, some of the *Thor*'s guns were so hot that they jammed, and her ammunition was running low, but she was unhurt. Suddenly the *Carnarvon Castle* turned away, listing and on fire. Kähler let her go. Ironically, Montevideo shipwrights made temporary patches for the *Carnarvon Castle*'s battered hull from plates removed from the *Graf Spee* hulk.

The *Thor*'s cruise continued. She replenished her ammunition and returned to the trade routes. Five months after the *Carnarvon Castle* battle, she tried to stop what appeared to be another large merchantman with a shot across the bows at just under five miles. At that moment her opponent's identity became apparent. She was another large auxiliary cruiser. Again the *Thor*'s gunners scored heavily, hitting with the first salvo and setting the *Voltaire* on fire within three minutes. Soon she was blazing fiercely but still firing. Then her rudder jammed and she swung in circles, still being hit but not hitting. One hour after the action began, the *Voltaire* showed a white flag, and Kähler came as near as he dared to the flaming ship to pick 197 survivors, including the captain, out of the water. The *Voltaire* sank within an hour.

The *Thor* was the only raider to engage British auxiliary cruisers. Her superior gunnery, small size compared to the high-hull converted passenger liners, and a good measure of luck provided her with the three overwhelming victories.

The raiders could not all be lucky. The most successful of all, the *Atlantis*, with twenty-two ships of 145,697 tons to her credit, was lying stopped in the South Atlantic on November 22nd, 1941. She had logged 622 days at sea and 102,000 miles. One engine was dismantled for piston replacement, *U126* was fuelling astern, and the submarine's commander was having a leisurely breakfast with Captain Rogge when the alarm bells went off. The heavy cruiser *Devonshire* was in sight at very long range and was seen to launch her spotter plane. The submarine dived and the raider began a charade with the cruiser and the aeroplane, hoping the submarine could manoeuvre for a shot. The submarine's temporary commander kept her near the *Atlantis*, waiting for the cruiser to close in. The cruiser kept well away, while the areoplane pilot studied raider identification material, including a copy of the *Life* magazine photograph made from the *Zamzam*'s boat. The cruiser captain hesitated for over an hour, radioing for information and checking with his aircraft pilot.

Finally assured that the *Atlantis* was not the merchantman she claimed to be, the *Devonshire* began firing 8-inch shells at a range of ten miles. Escape was impossible, despite a smoke screen. Rogge ordered abandon-ship as the shells tore into his vessel. The cruiser pulled out as the *Atlantis* sank, but almost the entire crew had been able to escape. The submarine surfaced and arranged the survivors in three groups: one on the submarine's deck, one below, and the other in the boats. The groups were rotated regularly until the survivors were picked up by the supply ship *Python* two days later.

A few days later the *Python* was caught with submarines around her by the *Devonshire*'s sister ship, the *Dorsetshire*. The submarines dived and one attacked unsuccessfully, so the *Python* was scuttled to avoid casualties when the cruiser opened fire. The *Atlantis*' crewmen were in the boats again, that time for a week. The submarines organized another rescue and Dönitz sent more submarines to help. All reached home safely, although one of them had to endure a depth-charge attack on the way. Rogge received the Oak Leaves to the Knight's Cross from Hitler at a reception for the *Atlantis*' re-united crew in Berlin.

The *Pinguin* was located in the Indian Ocean by the heavy cruiser *Cornwall*'s search plane one day after her twenty-eighth victim had sent out a raider report. The pilot almost accepted her disguise but was puzzled when no one came on deck to wave at him. The cruiser's captain was also confused by the disguise, so he closed in, firing warning shots. The raider waited for the range to close, then raised her gun flaps and opened fire, scoring one hit which put the cruiser's steering gear out of action temporarily, but the *Pinguin* was soon hit in her mine room and blew up after eleven minutes' action. Only sixty Germans and twenty-two prisoners survived. Captain Felix Krüder was not among them.

The *Kormoran* also met a cruiser. She was off the Australian coast when she sighted the light cruiser

Sydney heading directly for her. The cruiser was the namesake of the one which had destroyed the most famous German raider of World War I, the *Emden*, in the same part of the Indian Ocean. Captain Theodor Detmers turned his ship in an attempt to run but soon was forced to exchange signals with the oncoming cruiser. The raider claimed to be a Dutch ship, and the cruiser was apparently taken in by the deliberately prolonged exchange, for she ranged up towards the *Kormoran*'s starboard side for what her crew apparently took to be a routine merchantship inspection. Detmers was looking into the muzzles of eight 6-inch guns and at four torpedo tubes, but he noted that the cruiser's lighter guns were not manned and that some crewmen were lounging at the rail. He ordered a QQQ signal sent by radio and hoisted several more garbled flag signals in answer to the cruiser's persistent blinker signals. Finally the *Sydney* demanded the secret call letters.

The game was up, but the cruiser had come abeam at less than half-mile range and was slowing down. Detmers shouted. The battle ensign leaped to the masthead and the gun flaps swung away. Six seconds transformed the innocent merchantman into the deadly raider. One shot, then three more lashed out. The *Sydney*'s bridge and fire-control director burst open and her answering salvo went wide. Detmers could see men fall in the cruiser's torpedo battery and upper works under the hammering of his anti-aircraft guns. No gun could miss at such a range. Two torpedoes leaped out towards the cruiser. One hit her and lifted her bow bodily just as a shell tore off the second turret's roof and the two forward turrets went dead. The *Kormoran*'s gunners were firing salvoes every four to five seconds. The cruiser's seaplane caught fire, her aftmost turret was smashed, and fires leaped up on decks deserted by all but the dead. Only one turret still fired, and its two guns dealt heavy blows. The *Kormoran*'s engine room was hit and caught fire.

The *Sydney* turned as if to ram but lost speed and

passed astern, while the raider's guns continued to tear at her from bridge to waterline. The cruiser's last guns went silent, and, for a moment, so did some of the raider's as the crews cooled them with fire hoses. Then the *Kormoran*'s engines died, but the guns still spoke until about 500 5.9-inch shells had been fired. The cruiser finally loosed four torpedoes, but the nearest one missed astern by a hundred yards. Detmers ordered another torpedo sent after the flaming hulk. It missed, and the cruiser slowly pulled way into the gathering darkness.

For more than two hours, the *Kormoran*'s crew could see the *Sydney*'s flames in the darkness. She was never seen again. The *Kormoran*'s crew found their fire-fighting equipment destroyed by a shell, so the engine-room fire raged unchecked, killing the entire engine-room force. The crew abandoned ship shortly before the fires reached her mines and tore her apart. The survivors were picked up in the next few days, and eventually 315 of the *Kormoran*'s 400 men were saved by their enemies, but not one of the *Sydney*'s 644 men was recovered. While in captivity, Detmers was awarded the Knight's Cross of the Iron Cross.

One by one the *Orion*, *Komet*, *Widder*, and *Thor* made their way safely to German-held ports, until none was at sea in mid-November 1941. The *Thor* sailed on her second cruise late that month, leaving by way of the English Channel, as the Iceland Passages were considered too heavily guarded by radar-equipped cruisers. She was followed in March 1942 by the *Michel* and in May by the *Stier* ('Bull'), both of which had to fight their way down the Channel under heavy escort. The latter's passage cost two German torpedo boats and about 200 dead. The *Komet* tried to leave on a second voyage in October but was sunk by British destroyers in the Channel. In February 1943 the *Togo* tried to run the gauntlet but turned back damaged. Two more raiders never sailed.

The *Thor* had a long, successful cruise which ended in an overhaul at Yokohama. There she was joined by the supply ships *Uckermark* (the famous *Altmark* renamed) and *Leuthen.* Exactly one year after she had sailed from Germany, the *Thor* and her two companions were destroyed in an accidental explosion and fire.

The *Stier*'s cruise netted only three ships in five months. She was stopped at a rendezvous in poor weather when a large ship suddenly appeared out of the mists a little over two miles away. The *Stier*'s captain rang for full speed and quickly engaged the merchantman, which replied with a single antiquated 4-inch gun firing a 31-pound shell. Then began as classic a David-Goliath action as the *Kormoran-Sydney* battle. The American Liberty Ship *Stephen Hopkins,* her name an echo from the American Revolution's first scratch flotilla, shot her single gun magnificently against the *Stier*'s 400-pound broadside. Nearly point-blank range cancelled the raider's fire-control advantage, and she was immediately in a fight for her life. One shot smashed her steering gear; the next destroyed her engine oil feed. Thirteen more shells tore into her in the next ten minutes, leaving her stopped with uncontrollable fires raging. The *Stephen Hopkins* was also stopped and sinking. The crippled ships lay within sight of each other for nearly an hour until the *Stephen Hopkins* sank, after which her opponent blew up. The *Stier*'s captain paid the American the compliment of believing he had fought an auxiliary cruiser. The raider's supply ship had picked up survivors before the explosion, but the Liberty Ship's survivors made a thirty-one-day voyage to Brazil, which only fifteen survived out of an original crew of fifty-seven. Incredibly, the *Stier* lost only three dead, but she had thirty-three wounded.

The raider *Michel* cruised on and on. She was the only one at sea as the year 1943 began, and she left her trail of destruction behind her through the summer and into the autumn. She could not go home through the blockade. On October 18th she was only sixty miles from her new base, Yokohama, when she was attacked at night by the surfaced American submarine *Tarpon*. She tried to ram the submarine after being hit twice with torpedoes, but was finished off in two more attacks. The days of the mystery ships were over.

The nine ships' cruises were done, but their records stand: 129 ships totalling over 800,000 tons,* a toll nearly as large as a year's British construction; and that does not count the ships sunk by mines or the enormous indirect losses to British seaborne trade or the value of the prizes to the German war economy.

In the summer and autumn of 1940, which saw the disguised raiders at the peak of their successes, the prospects for ocean war were so bright that the almost-complete aircraft carrier was ordered to be finished, and a cruiser to be completed with a flight deck.

Air Force attacks on shipping were limited because of the Sea Lion operation, but Raeder continued to press for attacks on ports and shipping. In September 1940 a new type of aerial mine was ready in large numbers, and Raeder pressed for its use. A few weeks later Hitler assured him that the mines were being sown, but a month later Raeder was back, insisting on more aerial minelaying and aerial bombardment of British shipyards, especially those concentrating on escort-ship production.

At the end of October 1940 the first heavy ship was finally ready for a deep-sea cruise. The *Scheer* was named after the commander of the Imperial High Seas Fleet at the Battle of Jutland, Vice-Admiral Reinhard Scheer. She had been undergoing a complete refit since the beginning of the war. That included the removal of her square fighting mast, identical to the one her sister ship, the *Graf Spee*, had carried. In its place a far less

* All statistics are from David Woodward, *The Secret Raiders*, whose in turn derive largely from Captain S. W. Roskill, DSC, RN, *The War at Sea*, Vol I, pp 604–8, and Vol II, p 481. German sources credit the *Pinguin* with a slightly higher score than the *Atlantis*' score by adding the mine-damage totals to the ships' direct effects.

conspicuous, slim, round mast was fitted.

In early November the *Scheer* broke through the Denmark Strait, between Iceland and Greenland, undetected in weather so violent that she lost two men overboard despite all precautions. Three days later her aeroplane sighted a convoy whose departure had been known to the Naval Operations Staff and had been signalled to the *Scheer*'s Captain Theodor Krancke. As he guided his ship towards the convoy, the appearance of a small, lone ship confused him momentarily, but she was quickly stopped by warning shots and sent no raider signal, fortunately for the *Scheer*. The crew was ordered into the boats and picked up; the ship was sunk. The *Scheer* sped towards the convoy.

Late that afternoon the masts came in sight from the fire-control director atop the fighting mast. Then the lines of merchant-ship hulls slowly rose over the horizon. No warship led the merchantmen, although tense lookouts searchingly studied each silhouette. Then one merchantman hauled out of line towards the *Scheer*, trailing a smoke screen to shield the other ships and firing red rockets. A British radio wavelength came alive with a raider report. Behind the bold ship, the thirty-seven-ship convoy broke formation and scattered. The *Scheer* stood in towards her opponent, which was obviously an armed merchant cruiser. At ten-mile range the *Scheer* turned to bring all six 11-inch turret guns to bear and opened fire. Her 5.9-inch guns were ordered to fire at a tanker. Krancke kept the range open as he methodically shot the auxiliary cruiser to pieces. He preferred to use time and ammunition rather than risk damage so early in the cruise.

The enemy was the *Jervis Bay* under Captain E. S. F. Fegen, RN. He kept her between the *Scheer* and the convoy as long as steering and engines still worked, although the *Scheer*'s first hit had torn off one of his legs and smashed the other. The surgeon bandaged the stump and Fegen kept command. The bridge and the midship guns were soon destroyed, so Fegen dragged himself to the stern gun to direct its fire until the relentless bombardment sought it out. His posthumous Victoria Cross could but palely reflect his gallantry.

The sacrifice of Captain Fegen and 200 of his crew had forced Krancke to direct all his guns at the *Jervis Bay* and had gained an invaluable twenty-two minutes for the convoy. As the auxiliary cruiser's last gun went out and she settled deeper and deeper, Krancke saw the convoy disappearing into the growing darkness behind smoke screens. The *Scheer*'s secondary battery had set a tanker on fire. Her guns quickly hit other targets as they appeared briefly in the gloom. For over two more hours the *Scheer* cut through the scattered ships. The radar sought victims, and a searchlight or tracers impaled them until the heavy guns could smash them. Fires raced along ships' decks and explosions shook the raider as her victims flared up and disappeared. Here and there a gun crew resisted briefly, to no avail. A torpedo finished one ship whose cargo had buoyed her up after her side plates were torn open. Then the three-hour carnage was over. Five merchantmen had joined the *Jervis Bay*, and three more were damaged. One of them was an abandoned burning tanker, part of whose crew found her the next day, put out the fires, and brought her into port with a broken back.

It was time to go. The *Scheer* had used one-third of her 11-inch shells and half of her secondary ammunition. British Fleet units would soon converge on the area, and Krancke wanted to use the darkness to gain as great a lead as possible on the pursuers. Thanks to the *Jervis Bay*'s defence, the *Scheer*'s score was not as high as it might have been, but the whole British convoy system was disorganized for twelve days, during seven of which no convoy reached Britain. As a result of the attack, major convoys received battleship escort from that point on.

The *Scheer* went on to a 161-day cruise that, with a

smoothly functioning supply system, eventually took her to the Indian Ocean. Her experiences were generally similar to those of the auxiliary cruisers, but her disruptive effect was much greater. She added one trick to the raiders' methods. Painted like a British warship, she would rush towards enemy ships with two of her forward guns pointed up and one down, so she would look like the typical British cruiser with double turrets. The merchant-ship captains were so used to daylight cruiser checks that one of them paid no attention when the *Scheer* captured a nearby ship and discovered his mistake only when the German naval ensign went up and the guns were aimed at him a short time later.

On February 19th, 1941 Krancke tried to stop an uncooperative ship that had an American flag painted on her side. He finally signalled, 'Stop at once and don't force me to fire. You're behaving very suspiciously.' The merchantman answered, 'So are you. You're acting like a German.'* Then she sent an RRR call. The 'neutral's' false flag paint was still wet when Krancke's boarders went up the rope ladder that the British deckhands had reluctantly lowered for them. On another occasion he stopped a neutral Greek ship with 'Red Cross supplies' from New York aboard. A careful search revealed weapons in each crate under a thin veneer of cotton, and the ship was sunk.

In general, the *Scheer*'s cruise was like the *Graf Spee*'s in that her heavy armament usually forestalled resistance, so she inflicted very few casualties among the crews of her ten single victims. One ship briefly tried to shoot it out at night because her crew was blinded by a searchlight and could not identify her assailant.

The *Scheer* was nearly trapped in the Indian Ocean when two ships in succession sent raider reports before surrendering. Krancke was aware that powerful British forces were gathering, but a shadowing British plane lost

* Admiral Theodor Krancke and H. J. Brennecke, *The Battleship Scheer*, p 167.

contact and Krancke changed course to avoid a cruiser that passed very close that night. It was heard reporting by radar that it had failed to make contact. Two more cruisers were avoided when a nervous British merchantman saw them first, mistook them for German raiders, and sent out an RRR message describing them and their position – which was directly in the *Scheer*'s path. Altogether, seven cruisers and an aircraft carrier were in the ring, but the *Scheer* slipped through.

The award of the Knight's Cross to Captain Krancke was announced by radio, and the machine shop made one for a formal presentation on the quarterdeck, at which Krancke announced that the ship was homeward bound. Kranke ordered a radar part sent out to him, and the ship refitted in the South Atlantic for the breakthrough. In late March 1941 the *Scheer* sailed through the Denmark Strait, sighting and avoiding several British cruisers. Fortunately the next sighting, the 'battleship *Nelson*', turned out to be an iceberg, and the *Scheer* was safely in Bergen on March 30th, Captain Krancke's birthday. Two days later she arrived in home waters, completing the war's most successful voyage of a lone German warship.

The heavy cruiser *Hipper*, named after Raeder's commander at Jutland, had sailed a month after the *Scheer*. She broke through the Denmark Strait in early December 1940, covered by the confusion caused by the *Scheer*'s attacks as well as the usual winter weather. She cruised in the Atlantic, finding a troop convoy bound for the Middle East on Christmas Eve. A dawn attack was frustrated by a strong cruiser escort, which forced her to break off after an exchange of fire and a few hits for each side. She entered Brest two days later, the first major German warship to do so. When she had completed repairs to her damage and to her unreliable engines she sortied again on February 1st, 1941, sank a lone ship, and took part in the war's only successful coordination of a surface ship, aircraft, and a submarine in the Atlantic.

The submarine sighted and reported the unescorted convoy, five aircraft attacked, the submarine scored some torpedo hits, and finally the *Hipper* arrived to sink seven ships from the scattering group before returning to Brest for fuel on the 14th. A month later she sailed again, breaking through the Denmark Strait a few days ahead of the *Scheer*. Her fuel-hungry steam-turbine power plant and her frequent mechanical breakdowns made her a poor raider, and her French base had been subjected to heavy bombing attacks, which had not hit her but which made it inadvisable to leave her there.

Meanwhile attacks on targets accessible to destroyers and torpedo boats from French Atlantic ports took place with few successes other than the tying down of more British forces. By January 1941 all destroyers were under repair, mainly for maintenance of their experimental power plants.

Spring also saw improvements in Air Force cooperation, despite an argument in the last months of 1940 over using torpedo planes against the British. Hitler endorsed the plan after hearing about the success of the British torpedo planes against the Italian battleships during Taranto Night, while Raeder opposed it because Göring wished to use planes then under naval control in the North Sea. Raeder was too short of naval aircraft to spare any. It was unfortunate that the idea of torpedo planes, which Raeder favoured, was delayed because of Göring's ambitions. However, in the spring of 1941 the Air Force looked for easier successes than the Battle of Britain had provided and began to strike very hard with bombs at naval targets. The Navy had long been sure that the Air Force alone could sink 300,000 tons of shipping per month and destroy harbour facilities on a significant scale. In March, April, and May of 1941, the Air Force almost achieved that goal, reaching 296,000 tons in April, the high point. Most Glasgow shipyards were put out of action for from three to seven months, and Liverpool had half its docks destroyed. Just as things seemed best from Raeder's viewpoint, the Russian offensive called the Air Force away.

Meanwhile the battleships *Scharnhorst* and *Gneisenau* headed for the Atlantic, the first time in history for German battleships to do so. They had started from Kiel on December 28th, 1940, but had had to turn back because of storm damage. On January 23rd they came out again, moving north along the Norwegian coast and then breaking for the Iceland-Faeroes Passage. They reached a point south of Iceland, where they sighted a cruiser at first light and promptly retreated to the north-east at high speed, shaking off the cruiser. Admiral Günther Lütjens had avoided a daylight battle with the Home Fleet, which was awaiting the German sortie. A week later the battleships came south again and successfully negotiated the Denmark Strait without being sighted by the British.

A few days' run southwards brought them to the Halifax convoy route, where their admiral's greatest hopes were fulfilled. A loaded eastbound convoy came in sight. Lütjens split his force, one ship to the south and one to the north of the convoy, and closed in. Then came the unpleasant surprise: the fighting top of an R-class battleship came into view. She was old and ponderous but carried the 15-inch guns that German sailors rightly feared, remembering the damage done to the *Gneisenau* by the *Renown*'s few hits off Norway not many months before. Lütjens' instructions, which Naval Operations Staff later admitted were too rigid, caused him to call off both ships rather than try to lure the escort away with one ship and attack the convoy with the other.

Two weeks later, the ships were back on the same route but farther west, where westbound convoys often were unescorted as they dispersed to various destinations. There they found and sank five ships in one day, but the British were alerted and the hunt was on again. Lütjens shifted far to the south and east to strike the route around the bulge of Africa. Again a convoy was sighted, and again a battleship accompanied it, that time the *Malaya* of Jutland fame. Lütjens called in three submarines to try to eliminate the battleship. They sank four merchantmen but failed to damage the *Malaya*. The alarm had been given, so Lütjens' force disappeared into the west sinking a lone ship on the way.

Back on the Halifax route with two supply ships to form a 120-mile-wide scouting line, the *Scharnhorst* and *Gneisenau* sank thirteen unescorted ships in two days and sent three in as prizes. Then they headed for Brest to prepare for an even bigger operation scheduled for the next month. The *Gneisenau* avoided another battleship, which sighted her briefly. The two ships also were sighted twice by aircraft but nevertheless were able to reach the French coast safely. The two-month cruise had included nine refuellings at sea. The loss to the British was 115,622 tons of shipping as well as a major disruption of convoy cycles. The battleships had diverted British forces from the operations of the *Hipper*, the *Scheer*, and the distant secret raiders. Finally their run to Brest had indirectly covered the return of the *Hipper* and the *Scheer* to Germany. The cruise was disappointing only because of the battleships escorting the convoys. Finding targets had been a problem because of British diversive routing and limited German search capability. Radar-fitted supply ships and special radar-equipped search submarines were therefore planned for the next raid when the battleships reached Brest on March 22nd, 1941.

New plans were being readied, for the greatest operation of all was yet to come, and the greatest warship in the world was preparing for sea. The battleship *Bismarck* was a paradoxical ship from the first. At Hitler's command she was named after the 'blood and iron' chancellor who had created the German nation but who had despised the Navy. Her consort was to be the new heavy cruiser *Prinz Eugen*, a ship named to honour the Austrian Navy – an important force until the end of World War I, whose river-based remnants had been absorbed by the German Navy at the Anschluss. Ironically, she was named after the Austrian ally of the Duke of Marlborough, the ancestor of Winston Churchill. Of the two ships, the *Prinz Eugen* was destined to become the Navy's 'lucky ship', while the *Bismarck* was to become its most famous and most tragic warship.

From the start, the plans were beset by misfortune and delay. The *Scharnhorst* needed engine repairs which would keep her in Brest, out of the operation. In April the *Gneisenau* received first torpedo and then bomb damage from the persistent British Navy and RAF, so she too could not sail. The new battleship *Tirpitz*, sister ship of the *Bismarck*, was months away from completion of crew training and mechanical shakedown. The *Hipper* and *Scheer* were refitting after their Atlantic cruises, and the *Lützow*'s Norwegian campaign damage was still being repaired. The *Bismarck* and *Prinz Eugen* would have to sail alone, and Raeder was anxious to get them to sea while the Arctic nights were still long enough to help cover the breakout. Mechanical problems delayed the *Bismarck*. Then the *Prinz Eugen* ran over a magnetic mine in late April, which set the timetable back another two weeks.

Admiral Günther Lütjens came north from Brest, fresh from his successful cruise with the two smaller battleships. He was troubled by the lack of support his new commands would have and by the strength the British were deploying in the Atlantic. He requested Raeder to delay the sortie until the *Scharnhorst* or even the *Tirpitz* could join, but Raeder refused. Heavy ships were needed immediately in the Atlantic. Not only was the German submarine fleet too weak on the North Atlantic trade routes, but diversions of British Fleet strength from the Mediterranean were essential to aid the passage of convoys to the Afrika Korps and to assure success of the daring Crete invasion which was scheduled for late May.

Behind all those urges to action lay the greatest threats: what if the United States should enter the war? What if refinements in ships' search radar should make breakout impossible in the near future? Would Germany's greatest ship be doomed to impotent menace in the backwaters of German coastal waters as had the Kaiser's vaunted High Seas Fleet?

Lütjens was well aware of the arguments over tactics and the extent of a fleet commander's freedom of action, which had led to the removal of the two previous fleet commanders, Admirals Hermann Boehm and Wilhelm Marschall. If he vigorously opposed the plans he would be expected to carry out, Raeder's reaction was certain. Lütjens did not wish to be the third fleet commander relieved of his command.

On May 18th, 1941, the doubts and debates were history. The *Bismarck* and *Prinz Eugen* sailed for the Atlantic. On his bridge, Admiral Lütjens stood determined to take his ships out and follow orders, no matter what the consequences. His orders were clear: attack the North Atlantic supply line, which alone kept Britain in the war; break through and carry on without combat if possible, but fight all-out if action was joined; destroy merchant tonnage as the primary goal; operate as long as combat readiness could be maintained; and return to Germany.

The two ships sailed through the Great Belt between the Danish islands, through the Kattegat, then through the Skagerrak north of the Jutland Peninsula, which had given its name to Germany's greatest naval battle twenty-five years before. All seemed peaceful as the ships sailed up the coast of Norway and into a quiet fiord near Bergen to refuel on May 21st. Air reconnaissance the previous day had reported the British Home Fleet at anchor in Scapa Flow, but that morning an intercepted British radio message ordering aircraft to search for two battleships and three destroyers heading north showed that the British were alert, although their intelligence

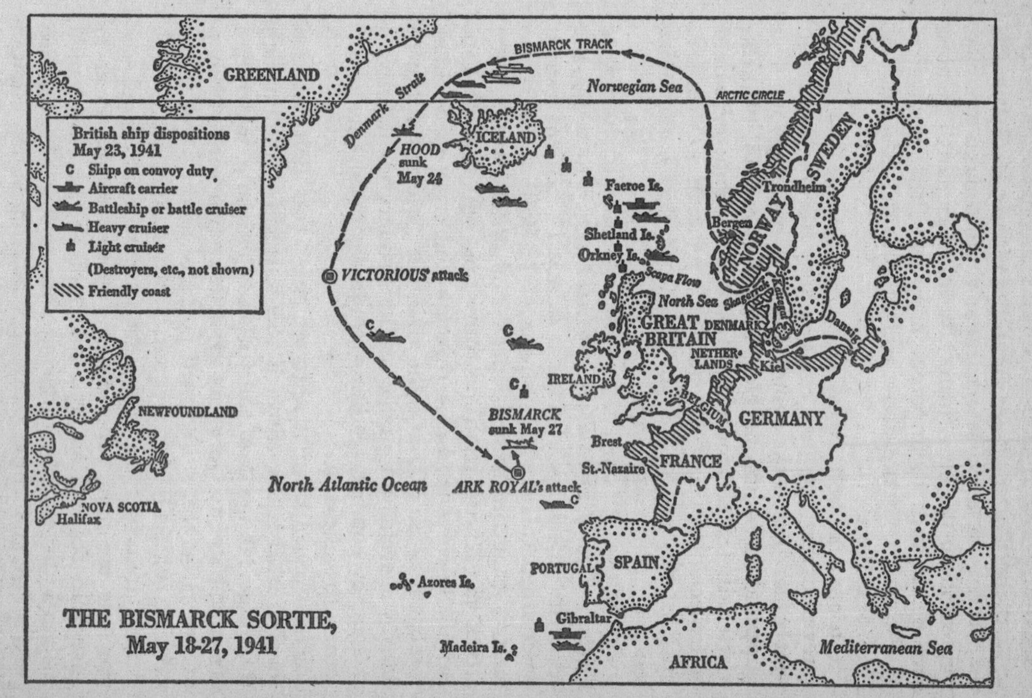

THE BISMARCK SORTIE, May 18-27, 1941

was inaccurate. The first report had presumably come from a British agent on the neutral Swedish coast. The British confirmed it by aerial reconnaissance photographs which identified the ships. By midnight the *Bismarck* and *Prinz Eugen* were gone. The chase had begun.

Far to the north and west they sailed, dismissing their destroyer escorts at the latitude of Trondheim and heading for an immediate breakthrough under cover of the prevailing stormy weather. Speed was of the essence, for not until they reached the open Atlantic would their support ships be available. Two scout ships, two supply ships, four tankers, and six submarines had sailed earlier, and were waiting for the warships to break out. Speed might enable them to pass the Denmark Strait before British heavy units could arrive. An erroneous aerial reconnaissance report that still showed the entire Home Fleet in Scapa Flow apparently encouraged the move to that distant, icy strait; for the far broader passages between Iceland and the Faeroes and between the Faeroes and Shetlands were far closer to the British base.

All that day and far into the 23rd the *Bismarck* and *Prinz Eugen* pushed on through rain squalls and heavy clouds near the ice line that ran close to the Arctic Circle. A few miles of visibility terminated sharply in dense fog banks to the south. As the vessels neared the north-west coast of Iceland, the ice-free passage narrowed to eighty, seventy, and finally sixty miles. Night was little refuge in seas so close to the midnight sun, but the weather, closing in more and more, was almost a perfect substitute. Almost perfect – but the heavy cruiser *Suffolk* suddenly appeared at the edge of the fog belt seven miles ahead of the *Bismarck*. The British ship quickly turned into the mists, circled to the rear of the German force, and began sending radio signals that announced the hunt was on. The *Bismarck*'s radiomen intercepted the British contact reports, and, more ominously, the electronics specialists manning radar search receivers recorded their own entrapment in the net of the *Suffolk*'s new tracking radar.

One month earlier, when the sortie had been expected to start, the *Suffolk* was just having her search radar fitted at her captain's behest. At that time, no British cruiser on Arctic patrol had possessed such equipment, so the Germans could easily have evaded the British patrols. The new British radar presented the *Bismarck*'s officers with their first surprise.

An hour later another British heavy cruiser broke clear of the fog ahead of the *Bismarck*. That ship, the *Norfolk*, was only six miles away when the *Bismarck* greeted her with 15-inch shell salvoes, three of which straddled the cruiser, spraying her with steel splinters. Luck, smoke, and a rapid retreat into the massive fog banks saved the *Norfolk* from damage. She took station in the fog off the *Bismarck*'s port quarter.

Admiral Lütjens ordered speed increased to 28 knots for the night run through the Denmark Strait. He sent the *Prinz Eugen* speeding ahead to change places with the *Bismarck* so his battleship's guns could continue to threaten the British cruisers. Increasing snow and fog intermittently hid the pursued and pursuers from each other, but the persistent British radar pulses damped German hopes of a quick escape. Lütjens decided against an attempt to turn to destroy the cruisers at close range. Perhaps he feared a torpedo attack in a moment of low visibility or desired to gain manoeuvring room in more open waters. Whatever his reasons, his ships stood on steadily to the south-west.

A black smudge of smoke, then a silhouette and, quickly, a second, became visible to German lookouts early the next morning on a bearing just forward of the port beam. Fire-control directors and turrets were trained, and the *Bismarck*'s eight 15-inch rifles and the *Prinz Eugen*'s 8-inch main battery were angled sharply upwards for a long-range battle. Lookouts identified the leading ship as the battle cruiser *Hood*, equal to the *Bismarck* in guns, size, and speed, but more than twenty years old and weak in deck armour. The second, following in close order, was a modern ship of the *King George V* class, a formidable foe with ten 14-inch guns.

The two continued to close in, nearly bows on; for the old *Hood* was vulnerable to long-range plunging fire, and her consort's inexperienced crew could not be expected to hit elusive targets at great distances. The headlong dash, however, masked eight of their eighteen heavy guns. The British ships were plunging heavily into the swells, which threw masses of spray over their forecastles and blinded the main turret range finders. Neither radar nor spotter planes had revealed the presence of the British capital ships, nor had radio been used to give the two heavy cruisers or six nearby destroyers time to close in on the Germans. All those decisions had apparently been taken in a vain attempt to achieve surprise against a fully alert German squadron on a day in which visibility had increased rapidly to over twelve miles. Vice-Admiral Lancelot Holland had allowed two-to-one superiority to become less than parity before a shot had been fired.

The *Hood* fired first at about twelve miles' range, followed immediately by her consort, the *Prince of Wales*, and by the two Germans. Lütjens ordered fire concentrated on the leading enemy ship, the *Hood*. Admiral Holland also ordered fire concentrated on the leading heavy ship, believing that the *Bismarck* was in the lead. The error was caused by the similarity of the German ships' silhouettes and their change of position since the shadowing cruisers' last visual-contact report. The *Hood* therefore opened fire on the *Prinz Eugen*; but Captain J. C. Leach of the *Prince of Wales* recognized Admiral Holland's error and ordered his crew to fire on the *Bismarck*, disregarding his admiral's order.

The *Prinz Eugen* hit the *Hood* after a few ranging salvoes and started a large fire amidships. The *Bismarck*, firing salvoes every twenty-two seconds, was on target at about the same time. The *Hood*'s gunners took only three salvoes to find the *Prinz Eugen*'s range, but the *Prince of Wales*' inexperienced crew, although undisturbed by

German shells, missed the *Bismarck* by half a mile with the first salvo and required six more salvoes to find range. For three minutes, Admiral Holland held on for his foes at 28 knots, his ship being struck repeatedly. Then the British ships were turned to port to unmask their aft guns. Slowly the British formation swung towards its new course, with the *Hood* on fire aft and closely patterned German salvoes tearing at her. Four minutes – five minutes the battle lasted, until another salvo of 15-inch shells straddled the *Hood*. A moment later flames shot out of her to mast-top height, followed by explosions and an enormous cloud of flame: a fireball flecked with steel turrets and debris billowed upwards and was quickly covered with oily black smoke. The bow and stern stood out for a moment against the inferno, then they buckled inwards and plunged into the depths, carrying all but three of the 1,419-man crew to their deaths.

The *Prince of Wales* turned sharply to starboard to avoid the sinking wreck and within a minute came under the same heavy and accurate fire. The range was down to nine miles, and the tight British formation had allowed a rapid German target shift. Shell splashes, some of them 200 feet high, surrounded her to such an extent that her spotters had great difficulty in observing her own fire effect. The *Bismarck*'s 5.9-inch secondary battery joined the assault, and was answered by the British 5.25-inch guns. A 15-inch shell hit the *Prince of Wales*' bridge, striking down everyone but the captain and a signalman and destroying some of the fire-control system. Her guns, delivered just three weeks before the battle and still being serviced by dockyard personnel, broke down repeatedly, so she was firing salvoes of about three shells instead of ten. Two hits below the waterline let in 600 tons of water aft, while others, one of them an 8-inch round that penetrated a magazine but failed to explode, tore through the armour. The range was down to seven miles when the *Prince of Wales* received her seventh hit. She turned sharply away, pouring out smoke to blind the deadly

German gunners. As she heeled in the turn, her aft quadruple turret broke down. The *Bismarck* and the *Prinz Eugen* ceased fire when the range opened to more than ten miles; the twenty-minute battle was over.

Admiral Holland had fought a very poor battle, and it was Captain Leach's insubordination that had saved it from being completely futile. His decision to fire at the *Bismarck* despite orders had given his inexperienced crew over five minutes to range on the *Bismarck*, rather than on the less important *Prinz Eugen*, during the period when his ship was not being disturbed by German fire. Two 14-inch hits had been scored on the *Bismarck*, reducing her speed from a maximum of nearly 31 knots to 28, dropping her bow one degree, and, most important of all, causing her to lose fuel oil.

Admiral Lütjens reported Germany's greatest and most startling victory to a delighted homeland while Rear-Admiral W. F. Wake-Walker of the cruisers took the battered *Prince of Wales* under his command and resumed shadowing. The *Suffolk* soon reported a drop in the Germans' speed to 24 knots, and the *Bismarck*'s large oil slick.

On the *Bismarck*'s bridge, a sharp disagreement took place as the *Prince of Wales* disappeared. Captain Ernst Lindemann wanted to finish off the damaged enemy and then return to Germany for repairs, but Admiral Lütjens ordered the ship to stay on course south-westward into the Atlantic. Many factors may have influenced him, among them the *Bismarck*'s loss of speed relative to the apparently still speedy *Prince of Wales* and the conviction that his enemy was the Home Fleet flagship *King George V*, which would draw him towards the rest of the Home Fleet if he continued the fight. He disliked entering smoke screens or cloud and fog when torpedo-carrying cruisers and possibly destroyers and torpedo planes were in the vicinity. He knew that further battle would force him to run for a home port for repairs, fuel, and ammunition when he had already succeeded in breaking through to the Atlantic. The breakthrough had been considered the most difficult part of the operation by German tacticians, and a return through those narrow passages, with the aroused British Fleet operating on interior lines, was viewed as a very risky enterprise. His ignorance of his second enemy's identity probably was a major factor in his decision. Ironically, by that night, Admiral Alfred Saalwächter's Group West could radio from Paris that the *Prince of Wales*, not the flagship, had probably been Admiral Lütjens' morning opponent. In the event, Lütjens decided to obey his general order – to get into the Atlantic for commerce war – and ignore two more specific ones – to fight all out if a fight was forced on him and to return to Germany rather than the French ports, which were threatened by air assault.

Within two hours he announced his intention of putting into St-Nazaire, the only French port with a dry dock large enough to hold the *Bismarck*. By early afternoon his plans were refined. He intended to release the *Prinz Eugen* for independent commerce war and, if the *Bismarck* could not shake off her pursuers, to lead them through a submarine ambush south of Greenland as a means of doing so. He realized that Admiral Sir John Tovey, Commander-in-Chief of the British Home Fleet, was concentrating all his strength to destroy the *Bismarck*, and that escape from his pursuers was essential. Group West suggested withdrawal to a remote area if it were possible to shake off the pursuit.

In the evening the *Bismarck* turned on her pursuers and fired a few salvoes, forcing them to open the range and allowing the *Prinz Eugen* to escape southwards in a heavy rain squall while the *Bismarck* led her pursuers south-south-west towards a dawn contact with the submarine line. An hour and a half later, however, apparently despairing of an opportunity to get free of the radar tracking and plagued by a worsening fuel shortage, Admiral Lütjens ordered the ship turned southwards, giving up hope of the submarines' aid or of succour from a tanker.

Admiral Tovey's measures became more obvious just before sunset, when nine Swordfish torpedo planes attacked from three directions through the *Bismarck*'s fierce anti-aircraft fire. Only the failure of the shells to explode when they tore through the canvas-covered wood-and-metal frames can have saved those 85-knot biplanes from destruction. Their pilots, crouched in open cockpits, pushed in to half-mile range to hit their target once on the 15-inch-thick armour amidships. The battleship ploughed on, hardly affected by the hit, her officers wondering why so few planes were in the assault.

That assault illustrated the lengths to which the British Admiralty had been going ever since a daring pilot had flown through abominable weather to report the German ships gone from their Norwegian refuelling stop on the day after their departure. The alert cruiser patrol in the Denmark Strait had been one of the moves. So had the placing of the *Hood–Prince of Wales* force to the south of Iceland, ready to counter a move through the passage to the east or to the west of that island. Another move had been the holding back of the new aircraft carrier *Victorious,* freighted with fighter planes for Malta and with only the nine Swordfish newly arrived on board. The *Victorious* had sailed in company with the *King George V,* carrying Admiral Tovey, and was soon joined by the battle cruiser *Repulse*. They were escorted by four light cruisers and seven destroyers. Their assignment had been to cover the passages east of Iceland. On the day of the *Hood*'s disaster, the carrier had been rushed forward with the cruiser escort for her evening attack, while the Admiralty had attempted to gather forces from convoy escorts all over the Atlantic and even from the critical Mediterranean, calling out the Gibraltar Fleet (a fact reported to Admiral Lütjens by Group West), so serious was the *Bismarck*'s threat. By the next morning, Admiral

Tovey expected to come up with his quarry, hopefully slowed by the *Victorious*' torpedo attack.

An hour after the torpedo-plane attack, the *Bismarck* fired a few more salvoes at her pursuers without result. Still later that night, Lütjens ordered her turned to a direct course for France. Hour after hour the *Bismarck* pushed south-eastwards. Dawn of May 25th came with no attack and no British ship visible, but the invisible radar beams registered with monotonous persistence on the German instruments. Held so firmly in the electronic trap, Admiral Lütjens permitted himself a luxury rare in war – a long radio message describing the Denmark Strait battle and commenting on his situation relative to the following British radar. Group West flashed back the news that the British had apparently lost contact six and a half hours before. Their radar beams were reaching the *Bismarck* but were no longer bouncing back to the *Suffolk*'s receiver. The *Bismarck*'s technicians, concerned with their radar search receivers, had failed to note the absence of position reports in the *Suffolk*'s regular transmissions. For six and a half hours the *Bismarck* had been free and had not known it, then she trapped herself with her own radio message.

The British Admiralty rushed the raw radio-direction-finder data to the flagship, *King George V*, where eager navigators plotted them on a Mercator chart and discovered that the quarry apparently had changed course sharply to the north-east – towards the Iceland-Faeroes Passage and a breakthrough into the Norwegian Sea and back to Germany. Immediately Admiral Tovey and the Admiralty issued a flood of orders, redirecting fuel-short heavy ships towards the unguarded northern blockade line.

Tired German lookouts scanned the horizon while officers calculated the fuel reserve and speculated on British failure to re-establish contact as the *Bismarck* continued on course, not to the north-east as the British thought, but towards France. There appeared to be no point in radical evasive moves. The British, they were sure, knew their approximate position. With fuel short and time working for their enemy, the shortest course and moderate speed seemed the best. The day continued to be very quiet. In the midst of war there was time for Admiral Lütjens to appreciate birthday greetings from Grand Admiral Raeder, coupled with hopes for continued success. A few hours later a similar message arrived from Hitler.

Lütjens used the quiet time to address the crew over the loudspeaker system. He thanked the men for their birthday wishes and commented on the victory over the *Hood*, but then he went further: he warned them that the worst was yet to come, that the British would gather all their forces to hunt the vanquisher of the *Hood*, and that a win-or-die struggle impended. A chill air of foreboding ran through the previously self-confident ship's company, but sea and sky remained clear of enemies.

No such respite was granted the British, whose flagship had been only a hundred miles away from an interception when contact had been lost, and whose grim frustration mounted hourly. During the afternoon and into the evening all British reports were negative. For seven hours, the chase into the empty northern wastes continued, until information from a new set of radio-direction-finder bearings caused Admiral Tovey's staff to recalculate the old bearings on a properly calibrated Polar Coordinate chart instead of the Mercator chart to discover their error.* The Admiralty reached a similar conclusion at about the same time. Once more the ships turned, but not all could make the run to the south-east. Most of the destroyers were gone, making port on the last fuel in their tanks. Some of the cruisers and the carrier *Victorious*, far behind and with fuel low, also gave up the chase, as did the

* Further confounding the story is the fact that the German records show no message from the *Bismarck* from early morning until late evening. The identity of the ship that transmitted the message, on which the second set of bearings was made, is not known.

damaged *Prince of Wales*. More convoys were rerouted out of the *Bismarck*'s projected path. The slow but powerful battleship *Rodney*, with nine 16-inch guns, had been called from convoy duty and had crossed ahead of the *Bismarck* in a perfect interception position that afternoon, but she too had cleared the way by sailing on the false track. She turned towards a junction with the *King George V* on her long stern chase; but the flagship was 150 miles behind her quarry, and the *Bismarck*'s location was only an estimate.

Dawn of May 26th revealed a sea still empty of enemies to the *Bismarck*'s watch. Men who had been sleeping in snatches near their battle stations assured each other that one more dawn would bring them into the orbit of the promised air cover, submarine patrol line, and destroyer escort. By midmorning there had been no hostile contact for over thirty hours. Then a low-flying Catalina flying boat came briefly into view through a break in the heavy cloud, was smothered by anti-aircraft fire, disappeared into the cloud, and lost contact. Shortly afterwards, two long-range carrier aircraft appeared to take over the shadowing, and in mid-afternoon the light cruiser *Sheffield* fell in astern to begin radar tracking. The *Bismarck* had been found again – but apparently too late for the British pursuers.

Meanwhile, *U556* was labouring through the high, steep seas to reach her assigned position in a patrol line designed to cover the *Bismarck*'s entry into the Bay of Biscay. Lieutenant-Commander Herbert Wohlfahrt (meaning 'welfare'), on her tiny, wave-swept bridge, had a very special concern for his assignment. Months before, in a spirit of lighthearted camaraderie, he had presented the *Bismarck* with an elaborate certificate proclaiming the 770-ton *U556* 'godfather' to the 41,700-ton behemoth and promising to see that she came to no harm. Late in the afternoon his opportunity came. Enemy warships appeared. *U556* crash-dived and came to periscope depth in time to see the battle cruiser *Renown* plunging through the massive seas at high speed and the aircraft carrier *Ark Royal* pitching wildly but with torpedo aircraft on deck. It was the Gibraltar Fleet, the only capital-ship group in a position to intercept the *Bismarck*. Commander Wohlfahrt's war diary tells the story: *

> 1948. Alarm. A battleship of the *King George* class [an error] and an aircraft carrier, probably the *Ark Royal*, came in right from the mist from astern, travelling at high speed. Bows to the right, inclination 170 degrees. If only I had had a few torpedoes! I would not even have had to manoeuvre – I was just perfectly placed for an attack. No destroyers, no zigzagging! I could have stayed where I was and got them both. Torpedo-carrying aircraft observed operating from carrier. I might have been able to help the *Bismarck*.

Still the *Bismarck* appeared to be in little danger. The battle cruiser *Renown* was older and more weakly armoured than the *Hood*, and the Admiralty ordered Vice-Admiral Sir John Somerville not to attack the *Bismarck* with her until other capital ships could come up – if they could. Only the *Ark Royal*'s Swordfish had a chance to slow the *Bismarck* with their torpedoes. In seas so violent that German destroyers were held in port, and that caused the *Ark Royal*'s flight deck to pitch through a fifty-six foot arc, fifteen Swordfish struggled off her flight deck. One turned back, but the rest slowly battled the head-winds, storm, and cloud to locate the target, form into groups, and come in to the attack from different angles off her bows. Eleven launched torpedoes and pulled up, wondering at the lack of anti-aircraft fire, then in sudden horror realized that their torpedoes were running towards

* Karl Dönitz, *Memoirs*, p 169. The *U 556* sighting occurred after the launching of the *Ark Royal*'s second torpedo-plan attack. (Wohlfahrt's description indicates before, but later correlations indicate after.) The incident is related at this point in order to keep in sequence from the German viewpoint.

the *Sheffield*. Five of the torpedoes exploded prematurely, and the wildly slewing *Sheffield* avoided the others. Three Swordfish pilots recognized their target just in time to break off the attack.

Time had been lost, but the near tragedy provided valuable information. Defective magnetic detonators were replaced with contact detonators on the aerial torpedoes for the next assault, and once more intrepid British pilots braved the elements in their fragile canvas-covered biplanes to make the last attack possible before sunset. That would be the last chance for the British. Their capital ships were too low on fuel to venture much farther, and, by dawn, the *Bismarck* would be close enough to France to be protected by land-based planes. The fifteen Swordfish flew to the *Sheffield*, which coached them to the assault against the fifty-six anti-aircraft guns of the alert colossus. The violent sea helped upset the aim of the tiring German gunners, and the planes' own flimsy structure spared some of them fatal damage from the myriad shell splinters which slashed through them. Determined defence failed to stop the fifteen from closing in and attacking. Eleven were failures as their torpedoes missed. Two could not launch their missiles. The fourteenth torpedo struck amidships but caused no damage.

The fifteenth attack was not deadly either – or so it seemed. The torpedo smashed the steering engine room; the *Bismarck*, however, had three propellers and normally could steer herself to harbour by alternating the speed of her engines. Nevertheless, the German Navy's proudest ship was doomed. The rudders had been hard over when the torpedo struck, and nothing could move them. The *Bismarck* swung broadside to the *Sheffield* and began hurling half-salvoes at the surprised British cruiser, which had failed to turn as the *Bismarck* turned. As the *Sheffield* sheered desperately away under smoke, with three dead, nine wounded, and her radar smashed, she quickly sent the news that was to dismay Germany and delight Great Britain: the *Bismarck* was circling, then steadying at slow speed on course north-west, into the massive seas and towards her pursuers.

Desperate attempts by divers working in the flooded steering engine compartment failed to blast the rudders loose. When their efforts failed, the end was certain. Only the means were yet to be decided.

Aboard the *Bismarck* there was time for the dramatic gesture. Admiral Lütjens signalled, 'We fight to the last shell. Long live the Führer,' and, a few minutes later, 'To the Führer of the German Reich Adolf Hitler: we fight to the last in our belief in you my Führer and in the firm faith in Germany's victory.' Hitler answered, 'To Fleet Commander: I thank you in the name of the German people. To the crew of the battleship *Bismarck*: the whole of Germany is with you. What can still be done will be done. The performance of your duty will strengthen our people in the struggle for their existence.'*

There was time, too, for the small touch. Admiral Lütjens asked Admiral Raeder to reward the *Bismarck*'s gunnery officer for sinking the *Hood*, so Commander Adalbert Schneider, a man with but hours to live, received the Knight's Cross by order of the Führer.

There was also time to look towards the future, a future few aboard could hope to see. The Arado float planes were prepared for launching to take the war diary and other documents to France, but one of the unimportant hits amidships had damaged the compressed-air system, preventing the take-off. Later, Admiral Lütjens radioed for a submarine to take off the war diary; but none arrived in time. The war diary, with all its information about the war's most famous cruise, stayed aboard to the end.

The German Navy did what it could to intervene, ordering all nearby submarines into the conflict. Only *U556* was in the vicinity. Without torpedoes, her crew sent homing signals for other submarines and watched starshells burst high above the sea.

* 'Führer Conferences on Naval Affairs', *Brassey's Naval Annual, 1948*, p 213.

Shortly after dark, the *Bismarck*'s radar began to pick out British destroyers closing in, obviously for torpedo attacks. There were five of them, under command of Captain Philip Vian, hero of the *Altmark* affair a year before. Called out of a convoy escort to screen the Home Fleet, Captain Vian had 'steered to the sound of the guns' on his own initiative. Again and again the battleship met the destroyers' lunges with accurate 15-inch and 5.9-inch shell salvoes, the first combat use of night radar ranging. Hour after hour her radar men saw the destroyers dodge out of range, then come in again. From her bridge, only sporadic gun flashes marked the destroyers' positions, while their starshells burst brilliantly to light the stormy battlefield, then as suddenly left it black and empty. Lookouts strained against their own guns' blinding flash and the blinding dark that followed, while officers dreaded the unseen menace of the torpedoes they could no longer evade. Before dawn, the destroyers withdrew. Neither side had scored. The destroyers had enjoyed the lucky freedom from damage that had favoured all the British lighter ships in the campaign, and they had tired the German gunners and made the British heavy ships' job an easier one.

With the light came the Home Fleet. The Gibraltar Fleet's thin-skinned battle cruiser *Renown* was kept out of the fight, to forestall another disaster. The flagship *King George V*, a sister ship of the *Prince of Wales*, had barely enough fuel to bring her into the battle and still get home. The *Rodney*'s deck was encumbered by crates of parts needed for a refit in the United States, and she had 500 invalids aboard who had expected a quiet voyage across the Atlantic. Those two ships, mounting ten 14-inch and nine 16-inch guns, respectively, were joined by the heavy cruisers *Dorsetshire* and *Norfolk*, with eight 8-inch guns each.

The *Norfolk* was the first ship to be sighted by the *Bismarck*. She sailed to within eight miles but then retreated into the stormy seas as rapidly as she had come. Soon the two battleships appeared ahead, and the *Bismarck* managed to turn slightly to starboard with her engines to allow all eight heavy guns to bear on them. The British fired first at 8.47 AM as they closed in with only their forward turrets bearing. The *Bismarck* held her fire briefly, then lashed out at the *Rodney*. Her third salvo was a straddle, remarkable shooting for a tired crew, and the *Rodney* sheered out to bring all her guns to bear. The *King George V* closed in rapidly. The *Norfolk* opened fire from ten miles ahead.

The *Bismarck*, unable to 'chase salvoes' as the British were doing, made too good a target. An early salvo from the *Rodney* scored a hit on her second turret. Blast and splinters swept the bridge, killing almost everyone there, just as a *Bismarck* shell had destroyed the *Prince of Wales*' bridge at dawn three days before. The *Bismarck*'s fire-control system was destroyed, and the gun turrets, firing independently in local control, quickly became inaccurate. The *King George V* swung parallel to the *Bismarck* on a reverse course at eight-mile range, and her aft quadruple turret joined in the battle. Another foe, the *Dorsetshire*, appeared on the opposite side. She opened fire from ten miles away. A fire was started on the *Bismarck*'s after deck, then another amidships. The British ships closed the range as the German fire slackened.

Shell after shell smashed into the upper works. Masts, funnel, and bridge were shredded; turrets were torn open; silent guns pointed at sea or sky – but the two 15-inch guns of the third turret still fired sporadically. The British battleships' 5.25-inch and 6-inch secondary batteries opened fire as the range closed; the *Rodney* and *Norfolk* fired torpedoes without effect; and finally the battleships stood in to two-mile range to pour in salvo after salvo, the 1-ton shells bursting in clusters on the *Bismarck*'s deck. There was no reply. The *Rodney* fired two torpedoes, scoring the only torpedo hit ever made by a battleship on another battleship; and then the two British battleships turned away, too short of fuel to stay for the end, leaving the *Bismarck* helpless but still moving.

Despite the nearly complete destruction topside, the armour had held throughout the two hours of carnage: watertight integrity was maintained, and the engines were unimpaired. The *Norfolk*, which had helped begin the campaign in the Denmark Strait, tried to end it with four torpedoes, one of which probably hit. The *Dorsetshire* fired two torpedoes at the starboard side of the flaming wreck, obtained one hit, then circled and hit it with another on the port side. It was the seventy-first torpedo fired in the campaign, and at least the seventh hit – yet the *Bismarck* did not sink. The torpedoes were ineffective against the armour. Fearing that the British might try to board their ship, her crew opened sea valves and exploded scuttling charges as the last act of the drama. The German Navy's greatest tragedy ended when the *Bismarck* capsized to port and sank, with the flag flying, at 10.40 AM on May 27th, 1941.

A submarine provided the final brutal irony for the *Bismarck*'s survivors. The violent seas had prevented *U74* from reaching the battleship to get her war diary or from attacking the British. As she cruised through the battle area at periscope depth, she was sighted by the *Dorsetshire* and a destroyer which were hove-to, rescuing survivors. The British worked up to high speed, taking 110 survivors with them but leaving hundreds in the water. *U74* could rescue only three. Over 2,200 men died, including Admiral Lütjens and Captain Lindemann.

After adjusting to the shock of the catastrophe which followed the victory over the *Hood* and *Prince of Wales* so quickly, and after answering some second-guessing by Hitler, the German Navy drew its conclusions. Broad Atlantic sorties were over. The aircraft carrier would not be finished, for she could not hope to break through into the Atlantic. Right after the *Bismarck*'s destruction, the British systematically hunted down nearly all the supply ships in the North Atlantic, destroying the raiders' logistic system. Air power and radar – the one of which the Germans lacked, the other of which the British had developed only too well – had done their work. The limited British forces had extended their eyes and striking power all too far. Yet the great ships had done their part. They had forced the diversion of British forces from the Mediterranean. They had carried on the war at sea while other forces gathered.

The submarines' turn had come.

Chapter 7

THE NORTH ATLANTIC

The submarine offensive June 1940–May 1943

As the fall of France brought the surface forces of the German Navy their 'golden age', so too that event gave their submarines their first opportunity. All the harbours of western France became available as submarine bases, shortening enormously the submarines' time in transit to the focal point of the crucial trans-Atlantic route, the area west of the British Isles known as the Western Approaches. The Gibraltar route, along which sailed all the traffic of the South Atlantic and Indian Oceans, was flanked. No blockade by mines and patrols, such as the one which had blocked the North Sea exits to the submarines towards the end of World War I, could be attempted.

The effect was cumulative. The shortened transit distance enabled even the small submarines to operate in the Western Approaches and the larger ones to remain there longer. The use of French repair facilities, which were later completely protected by enormous concrete buildings, relieved the congestion of German dockyards so more submarine building could be scheduled at home. The more submarines on station, the greater the likelihood of locating convoys, and thereby the more successes.

Immediately after the fall of France, the British shifted their convoy routes into the channel north of Ireland known as the North Channel, adding more strain to their west-coast harbour facilities. With the French Fleet out of the war and a large number of British escort vessels tied down by the invasion alert and by the need to escort Fleet units in their numerous sorties, the opposition to the submarines was noticeably thinned.

On May 15th, 1940, after a lapse of three months caused by the Norway campaign and by the need to repair and refit the submarine fleet, the first submarine set out to patrol the Western Approaches. Despite some torpedo failures, which resulted in the elimination of magnetic detonators for several years, *U37* found good hunting and weak escorts. She sank over 43,000 tons of shipping. The next submarines out confirmed the trend, finding many single targets and convoys. Usually the convoys were so close to the British Isles when sighted that the submarines did not have time to form packs. Group tactics, however, were not really needed with such easy targets, and radio silence was desirable; so Dönitz made relatively little effort at tight control, relying mainly on individual captains' good judgement and initiative once in an assigned area. As the German radio interception service only occasionally located convoys, dependence on submarines which maintained radio silence for finding targets was necessary.

With almost no restrictions on their actions, the submarines wrought havoc. They changed from submerged to surface attack, from day to night, from long-range spreads of torpedoes to short-range single shots fired within the escort ring. Sometimes, when positions ahead of convoys or fortuitous convoy course changes gave them the opportunity, they operated between the columns of merchantmen in the convoys. Captured French documents and equipment increased their knowledge of British anti-submarine methods and encouraged bold tactics. Aggressive submarine commanders exploited their opportunities to the full. It was the first 'happy time', the time of the great aces. Leading them was Lieutenant-Commander Otto Kretschmer, whose deadly aim and 'one torpedo, one ship' policy soon raised his score to 200,000 tons.

At Dönitz's and Raeder's headquarters, satisfaction over totals of sunken tonnage was countered by concern over the submarine building programme. Production was still far too low one year after the war had begun. In late May, in the midst of the Western Front battles, the submarine situation had been discussed at length with Hitler, and the decision made to concentrate on a long-range programme of construction and training rather than on an all-out effort by all submarines for a short time. That seems strange in view of Hitler's hopes for an early peace; but he apparently realized that committing the training submarines to battle, while not changing the situation much at sea, would endanger the long-range potential of the submarine effort. The decision had been a correct one. At the same conference, Hitler had promised to concentrate on submarines and aircraft when the campaign in France ended. That promise was repeated on June 4th in answer to Raeder's questions about lagging submarine construction. Later in the month, the campaign in France drew to a victorious close, so Hitler approved acceleration of submarine construction – but that was not the last word on the subject.

In July, as the first submarines began using Lorient for a base, Hitler agreed to intensify the submarine war again by declaring a submarine danger zone almost identical to the large area off western Europe forbidden to Americans by Presidential order. Within it, except for hospital ships and neutral ships on scheduled routes, unrestricted submarine warfare was permitted, although that phrase was not used.

At the end of the month, the Italians, who had sent single submarines into the Atlantic, offered to station a group there permanently if the Germans would provide a base. The offer was eagerly accepted, although Hitler refused to permit the German Navy to command the group, so the Italians would not have a precedent to ask for command over German units. Coordination at lower levels was quickly achieved between Dönitz and the

Italian commander, Rear-Admiral Angelo Parona, while Italian officers embarked in German submarines for practical experience in North Atlantic warfare. The Italian submarines were then each sent on one patrol to the Azores area, after which they were assigned to North Atlantic areas by Dönitz. Although they doubled the number of submarines available in the operating area, their performance was a disappointment. They were technically inferior to the German submarines and their training was so different and old-fashioned that they found few convoys, attacked none, and guided no German submarines to any. Eventually they were shifted to separate areas south of the German area and to the Gibraltar and West African areas, where they had individual successes, usually in daylight submerged attacks or in gunnery engagements. Over thirty of them participated from September 1940 to May 1941, when heavy commitments in North Africa and Greece led the Italian High Command to recall them to aid in the coming Mediterranean convoy and fleet battles.

In September, the British exchanged naval air bases for fifty old American destroyers in the famous 'Destroyer Deal', which led to unpleasant comments regarding America's becoming a hostile neutral at Raeder's next conference with Hitler. For Britain, however, the destroyers could do little more than cushion the shock of the first large-scale sustained convoy battles in the Western Approaches, which took place in September and October. In three nights in mid-October, eight submarines sank thirty-eight ships from three convoys. The whole operation became known as 'The Night of the Long Knives' in the jubilant German Press. Those operations fully justified Dönitz's hopes, so at the end of October he could sum up the experiences, confidently endorse the methods, note the weakness of British patrols, and again stress the need for more submarines. The need, he knew, had to be met if the initial German group successes were to lead to ultimate victory. A year of war had cost twenty-eight submarines, which had been balanced by twenty-eight replacements from the builders' yards. The small submarines were transferred to the Baltic training flotillas, so the combat fleet was reduced to twenty-two submarines in February 1941.

In the winter of 1940–41, the submarines were gradually forced away from the coasts of Great Britain by improved British air cover. That increased the problems of the submarines somewhat, for darkness and storm, coupled with greater distance between submarines, made it possible for convoys to slip between them. With the average number of submarines on station being only four to six from November to January, and reaching an all-time low of one at Christmas, very few coordinated attacks were possible, even though the submarines were stationed far enough from Britain to follow a convoy for more than one day. When contact was made, submarines often fired all their torpedoes and went back to base, leaving more gaps in the reconnaissance line.

In October 1940 Dönitz moved his headquarters from Paris, where he had been stationed in readiness for Sea Lion, to Kernevel, near Lorient, in order to put into effect the system of close contact with the operating forces that he always favoured. There, in daily conferences, he put into practice the plans he had developed for more than five years. Each day reports came in and orders were issued. Information from submarines at sea and the little from other sources, such as radio intercepts and spies, was analysed and fitted into the total strategy. The reports of the captains were also studied after each cruise, and all captains were carefully interviewed by Dönitz.

With enough submarines for regular group tactics finally anticipated within the next six months, regular patrol lines could be planned. The North Atlantic was the decisive theatre of the war and the submarines were to concentrate there, but they were to shift position away from any area in which British patrols were so strong that they caused the average tonnage sunk per submarine per day at sea to decrease. They would remain in a new area as long as that crucial figure stayed up – as long as they could assemble, manoeuvre, and fight. As soon as an area was chosen, a patrol line would be established in which submarines would sail towards expected convoys during the day and on the opposite course at night to prevent convoys from slipping through their cordon. A submarine finding a convoy would send beacon signals, and the attack would begin on the night the submarines assembled. One submarine would serve as the beacon-signal craft as needed, although this duty could often shift from one submarine to another during a battle. Dönitz's basic strategy was to sink British shipping in the most efficient way possible. The area, the route, the cargo or lack of it, were minor considerations at best; total shipping tonnage on the heavily travelled North Atlantic was to be decisive.

After operating for almost two years with practically no air support or reconnaissance, enough pressure was applied by the Navy so that a conference between Dönitz and Jodl of the OKW could be arranged by Raeder. Dönitz succeeded in convincing Jodl that the submarines had to have enough long-range aircraft under control of the submarine command to have twelve airborne daily. On January 7th, 1941, one air group at Bordeaux with long-range aircraft was subordinated to Dönitz by the OKW. Göring attempted to get the group back when he returned from a hunting trip, but Dönitz refused the demand. Göring then tried a different tack and created a new Air Force position – Air Commander, Atlantic – to control the reconnaissance activities. Fortunately, co-operation between the new officer, a former Navy flyer, and Dönitz was excellent.

In practice, two planes a day – rather than twelve – were usually available, one of which flew from Bordeaux to the Western Approaches and landed at Stavanger, Norway, while the other returned by the same route. The aircraft found some convoys in the Western Approaches, but their reports were often inaccurate, and distance and time usually defeated attempts at direct cooperation with the submarines. As the submarines moved farther to sea, they went beyond aircraft range, so the main function of aircraft was to give general information about convoy movement patterns, in itself a valuable asset to Dönitz.

Aircraft cooperation with the submarines and occasionally even surface ships was sometimes achieved in the Bay of Biscay–western Spain area. There, all three types of forces were used against shipping first located by any one of them. The tiny number of aircraft limited even those successes.

In the North Atlantic the number of submarines on patrol slowly crept past ten in the early months of 1941. The commanders, old and new, had good hunting: they sank nearly 100,000 tons in January, and forty-two ships of over 200,000 tons in February. The total dipped slightly as some submarines left to create a diversion in more southerly hunting grounds, but it topped 200,000 tons again in June. In January 1941 British imports were less than half their January 1940 totals.

The Naval High Command had reason to be optimistic at that time. The surface raiders were meeting success. Soon, it was expected, the Air Force would be capable of sinking 300,000 tons of shipping per month. That would put Germany in striking distance of the monthly average of 750,000 tons which, it was estimated, would force Britain out of the war if maintained for a year. Already total sinkings were estimated at 400,000 tons per month, with the British building only an estimated 200,000 tons per month. The time appeared ripe to crush the British – before Anglo-American building increased to the 500,000 tons per month which was estimated for 1942.

In the Atlantic, 'Silent Otto' Kretschmer continued to score. Three auxiliary cruisers, two of them sunk in one night, were numbered among his successes. Those large ships patrolled at modest speeds and some of them fell victim to practically every class of German warship: the *Rawalpindi* sunk by the two small battleships, the *Jervis Bay* destroyed by the *Scheer* after heroic resistance, three more defeated by the tiny raider *Thor*, and six sunk by submarines. Kretschmer led Prien (the 'Snorting Bull' of Scapa Flow) and Lieutenant-Commander Joachim Schepke in the friendly rivalry for tonnage-sunk honours. All three were at sea and cutting into convoys south of Iceland in early March 1941. Prien and Kretschmer had accidentally met while approaching a convoy and had exchanged signals. On March 8th Prien's submarine was sunk in a depth-charge attack with the loss of all on board. Just over a week later, Schepke's *U100* was caught by destroyers after leaving a badly battered convoy. Forced to dive, then depth-charged, she came to the surface out of control. A British destroyer rammed her amidships. Schepke was crushed by the destroyer's bow, and the submarine sank with him.

At the same time, Kretschmer had left the same decimated convoy after expending his last torpedoes on six ships. He had made his escape through the escorts and gone below when the officer on watch sighted a destroyer. He mistakenly assumed that *U99* had been seen, so he ordered a crash dive. One of the destroyers that had just destroyed *U100* picked up an Asdic contact and followed it with depth charges. Kretschmer's craft was badly hurt, and sinking towards the depth where her hull would be crushed. He had no choice but to blow his ballast and surface. Without torpedoes, helpless to fight back, he ordered one last radio message: 'Destroyer depth-charged; 50,000 GRT; prisoner of war. U-Kretschmer.'* He was announcing the sinking of 50,000 tons of shipping and his own imprisonment. Then he ordered *U99* scuttled. All but three men were saved by their enemies and joined the five survivors of the *U100*. Kretschmer was the war's greatest ace, holding the Oak Leaves to the Knight's Cross for his record of one

* Harald Busch, *U-Boats at War*, p 55.

destroyer and forty-four merchantmen sunk, a total of 266,629 tons.

Two more submarines were also sunk in the first weeks of March. Alarmed by the losses, Dönitz ordered the remaining submarines to move farther out to sea, in case the British had developed new anti-submarine devices. As soon as it was realized that the heavy losses were merely coincidences, the submarines were moved back again to the North Channel area and to the route from Great Britain to Gibraltar.

At Naval High Command, the mood of optimism about the Battle of the Atlantic faded in the spring of 1941. Preparations for the Russian operation in June called the Air Force away from its attacks on shipping. The *Bismarck* sortie in May was the last Atlantic operation of the heavy surface ships. The auxiliary cruisers continued to operate but on a slowly diminishing scale as some of them were sunk and others returned to port. Obviously, the submarines would eventually be left to carry the burden alone.

In late summer, British anti-submarine defences near the British Isles were becoming noticeably stronger, particularly in aircraft, and Dönitz's Fleet was growing larger, so it was possible to shift to the west again in September and to set up scouting lines of ten, fifteen, and eventually twenty submarines wherever radio intercepts or other information suggested convoy traffic. Submarines were still too scarce to cover all possible routes, so many convoys escaped. However, when a convoy was found and shadowed by day, and attacked by increasing numbers of submarines night after night, the escorts were often outnumbered by the submarines and the merchant ships took staggering losses. In mid-September, for instance, a convoy lost sixteen ships in two nights south of Greenland and was saved from further losses only by fog, which prevented the submarines from maintaining contact. September's successes totalled fifty-four ships (208,822 tons).

The submarine construction programme finally began to produce adequate numbers of new units for the Fleet. In June 1941 the delivery rate of fifteen per month was reached for the first time. Not only long building time, but shakedowns, trials, and training, made submarine delivery to the fighting commands a slow process. Shipyards were spending less than half their time on new construction (a sore point with Dönitz), and over half their time on repairs and refits of surface ships and submarines. Problems of material priorities, building rates, shipyard schedules, and similar questions appeared with monotonous regularity in Raeder's discussions with Hitler, yet no really satisfactory programme was agreed upon. Hitler always agreed with Raeder and promised relief, but projects of the other Services always received priority. Finally the naval war was guaranteed priority after the Russian operation, which was to have been concluded in the autumn of 1941!

The Naval Operations Staff had long favoured the use of submarines in distant waters to augment the efforts of the surface raiders. In June 1940 the first submarine had been sent to the South Atlantic, and several others followed in the next six months. They were larger craft than those preferred for North Atlantic operations and their basic purpose was to disrupt British shipping, causing delays and dispersing escorts. They and the first group of submarines which went to the Freetown, West Africa, area in February 1941 did well, but their tonnage-sunk-per-day figure was lower than that of the smaller submarines in the North Atlantic because of their long transit times. They were supplied by supply ships sent from Germany, blockade runners from neutral ports, and surface raiders. Although other groups were sent, Dönitz resisted the Naval High Command's desire to send many submarines on distant forays, arguing successfully that the North Atlantic yielded better results and that many submarines were needed to find convoys.

In June 1941, after the *Bismarck* sortie, the British hunted down almost all the supply ships at sea, and in July the submarines were deprived of the very limited use they were making of the Canaries as supply points because of British diplomatic pressure and Spanish reluctance to become too much involved with Hitler. Submarines, therefore, could not remain long off West Africa. It was not until the autumn of 1942, when tonnage sunk per submarine per day in the North Atlantic had declined somewhat because of the growing British defences, and a submarine tanker was available, that a group of submarines could be sent to the Cape Town area and even into the Indian Ocean, where it had considerable success.

The submarine tankers, first introduced in the late spring of 1942, were specially constructed submarines which provided the attack submarines with fuel, spare parts, food, clothing, ammunition, torpedoes, water, medical care and equipment, and crew replacements. In effect, a submarine tanker enabled the attack submarines to double the length of time they remained on patrol.

While submarine tankers made South African operations possible, the submarines found a better system when, beginning in the spring of 1943, they began operating from the Japanese base at Penang, on the western coast of the Malay Peninsula, and even operated a tanker in the Indian Ocean from that base. That arrangement continued until close to the end of the war.

One of the gravest problems to Dönitz was the tendency of Hitler and the Naval Operations Staff to employ submarines in tasks unsuited to their capabilities. They served as weather stations in the Atlantic; they guarded coasts against invasion attempts that never came; they convoyed surface ships; and, worst of all, they attempted to intervene in particular theatres of war in emergencies. In all those roles they tried to substitute for scarce or non-existent surface forces, aircraft, or bases. All such operations removed submarines from the vital scouting lines in the crucial North Atlantic and reduced the critical figures of tonnage sunk per submarine per day at sea. In addition, some of those duties resulted in much higher rates of loss to the submarines.

Two submarines were usually on weather patrol in the Atlantic throughout the war. That was a minor drain on resources, but in January 1941 Hitler became seriously worried about a British move on Norway, which he considered the decisive area of the war, so he ordered all the submarines there. The order was modified to twenty submarines, still a very serious blow to Atlantic operations. They were placed under the admiral commanding in Norway in March so coordination with other units could be better organized. The number in that area varied throughout the war, dropping in the summer of 1941, then rising sharply as Hitler's worries returned in the last few months of 1942. The Naval Operations Staff agreed with Dönitz that the submarines could sink more shipping in the Atlantic but felt the redeployment was warranted because the Allies had sufficient strength to attempt an invasion of Norway. The submarines could do double duty by aiding in the attack on Murmansk convoys. To the arguments that sinkings in the Atlantic tonnage war were the best guarantee against invasion and that submarines could do no more than harass invasions after they had begun, the Naval Operations Staff had no reply. There was, however, little to send to Norway or anywhere else in an emergency except submarines. Hitler seemed confused about his policy. After talking about the tonnage war one moment, he would refer to the importance of striking at the Murmansk convoys, two incompatible ideas because the Murmansk convoys sailed so infrequently that most Arctic patrols found no targets. The submarines did score some successes in the Arctic, particularly noteworthy being their cooperation in the destruction of most of Convoy *PQ 17* in July 1942, but the tonnage sunk per day at sea there was always low because of the scarcity of targets and the increasing

British defences. By December 1942 the number of submarines in the Arctic was again reduced, following the North African invasion.

Raeder could usually prevail against an occasional idea of Hitler's such as the one to have transport submarines built for an assault on Iceland, or the one to use submarines to prevent Allied invasions of the Atlantic islands. However, diversions for convoying blockade runners and raiders had to be made, despite their doubtful value, for there were practically no other forces available. In June 1941 some submarines were sent to the Baltic, where they were needed to prevent Russian naval moves, but they were withdrawn at the end of August, as the Russian Fleet remained rather quiet.

The worst drain of all, however, was to the Mediterranean theatre. From April to July 1941 Raeder was able to prevent Hitler from transferring submarines to aid the African campaign; but a check on whether the Italians would make a base available was decided on by Hitler in July. In August an order was issued, and despite naval protests six submarines were sent into the Mediterranean in September, six in November, and more in the following months. Their diversion reduced the very successful Atlantic operations to a fraction of those of preceding months. Dönitz protested regularly and Raeder supported him in the main, although he believed in the need for some activity in the Mediterranean to aid Rommel and forestall British action in north-western Africa. Dönitz pointed out that British strength made successes relatively unlikely and that, because of tides and eastward-flowing currents, any submarine sent into the Mediterranean had little chance of moving back into the Atlantic in the face of ever-increasing British forces at Gibraltar. By December, practically all Atlantic submarines were in the Mediterranean or to the west of Gibraltar in response to an order to have twenty-five submarines on station in the vicinity of the Rock.

The submarines did have isolated successes in the

Mediterranean, sinking a battleship, an aircraft carrier, and a cruiser as well as some merchantmen, but the losses were high because of calm waters and the large British escorts which accompanied all shipping. When the submarines off Gibraltar were finally released to attack the Gibraltar-to-Britain route in mid-December 1941, they did not fare well either, for the seas were too calm and British anti-submarine defences, which included an escort aircraft carrier for the first time, were too strong. The submarines sank the carrier, a destroyer, and two merchantmen, but lost five of their number. In January 1942 orders came through from the Naval High Command that, after sending two or three more submarines into the Mediterranean, the remaining submarines west of Gibraltar could be deployed again for commerce war in the North Atlantic.

As the United States increased its rate of shipbuilding and began to give more aid to Britain, Raeder urged Hitler to lift restrictions on attacks within the American neutrality zone. Even when Americans began convoying ships to the Iceland area and shadowing submarines, however, Hitler refused to do anything to antagonize the United States at sea, remembering that submarine warfare had been the key issue leading to American entry into World War I. American ships were not even subject to normal search and seizure. When a submarine sighted and chased the American battleship *Texas* inside the American-proclaimed war zone in June 1941, Hitler issued an order that submarines were not to attack any warship below cruiser size, and to attack large ships only if they were clearly identified as hostile. Those orders gave the submarines' most dangerous enemies, the escort vessels, immunity from attack. A slight relaxation of the regulations – that submarines could defend themselves against attack – was soon approved, but that left all the initiative to the enemy. Otherwise, Hitler insisted on preventing any incidents, although he refused to recognize officially new American security zone extensions which carried the area patrolled by United States warships hundreds of miles to the east – to a line just west of Iceland in February 1941, then to a line just east of the island in July.

Increasing American action inevitably led to clashes. The first was the *Greer* incident in September 1941. *U652** was pursued by a destroyer. When depth charges exploded, the submarine commander assumed that the destroyer was responsible, although actually a British aeroplane had dropped the charges. The submarine fired two torpedoes, both of which missed. The commander did not find out that the destroyer was the American *Greer* until the next day. By then the skirmish had been transformed into a major incident which brought forth Roosevelt's 'rattlesnakes of the Atlantic' comment and led to his issuing shoot-on-sight orders to his naval commanders. In October, one American destroyer was damaged in a convoy battle, and three weeks later another destroyer was sunk in a similar action.

On December 11th, 1941, Germany and Italy declared war on the United States, four days after Japan's attack on Pearl Harbor. Because the German leaders were not told of the Japanese attack in advance, they were unable to take full advantage of it. No submarines were immediately available for the American theatre, where Dönitz wanted to concentrate his forces for maximum sinkings before American defences were strengthened. He expected little or no American convoy organization, no anti-submarine experience, and very few escorts because of the enormous area requiring protection. He planned to strike in an area until its defences improved, then shift to a fresh area. Submarines were to operate singly, for the few convoys were expected to find haven quickly when attacked.

About thirty submarines out of the ninety available

* Submarine numerical designations do not reflect the number of submarines produced by a specific date.

were operating in the Mediterranean or off Gibraltar, however, and many others were needed to relieve them and to replace their losses; so Dönitz's request for twelve submarines to operate off the American coast was halved. From the day in mid-January that those limited forces began to operate between the St Lawrence River and Cape Hatteras, the campaign, which the German submarines called the 'American Shooting Season', was an enormous success. The submarines often operated right off American harbours. They waited just off the shipping channels for fat targets to be silhouetted by the city lights, then they picked the most valuable ships for their precious torpedoes. Tankers were specified as preferred targets, followed by freighters of 10,000 tons. Gunfire dispatched many smaller ships and cripples. Shore dwellers saw flashes in the night, heard the dull booms of explosions, and watched bodies and wreckage drift onto the beaches the next day. Long after the submarines had returned triumphantly to France, canted masts and bows stood above the waves and sticky black oil fouled the beaches.

To the submarine commanders it was the second 'happy time', reminiscent of the successes off the British coast in late 1940. One of them celebrated his successes in a radio message to Dönitz:

> The new-moon night is black as ink.
> Off Hatteras the tankers sink
> While sadly Roosevelt counts the score –
> Some fifty thousand tons – by Mohr.*

Not content with the havoc wrought within sight of American coastal cities, a group of smaller Atlantic submarines was sent to the Nova Scotia-Newfoundland area, and a group of large ones to the Trinidad-Aruba-Curaçao oil area, to cut American war potential directly. The unready Americans inadvertently aided the submarines by radio chatter and the maintenance of peacetime coastal

* Wolfgang Frank, *The Sea Wolves*, p 162.

lighting. Belatedly they responded to the submarines' challenge and fought back by organizing convoys, escort groups, and air patrols, the same methods that were bringing the British slowly increasing successes. Still, the first submarine was not sunk off the American coast until mid-April, three months after the campaign had begun.

The Caribbean was struck in February, and from then on new groups were shifted to areas of opportunity, such as the Gulf of Mexico and the western Caribbean. Their numbers were always small because of Hitler's insistence on diversions to Norway. No more than fifteen were on patrol at one time, but by the end of April the first submarine tanker had arrived to more than double the effectiveness of submarines in its area. In its first six months, the American campaign destroyed over 400 ships totalling over two million tons, about half of that being tanker tonnage. Slowly, better Allied anti-submarine measures, which forced the Germans to operate at increasing distances from their bases, led to diminishing returns. While some submarines were maintained off the Americas for their diversionary effect until practically the end of the war, in May 1942 some submarines were again operating in the North Atlantic, and in July that became the main theatre of operations once more.

Unrestricted submarine warfare also was gradually introduced against the ships of Latin American countries, usually for the reason that hostile acts were being committed by those countries. That had little effect on the overall war situation.

When the submarines moved back to the North Atlantic, the greatest convoy battles of the war began. They lasted with constantly shifting fortunes for a full year, at the beginning of which the submarines appeared to retain their ability to find their targets with the aid of a superb radio interception and decryption service and to strike hard with ever-increasing numbers. The war became not only a race between the submarines and the builders of the escorts and merchant ships, but also a technical race between detection and deception devices and between rival techniques of destruction.

At first, British techniques were mainly those of World War I, improved and expanded somewhat by aerial patrol. The submarines had fairly good chances of success against depth charges, underwater listening gear, disguised gunnery ships, new starshell and parachute flares, and the new underwater echo ranger, or Asdic. Land-based aircraft patrols forced submarines to dive and often lose contact with convoys, so the submarines moved farther to sea to avoid them. Beyond air-patrol range was the Mid-Atlantic Gap, or 'Black Pit', as the Allies termed it. The Gap closed very slowly as aircraft ranges and numbers increased, but it was still 600 miles wide in mid-1942. The British tried many expedients to cover it temporarily, such as catapulting expendable aircraft from merchant ships; but the first merchant ship converted into an auxiliary aircraft carrier was promptly sunk, and it was not until early in 1943 that small aircraft carriers regularly escorted convoys. More escorts for each convoy made a difference too, especially when the added escorts could form a large-diameter outer ring, preventing submarines from approaching the convoy by day and reinforcing the inner screen at night. More escorts meant that a submarine, once located, could be chased for prolonged periods of time, a tactic which increased submarine losses. The number of escorts was increased by mass production of special escort vessels, the destroyer escorts and corvettes. When the number of submarines attacking a convoy increased from day to day, the Allies provided special escort groups to reinforce the convoy's escort. The provision of anti-torpedo nets for ships was also tried.

A lucky event of August 1941 had given the British a first-hand view of their adversary. South of Iceland, a long-range Type IX C submarine, *U570*, had been bombed and damaged as it surfaced. Her commander had waved a white shirt to surrender! Aircraft had circled her, the pilots using blinker-light signals to threaten her crew until surface units could arrive to tow her in. By the spring of 1942, the knowledge gained from study of her design and capabilities, such as her speed, rate of dive, and maximum depth, was being used to hunt her sister ships, and she was refitted to fight against her builders.

Against the Allied combinations of anti-submarine techniques, quite a few ideas were tried by the German submarine command. The first, available early in 1942, was an Asdic decoy, a chemical discharge that created bubbles and returned Asdic echoes similar to those of a submarine. Then came a torpedo that would zigzag through a convoy until it hit a target. After two years of experimentation following the Norwegian campaign torpedo fiasco, a fully reliable depth torpedo with magnetic detonator was finally provided. The new technique had the advantage of sinking ships with only one torpedo by breaking their backs, causing higher crew casualties because the ships sank quickly. Hitler particularly appreciated the latter effect.

Starting in July 1942, the British countered the submarines that were sending beacon signals from behind convoys by fitting their escort ships with high-frequency direction finders. The escorts could then listen for the submarines' radio messages and sweep far astern of their convoys to force the submarines down. With perseverance and luck, that tactic could break the submarines' contact with convoys, or at least make the mass attack harder to organize.

Of all the new defensive weapons, one was decisive. As early as December 1941, Dönitz began to suspect that British destroyers were using radar to detect the approach of German submarines to the convoys. In the first months of 1942, submarine losses in the Bay of Biscay suddenly went up. The submarine commanders and technical experts doubted that radar was used, but in June the first air attacks on submarines at night began, with aircraft flying in to close range and then directing searchlights on to the submarines just before releasing bombs. Later the technical experts found proof of British use of airborne radar and suggested as countermeasures the installation of radar search receivers, complete radar sets, or non-reflective anti-radar coatings for conning towers. Radar search receivers were available and were soon installed, complete with clumsy, removable aerials – the 'Biscay Crosses'. The sets gave only a rough bearing and no range, but they did enable the submarines to dive in time to avoid attack. Diving reduced the efficiency of the submarines, which operated best on the surface, but it also cut losses. While the receivers were being prepared, the submarines had orders to cross the Bay of Biscay submerged as much as possible, and Göring was persuaded to provide twenty-four aircraft to escort crippled submarines back across the Bay. The submarines were also fitted with multiple heavy machine guns for extra anti-aircraft firepower. They weathered the first radar assault, but their mobility was reduced.

Through the summer and autumn of 1942 the Battle of the Atlantic reached a crescendo. In July, August, and September the long-cherished goal of thirty new submarines a month reaching western France was finally achieved, and the size of the force jumped from just under 100 in January to over 200 by the end of the year, despite the loss of 87 submarines in the same period. Their thoroughly trained crews were provided by the organizational genius of Rear-Admiral Hans Georg von Friedeburg, second-in-command of submarines. By October, two long patrol lines were always available in the Mid-Atlantic Gap: one in the east to intercept westbound convoys, and the other in the west for eastbound shipping. The distance between submarines in a patrol line was reduced to fifteen or twenty miles, so convoys had little chance of slipping through unsighted. The submarines sailed towards suspected convoys in daylight and away at night, so darkness was no help to the convoys. From five or six, the number of submarines that attacked a single convoy grew to nine, ten, and sometimes over twenty, and they hung on doggedly to renew the attacks for up to eight days and 1,000 miles. Often submarines left one westbound-convoy battle as they approached the western Allied air-patrol zone, and went immediately into an eastbound-convoy battle.

Their successes, coupled with continuing attacks in the American area and new forays into the South Atlantic, resulted in sinking over 400,000 tons a month from May through November 1942, despite the fact that tonnage sunk per submarine per day at sea continued to decline. The high point was 118 ships (743,321 tons) in November. By the end of the year, the Allies had lost almost eight million tons of shipping, most of it to submarines, but Allied merchant-ship construction had jumped to about seven million tons. The submarines were winning the Battle of the Atlantic – but the margin was narrow. In addition to merchant-ship sinkings, *U73* sank the aircraft carrier *Eagle* with a perfect four-torpedo spread in the Mediterranean, too late to affect the outcome of the El Alamein campaign, however.

The autumn of 1942 also saw an action which embittered both sides in the struggle. It started with the sudden violence and terror that were accepted almost casually by all but the victims at that stage of the war. Lieutenant-Commander Werner Hartenstein's Cape Town-bound *U156* sighted and chased the 19,695-ton liner *Laconia* 500 miles south of the bulge of Africa on September 12th. Hartenstein closed in on the surface after sunset and fired two torpedoes – or 'eels', as German sailors call them. Both torpedoes hit. The *Laconia* listed heavily to starboard, slowed as her engines failed, and began to sink. Her radio was functioning and her radio-men began to send out SSS calls.

As *U 156* cautiously approached the liner, lifeboats

could be seen. It became obvious that the ship was sinking, but to Hartenstein the ninety minutes she took to sink seemed a very long time. He wanted to get away from the area in which he had been reported, but he also wanted to verify the sinking; so he cruised slowly towards the hulk, past the rafts, boats, wreckage, and weakening swimmers. In a moment, all was changed. Cries for help were heard in Italian; and a startled commander ordered his men to haul some survivors aboard the submarine.

Then the extent of the tragedy struck Hartenstein. There had been 1,800 Italian prisoners of war from the North African campaign on board, of whom over 500 had been killed by explosions and flooding in the first moments of the attack as the torpedoes had hit the prison holds. Their guards had been 160 Poles, former Russian prisoners of war, who had tried to keep the Italians below decks long enough for the 800 British crewmen and passengers, among whom were 80 women and children, to take to the boats. As Hartenstein groped with his new problem, the *Laconia*'s bow dipped, her stern rose, and she plunged into the depths, taking her captain and 1,000 others with her.

Hartenstein was faced with a very difficult decision. Rescue of survivors entailed risking his submarine, and the security of one's own ship must always be a captain's first concern. While ordering the rescue effort to continue, he sent a signal to Dönitz, informing him of the situation. Dönitz, awakened when the message came in, faced the same dilemma as Hartenstein, with the additional concern of the touchy Italian Government's reactions to whatever he decided. After considering the various aspects of the problem – security from air attack, the submarine's interrupted mission, morale – he sent orders for the four other submarines in the Cape Town-bound group, in addition to two in a group off Freetown, and an Italian to aid *U156*.

Higher up the chain of command, Raeder's staff had the French informed, and they arranged to send surface ships from Dakar. Raeder approved the rescue provided that the submarines ran no risks, an impossible condition if adhered to literally. Hitler echoed Raeder and added that the Cape Town operation was not to be compromised.

Hartenstein spent the night picking up survivors, feeding them, and treating their injuries. Long before dawn, there were nearly 200 survivors on board a submarine designed to contain only her crew of fifty. Hartenstein sent out an uncoded radio message on several wavelengths: 'If any ship will assist the shipwrecked *Laconia* crew, I will not attack her provided I am not being attacked by ship or air forces. I picked up 193 men, 4°52′ South 11°26′ West. German submarine.'* Shortly afterwards, Dönitz's decision reached him, but it included a warning to be prepared to submerge. He spent the day pulling people out of the water and distributing them among the sound lifeboats, which were then towed astern.

The next day, certain of French aid for the rescue, Dönitz released the four other Cape Town-bound submarines to resume their cruises. They could not have arrived quickly enough to be of use. The third day of the operation, *U506* arrived and took aboard 132 survivors, halving *U156*'s burden. She then moved off to aid the collection of the sunken ship's boats. One day later, *U507* arrived to share the work, and the Italian *Cappellini* arrived a day later still.

The fourth day of the rescue operation, September 16th, was begun with the encouraging news that the French would arrive the next day. About midday an American four-engined aircraft appeared over *U156*. Hartenstein ordered a makeshift six-by-six-foot Red Cross flag draped over the forward gun. The anti-aircraft guns were not manned. A signal lamp told the aircraft crew that rescue was in progress. Then a British survivor was permitted to use the lamp to signal his identity and the fact that there were women and children aboard. The aeroplane flew off. Half an hour later it returned, dove

* Karl Dönitz, *Memoirs*, p 257.

at *U156*, and dropped three depth charges. They missed the submarine, but one hit a lifeboat just as Hartenstein ordered the boats cut loose. Another attack placed a delayed-action bomb below the submarine. Its explosion created a mining effect which lifted the submarine and damaged periscopes, communications gear, and the engines. Hartenstein turned towards the boats and ordered the survivors on board the submarine to jump overboard. As soon as they were clear, *U156* dove and left the area. She would have to return to France for dockyard work. Later that night, when his radio had been patched up, Hartenstein reported to Dönitz.

Submarine headquarters reacted violently to the news. Commander Günther Hessler, Chief of Operations, and Captain Eberhard Godt, the Chief of Staff, vigorously opposed the continuance of the operation, but all they could get from Dönitz was another order to the submarines to remain ready to dive and not to hope for enemy forbearance. Dönitz insisted on seeing the operation through, despite what he considered deliberate Allied brutality.

The reasons for the bombing attack were not so simple as the Germans supposed. The aircraft did not understand the submarine's blinker signals. Neither the aircraft crewmen nor their superiors at Ascension Island were aware of Hartenstein's rescue message. When the pilot saw the rescue work and the flag, he radioed for instructions. The commander on Ascension had been ordered to protect British rescue ships en route to the sinking area and was concerned about the damage submarines were doing at that critical point in the Battle of the Atlantic. He had no orders to respect the Red Cross flag, so he ordered the attack despite the fact that it would endanger the *Laconia* survivors.

On the morning of the fifth day of the rescue it was clear to all those in German submarine headquarters that the two remaining submarines were still overburdened with survivors. That was consistent with the prevalent submariners' tendency to underestimate the danger from the air. Dönitz reflected on the *Laconia* rescue and on the rapidly increasing number of air attacks on submarines in the preceding months. He considered submarines to be subject to air attack practically anywhere on the high seas and realized that no action could ever be thought of as 'ended'. He also recognized the corollary: submarines had to maintain fairly high surface speeds and minimal deck watches so crash dives would enable them to reach safe depths after sighting fast aircraft. Rescue operations violated those basic safety requirements. He drafted a comprehensive order taking the humane but dangerous choice out of his commanders' hands, but he did not send it. Then he waited for the operation to end.

At midday, *U506* was attacked, but was well below the surface by the time the bombs fell. Both *U506* and *U507* kept their survivors aboard and turned them over to the French ships, which arrived that afternoon. The French found most of the lifeboats in several days' search, and finally the Italian submarine turned over her passengers three days later. The rescued numbered 1,091 out of the original 2,732, but the intensive French search failed to sight two more lifeboats, which made four-week voyages survived by only 20 people out of 119.

Dönitz was greatly relieved at the news of the French arrival. He then issued his '*Laconia* Order'. It categorically forbade rescue except to take important prisoners of war. In the sequel, submarine captains occasionally carried out rescues despite the order, although such opportunities were few. At the Nuremberg Trials, Dönitz was accused of committing a war crime by issuing the order, which was interpreted as a 'kill survivors' order by the prosecution, but he was acquitted on that charge. The three German submarines that had participated in the rescue were sunk with all hands by aircraft on subsequent patrols. Hartenstein, an ace commander with an excellent reputation as a leader and a gentleman, had been scheduled to become Chief of

Operations in Dönitz's headquarters, replacing Hessler, another ace (who was, incidentally, Dönitz's son-in-law).

In late September 1942 a complete review of the submarine situation was held at Hitler's headquarters, with Raeder, Dönitz, and Admiral Werner Fuchs, the Chief of Naval Construction, and several technical specialists in attendance. Dönitz reported the successes and warned about probable future problems, emphasizing that the threat from the air might force submarines to give up surface attacks. Hitler discounted the air threat in so broad an arena as the Atlantic. Dönitz stressed the need for air support and discussed weapons coming into use. Experimental submarines with high underwater speed were approved by an enthusiastic Hitler, whose forces were still riding to victory on all fronts.

Whether as a result of Dönitz's strong presentation at the September conference, or the many disagreements about submarine dispositions, or some more personal reaction to Dönitz's growing importance as the submarines came to dominate German naval action, Raeder acted to restrict Dönitz's power despite the fact that Dönitz had been promoted to full admiral's rank in March. First he ordered that Dönitz was to be limited to operational matters. Dönitz called Captain Erich Schulte Mönting, Raeder's Chief of Staff, and told him that such a division of responsibility was unworkable and that the order could not be obeyed. That direct challenge to Raeder's authority went unanswered. The order was not carried out! Several months later Raeder again sent Dönitz a plan that would have separated submarine operations from training and support commands. Dönitz wrote to Schulte Mönting, pointing out the inefficiencies inherent in such a policy and threatening to resign if it were implemented. Godt went to Hitler's headquarters, on his own initiative but with Dönitz's approval, to brief Captain Karl Jesko von Puttkamer, Hitler's naval adjutant, on the situation. Hitler was not asked to step in, however, as Raeder again backed down when he was shown Dönitz's letter by his Chief of Staff. The submarine war went on unchanged.

On January 30th, 1943, Dönitz, who had expected to be retired only a few months before because of his disputes with Raeder, became Commander-in-Chief of the German Navy with the rank of Grand Admiral. Raeder was stepping down as the result of a quarrel with Hitler over surface-ship sorties. Dönitz retained command of the submarines, while Captain Godt and the submarine staff came to Berlin and controlled day-to-day operations.

With nearly 200 submarines available in the first months of 1943, the Battle of the Atlantic approached its crisis. December had been stormy, and January was stormier; but eight submarines destroyed seven out of nine tankers in a convoy heading for North Africa, a special success in that it directly affected the strategic situation by reducing Allied fuel supplies for the Tunisian campaign. Then the really big North Atlantic battles resumed and quickly dwarfed those that had come before. A six-day early February battle involved twenty-one submarines against sixty-three ships with ten escorts, which were quickly joined by two more. Twelve merchantmen fell victim to submarine torpedoes, and another sank after a collision, at the cost of three submarines sunk and four damaged. Ominously for Dönitz, only one submarine repeatedly broke through the escort screen; that one sank seven of the twelve ships. Skill, tenacity, and an increasing share of good luck were needed against reinforced escorts and wide-ranging air cover.

Through February and on into March the battles flared, with success sometimes on one side, sometimes on the other; but the tonnage sunk jumped sharply after the winter lull. February's 380,000 tons was eclipsed by March's 590,000 tons. In one March battle 141,000 tons was sunk in six days in history's largest convoy battle. Two convoys, one overtaking the other, were assaulted day and night by thirty-eight submarines, of which nineteen were able to fire torpedoes that sank twenty-one ships out of ninety-two. The desperate escorts were reinforced to eighteen during the battle but sank only one submarine and badly damaged two. The British Admiralty was close to despair.

The mid-March victory was the greatest, and the last, of its kind. Later the same month, an escort carrier was sighted in the columns of a convoy. Once again German submarines were attacked without warning while surfaced, despite the use of their radar search receivers. Convoys escaped from submarine concentrations. Submerged attacks had to be ordered because long-range aircraft made surfacing dangerous. So uncertain were German technicians about British search methods that they made wild guesses at the cause: treason, radiations from the radar search receiver, a completely new search method, or a different form of radar. The latter was the best suspect – and as it turned out, the correct one. It was a short-wave radar that the submarines' long-wave receivers could not detect.

Finally, the long struggle ended in 'Black May' of 1943, when forty-one submarines – one third of the submarines at sea – failed to return. Dönitz ordered the remaining submarines to withdraw from the North Atlantic and take stations south-west of the Azores, where defences were less strong. Dönitz says it best in his *Memoirs*: 'We had lost the Battle of the Atlantic.'* That battle, the last great turning-point battle of the war and in many respects the most important, was one that Dönitz was certain could have been won decisively had the German leadership placed the highest priority on a massive submarine construction programme early in the war. Germany's redoubtable foe, Winston Churchill, admitted: 'The U-boat attack was our worst evil. It would have been wise for the Germans to stake all upon it.'†

* p 341.
† Winston S. Churchill, *The Second World War*, Vol IV, p 125.

Chapter 8

SURFACE FORCES

To the frozen seas June 1941–May 1945

The *Bismarck* sortie was the turning point for the German surface forces in the Atlantic. After her loss in May 1941, the major German warships were inactive. Hitler issued orders establishing tight control over movements of capital ships. No capital ship was to risk action against an equal or superior ship; capital ships were to avoid contact if strong enemy forces were anticipated; no sorties to the Atlantic were to be allowed; movement of capital ships would require Hitler's personal approval; and no capital ship was to sortie if the British had an aircraft carrier in its theatre of operations. Against those crippling 'no unnecessary risks' orders Raeder protested in vain.

Raeder was not the only one who found that it was becoming ever more difficult to work with Hitler. As the events of 1941 unrolled, it became more and more evident that it was a year of crisis in the German High Command. The unbroken series of continental victories had been magnified by propaganda to the point that Hitler was glorified as the 'greatest general of all times' – and he apparently believed that he was. Such an attitude, coupled with a suspicious nature, made him very difficult to oppose. Many who had harboured doubts about him before the war were impressed by his successes, but others feared his ambition would outstrip German capabilities and lead to ruin. The Russian campaign sharpened the differences of viewpoint within the command structure, and Hitler reacted by taking more and more power into his own hands. In December 1941, after the failure of the drive on Moscow, Hitler removed the Commander-in-Chief of the Army and took the post himself. At the same time, the Army General Staff was restricted to work concerning the Eastern Front. The OKW, meanwhile, continued to decline in importance, becoming more and more an administrative office concerned mainly with secondary land fronts.

Operational command decisions were made in conferences at Hitler's headquarters two to four times a day at his call. Most of the men at those meetings, including the few naval representatives, merely reported and received orders. Only a few actually discussed matters with Hitler and really influenced his decisions. Leadership was centralized and very personal, and the Navy was virtually unrepresented in the day-to-day decision-making process. Periodic conferences with individual top leaders were also held. The results of the conferences were written up as directives by the OKW.

In that atmosphere, Raeder was gravely handicapped. He had never established a real *rapport* with Hitler, and the loss of the *Bismarck* cost him much of the respect he had gained by the Norway operation and the Fleet's successes against commerce. As usual, Göring benefited. By early 1942 he had finally gained control of the last land-based aircraft that had been assigned to the Navy. The loss of control made little practical difference, since the effort had always been minimal. In the field of war production, Albert Speer was assigned as Armaments Minister, but he was subordinated to Göring, and an Air Force field-marshal became Speer's Under-Secretary for Aircraft Production. No other group had equivalent representation in the Armaments Ministry.

Despite his problems with Hitler, Raeder was determined to use his remaining surface ships whenever possible. The *Bismarck*'s consort, the *Prinz Eugen*, had arrived in Brest on June 1st, 1941, after a cruise shortened by fuel crises and engine trouble. Even though the British had stripped their convoy escorts to concentrate on the *Bismarck*, the *Prinz Eugen* had failed to locate any ships. The *Lützow*'s Norway damage had finally been repaired, and later in the month Raeder was somehow able to obtain permission for her to sortie into the Atlantic, but she was hit by an aerial torpedo off Norway and had to return. The *Scharnhorst* and *Gneisenau* were damaged in Brest by British air attacks and had to remain there for the rest of the year.

As 1941 waned, the inactivity of the heavy surface forces continued, but the strategic factors slowly changed. To leave ships in the Atlantic as long as possible was most desirable, even if they served only as a fleet-in-being to keep pressure on the Gibraltar and Home Fleets. However, it was obvious that the British would do their best to make Brest untenable for the heavy ships there, and as early as May 30th, 1941, the German Naval Shore Commander for France suggested sending the three ships back to Germany by way of the English Channel. The advantages of the move were the short route, good air and sea escort possibilities, good emergency harbours, safety from British capital ships, and the possibility that British radar could be jammed while the ships were in transit. Those favourable factors had to be weighed against the difficulties of navigating and manoeuvring in shallow waters, within narrow mine-free channels and while under attack by torpedoes, bombs, mines, and shells launched by air and light naval forces. Raeder rejected the idea of sending the *Scharnhorst* and *Gneisenau* through because of the risk but ordered a study for passage of the *Prinz Eugen*.

Events, however, were forcing Raeder counter to his desires. The fuel-oil situation grew slowly worse through 1941, with Rumanian supplies cut off temporarily during the Balkan campaign and the requirements of all Services up for the Russian campaign. By December the Navy's quota was cut 50 per cent and surface-force operations were not permitted unless the circumstances appeared very favourable.

Meanwhile, in August the British had begun sending convoys to Murmansk, as that was the shortest supply route to Russia. In addition, Hitler was becoming very nervous about the possibility of a British invasion of Norway. The problem was thrashed out in conferences from September 1941 to January 1942. Raeder favoured using the Brest ships at sea in short raids against the Gibraltar–Britain convoys, as the *Hipper* had been used before. The *Scheer* he wanted to use in the Atlantic for her diversionary effect along with the auxiliary cruisers. In Norwegian waters he wished to use the new *Tirpitz* for the threat she could present to the Iceland Passages blockade and to British moves against Norway. Fuel for her was short. All those ideas were discussed in November, but Hitler was not enthusiastic about any Atlantic moves. In early December Raeder again pressed for operational freedom, pointing out the diversionary effect of Japanese entrance into the war and the possibility of the *Scheer* using Japanese bases. He also revived the idea of a base at Dakar.

The Navy's opinion about Norway reluctantly changed during December as reports of British attack potential mounted and the British launched raids against the Norwegian coast. Raeder wanted more air power moved to Norway and believed that aircraft, together with the *Tirpitz*, would effectively forestall an assault – or smash one if it were launched. The rest of the Fleet he still hoped would operate in the Atlantic in view of the additional strain placed on British capital-ship strength by Japanese entry into the war and British losses in the Mediterranean. Hitler, however, was adamant. He insisted at the end of December that the Brest force be brought home by the Channel route or face dismantling so that guns and crews could go to Norway. He held little hope for the ships safely negotiating the Iceland Passages and added that battleships were losing their value anyway. Raeder could not agree with either idea, pointing out that their mere presence at Brest imposed enormous strategic liabilities on British sea power. By mid-January 1942 Raeder had lost the argument. He made a last mention of his opposition and then presented detailed plans for Hitler's final decision. Hitler stressed that the ships would inevitably be destroyed where they lay and that a surprise breakout was the only chance of saving them. It was the type of operation which appealed to him, as it made maximum use of his insights regarding enemy reactions to unexpected events.

Planning for the sortie was secret and thorough. Everyone knew what to do, but practically no one knew why he was doing it. On the evening of February 11th, Brest was sealed off from all contact with the surrounding countryside. The ships raised steam so they could leave shortly after dark for as long a night run as possible, but a British air raid delayed them over two hours. Then the *Scharnhorst, Gneisenau,* and *Prinz Eugen* sailed, escorted by six destroyers for the high-speed run up the Channel. The lone British submarine on patrol – ironically, the *Sealion* – had pulled out about an hour before to recharge her batteries. Vice-Admiral Otto Ciliax's force was through the first British defence, without knowing it.

In the deep-water channel chosen to limit the mine danger, the ships tried to make up the time the air raid had cost them. They moved at top speed and the tide pushed them on. The clear, dark night shielded them from British eyes but permitted their lookouts to make out the marker boats which showed the swept passages through German and British minefields. By dawn they were nearly on schedule, and the weather began to close in. Visibility dropped to a few miles in cloudy weather with rainy patches. Lighter naval forces joined them from ports along the route, and aircraft circled overhead without interference from their adversaries. Just after noon, the Dover narrows were reached. More motor torpedo boats and minesweepers joined, raising the escort to nearly sixty ships. Still there was no indication that the British were aware of the sortie that had already covered over 350 miles. The outer ships of the escort laid a smoke screen to add to the mists, and jamming of British radar was brought to a maximum after days of calculated build-up. Finally the Dover batteries sent a few wild salvoes after the ships.

The British were beginning to react, long after Ciliax had expected to be heavily engaged. His air cover, provided by 250 aircraft in carefully planned waves, was reaching its high point when the first British ships and aircraft arrived. It was a pitifully small force of five motor torpedo boats, two motor gunboats, and six 85-knot Swordfish torpedo planes covered by a few fighters which were quickly engaged by the German air armada. The uncoordinated attacks were carried out with hopeless gallantry. The Swordfish assault particularly impressed the Germans. Attacked by fighters, lashed by ships' guns, the six planes dodged through the inferno at fifty-foot altitude with wings shredded, fuselages torn, and crews dying, to launch their torpedoes at the heavy ships before they were destroyed. The leader of this intrepid band, Lieutenant-Commander Eugene Esmonde, an Irish volunteer and veteran of the *Victorious*' attack on the *Bismarck*, received a posthumous Victoria Cross; five of his seventeen companions survived, but only one of them was unwounded.

Then came a two-hour lull in attacks on the ships during a period when they had to slow down in narrow swept passages over shoal water. Every minute, the English coast receded farther into the distance and the mists closed in. It seemed that the ships might get through unscathed. Two and a half hours after passing Dover, the *Scharnhorst* received a massive blow aft and came to an agonizing halt. She had struck a mine. Ciliax and his staff ordered a destroyer alongside and jumped onto her deck. For thirty minutes the battleship remained an inert target, but no enemy appeared. Then her crew completed emergency repairs and she steamed to catch up with the rest of the squadron. As Ciliax caught up with the main body, his destroyer was slightly damaged by an accidental shell explosion so that she lost speed. Another destroyer was called in; both stopped while a new air battle snarled overhead, and Ciliax was decorously piped over the side into a small boat from which he was piped aboard the other destroyer, to continue the cruise.

From the middle of the afternoon to sunset, several hundred British aircraft were sent against the German force, but bad weather and poor coordination led to such confusion that only thirty-nine bombers and a handful of torpedo planes found their targets and attacked. They came in alone or in small groups, covered only sporadically by the large number of fighters which attacked the German air umbrella, and they damaged only two torpedo boats. Five British destroyers of World War I vintage used the weather to close in enough for a gun and torpedo attack that left one of them crippled, but they scored no successes. Darkness ended the futile British attacks but not Ciliax's worries. During the night the *Gneisenau* struck a mine and the *Scharnhorst* struck her second mine in seven hours, shipping 1,000 tons of water; but the lucky *Prinz Eugen* escaped damage. By dawn, all were safe in the Elbe and Wilhelmshaven.

The exploit was an enormous propaganda victory for Hitler. He had been right. The British had expected a night breakthrough past Dover; so the surprise daylight dash through the Dover narrows had resulted in a confused throwing in of totally inadequate forces. *The Times* said: 'Vice-Admiral Ciliax has succeeded where the Duke of Medina failed . . . nothing more mortifying to the pride of sea power has happened in home waters since the seventeenth century.'*

Hitler's intuition had led to a tactical victory, but the operation was the final strategic retreat of the Navy's surface forces. Until the Channel dash, the British had been forced to continue battleship escort of convoys in the

* Captain S. W. Roskill, DSC, RN, *The War at Sea*, Vol. II, p 159.

Atlantic in addition to the cruiser patrols in the Iceland Passages against the threat of the *Tirpitz* breaking out. At that time, the Iceland patrols were backed by only one battleship at Scapa Flow. As soon as the German ships arrived in the North Sea, the British concentrated their forces to back the blockade line and released considerable forces to other theatres of war.

A few days after the Channel dash, the *Gneisenau* was extensively damaged by a bombing attack that took her out of the war permanently; and the *Prinz Eugen* lost her stern to a submarine torpedo two weeks later. Despite those setbacks, a formidable force was soon assembled in northern Norway. The *Tirpitz* had arrived at Trondheim in January, followed by the *Scheer, Lützow,* and *Hipper*; a light cruiser; and screening destroyers. Their effect was immediately felt. Despite the restrictions on their operations set up after the *Bismarck* sortie, despite the weak air reconnaissance provided, and despite a chronic fuel shortage and inadequate base facilities, Raeder determined that the ships should strike. In the face of the German Fleet threat, the British increased the Murmansk convoy escorts and their covering forces to enormous size, sending battleships, a carrier, and cruisers on each operation.

On March 6th the *Tirpitz* sailed with three destroyers against an outbound and an inbound convoy. In weather too wild for air search, she was reported by a British submarine, after which the forces on both sides steered search courses for two days. The *Tirpitz* came within sixty miles of three Home Fleet capital ships and an aircraft carrier which the Fleet Commander, Vice-Admiral Ciliax, did not know were at sea, and she missed the convoys by seventy-five miles. One of the German destroyers sank a single straggler. On her way back to Trondheim, the *Tirpitz* was attacked by the *Victorious*' twelve torpedo planes with such determination that Ciliax was convinced his flagship had been hit by at least one torpedo that failed to explode. Others missed the weaving giant by so little that three tracks were visible crossing her wake at the same time. She returned safely to port. The two-year horror of the Murmansk Run battles had begun.

The Naval Operations Staff appraisal of the sortie emphasized the air danger to the heavy ships and the need for a strong air arm to support their sorties and eliminate British aircraft carriers – themes which became monotonous in their repetition thereafter. A German aircraft carrier was considered the most desirable long-term solution to the air-cover problem. As an immediate consequence of the action, Raeder decided to withhold the heavy ships until all were assembled. Hitler approved the idea immediately. He also agreed to the completion of the aircraft carrier despite some hedging by the Naval Staff in April about suitable aircraft and technical problems. In May and June the plans were expanded to include the conversion of several large merchant ships to auxiliary aircraft carriers.

On the night of March 27th, 1942, the British reacted to the *Tirpitz* threat by an assault on St-Nazaire, the only French Atlantic port with a dry dock large enough to hold the battleship. The attack began at midnight, with a diversionary air attack on the city which drew German attention until the force was two miles from its objective. A signal light blinked a challenge from the shore. Searchlight beams dropped to illuminate a ship that looked like a German torpedo boat but was surrounded by eighteen motorboats. She was the destroyer *Campbeltown*, one of the fifty Destroyer Deal four-pipers which Roosevelt had traded to Churchill for bases. As soon as the German lights found the force, a fierce, close-range gun battle began; but the *Campbeltown* pressed on, her upper works torn but her guns answering. She turned slightly and slammed into the gate of the Normandie Dock. Her crew then scuttled her with her bow wedged firmly in the gate. Commandos went down ladders to carry out demolitions, while others were landed by motorboats under heavy fire. A brief, intense battle punctuated by demolition-charge explosions ended with the death or capture of almost all the commandos, the *Campbeltown*'s crew, and most of the motorboat crews.

The next morning, a large inspection party went aboard the *Campbeltown* to investigate her removal and the repair of the dock gate. Four and a half tons of explosives in her bow blew up, killing the Germans and destroying the gate. The dry dock was permanently out of the war. Some time later a formal parade was held at which the citation accompanying the Victoria Cross was read to the *Campbeltown*'s captain by the commanding officer of his prisoner-of-war camp! It was one of five awarded for the action.

Raeder's eyes, however, were not on France but on the Arctic seas. The next four Murmansk-bound convoys, and the returning convoys which sailed at the same time, were struck by destroyers, submarines, and aircraft, which finally included torpedo planes. Each convoy fought its way through, provoking a series of spirited actions as the various German forces made their attacks independently of each other. Both sides lost ships, but no action was decisive, since the German heavy ships were held as a background threat and the British became bolder each time a convoy got through.

Threats, to be effective, must be supported by a willingness to act; so all the available heavy ships, with escort, sailed against the early July outbound convoy, whose code letters were *PQ 17*. The fast force comprising the battleship *Tirpitz*, the cruiser *Hipper*, and four destroyers sailed from Trondheim to Vest Fiord and then north to rendezvous with the slower *Scheer*, the *Lützow*, and six destroyers from Narvik.

Three destroyers and the *Lützow* ran aground, but the other forces met at Alten Fiord, just west of North Cape, the northernmost point in Norway. They were ready for the leap at the convoy as it moved past the Cape. Heavy air reconnaissance and support were promised, submarines were on station, and the practically continual daylight was considered advantageous to aircraft and surface ships. They were to operate under the nearly crippling 'no unnecessary risks' orders, including the requirement that the enemy aircraft carriers be eliminated before the German ships attacked, but Raeder hoped that German aerial superiority in the vicinity of North Cape would continue to dissuade the British from moving capital ships to those waters. Raeder's hopes were fulfilled: the Home Fleet capital ships stayed well west as the convoy moved towards North Cape. Hitler hesitated but finally gave the word for a quick raid to be completed before the British could move their heavy forces in close enough for an attack by the *Victorious'* aircraft. The British were known to have withdrawn the convoy's cruiser support, making the convoy and its lighter escorts tempting targets.

The Fleet sailed on the afternoon of July 5th and was quickly reported by British submarines and an aircraft. A few hours later the ships were called back because an extraordinary event had occurred: the British had scattered the convoy the night before. They were unwilling to risk their capital ships near the Norwegian air bases, so the First Sea Lord considered the convoy helpless and ordered its break-up in hopes that single ships could best avoid destruction. The mere fact that the *Tirpitz* had left her base at Trondheim had been enough; she could have stayed in Alten Fiord and never have moved towards the convoy. What fear had forced on the British, the submarines and aircraft capitalized on. The hunt became a massacre. Two-thirds of the thirty-three merchantmen were sunk. The equipment of an army went down with them: 210 aircraft; 430 tanks; 3,350 vehicles; and just under 100,000 tons of other war material. The German cost was five aircraft.

In the face of the *PQ 17* disaster, the British stopped the Murmansk Run for two months. The Mediterranean, where Rommel was knocking on the gate to Cairo, drew the Home Fleet away from the support of Russia to the support of Malta. American Fleet units briefly furnished support to the over-extended British, but the American ships had to be withdrawn to build up Admiral Chester W. Nimitz's Pacific Fleet, which was still inferior to the Japanese Fleet even after the decisive American victory at Midway. The Germans were elated at their success but could do no more to follow it up than launch raids against Russian Barents Sea shipping and installations.

For the next pair of convoys, the German Naval Operations Staff planned to use submarines and aircraft against the heavily escorted outbound convoy and use surface ships against the return convoy to the east of North Cape, on the assumption that it would be lightly guarded. Rather perversely, the concepts of Dönitz's tonnage war were adopted for surface ships in the one theatre where cargoes destined for the Russian Army, not ships, were critical; but the idea did fit the 'no unnecessary risks' policy, which Hitler reiterated whenever action was discussed.

In early September, when Russia's situation on the Stalingrad Front was desperate in the extreme, *PQ 18* sailed. That time the submarines and aircraft found a different reception when they closed in on the convoy. A massive escort of destroyers, backed for the first time by an escort aircraft carrier and British aircraft operating out of northern Russia, made the air and sea very dangerous around the merchant ships and their lighter escorts. The battle raged for days, with little respite for the convoy in the long hours of daylight. Both sides suffered losses, but the convoy could not be shaken out of its tight defensive formation. The German aircraft shifted their attacks to the escort carrier *Avenger*, without success. Meanwhile the *Scheer*, the *Hipper*, and the light cruiser *Köln* had moved from Narvik to Alten Fiord as an additional threat.

The empty return convoy had waited until the escort forces could cover it. That information led Raeder to cancel the projected surface-ship attack and leave the convoy to the Air Force and submarines. They were hampered by bad weather, but the submarines made contact and scored repeatedly. When the entire operation was completed, the toll stood at thirteen outbound merchantmen lost out of forty; three out of fifteen empty ships; a tanker, a destroyer, and a minesweeper of the escort group; and four aircraft. In turn the German loss of four submarines and forty-one aircraft showed that the Murmansk Run battles were approaching equilibrium.

Once again Mediterranean events interrupted the Murmansk convoys by drawing off British naval forces. The turning-point battles at El Alamein and the decisive invasion of French North Africa were the beginning of the end for the Axis in Mare Nostrum. The German surface forces in Norway raided Russian waters and laid offensive minefields until the next trial of strength. It could not be delayed very long. The desperate Russian defence of Stalingrad demanded Anglo-American support. For three months, only single ships could be sent. They sought safety in the long nights of autumn and in poor visibility, but fewer than half arrived. An empty convoy from Russia sailed towards Iceland in mid-November. It was scattered in storms so fierce that German action was limited to a few submarine attacks; only two ships were sunk, while twenty-six got through. All those Arctic moves were mere preliminaries to the attempted passage of the winter convoys.

A winter convoy moved, in many ways, in a different world from its summer counterpart. Nearly total darkness reduced aerial sorties to a minimum, so most of the German aircraft were withdrawn to other fronts. Submarines were hard for the British to find or attack, but were nearly blind themselves and were unable to attack in stormy weather. Surface-ship reconnaissance was severely limited by a twenty-two-hour night and two-hour twilight dimmed by severe storms, snow, cold, and high seas. The British, with improved radar for search and fire control, and with a large number of torpedo-carrying ships which menaced German heavy units, made every operation hazardous. Hitler's 'no unnecessary risks' orders made bold decisions particularly unlikely in confused situations where boldness might be decisive.

One new element was contained in Raeder's orders for the next operation. In addition to the injunction not to rescue survivors, which was necessary because of the risks rescue operations would create, a statement that British rescue of survivors was undesirable added a harshly personal tone to the naval war. Crews were officially recognized as extremely valuable to the British war effort; but the new orders were really superfluous, as survivors' chances were very poor in the stormy dark and cold.

One convoy slipped through to Murmansk in late December without being attacked. The next was sighted by a submarine. Despite the poor conditions for surface attack, an OKW request for the Navy to aid the Eastern Front, added to Raeder's drive to action, encouraged a sortie by the *Lützow*, *Hipper*, and six destroyers. Hitler's permission was obtained, and the ships sailed promptly in order to strike the convoy during the two hours of light on New Year's Eve. An hour after the ships had left, Vice-Admiral Oscar Kummetz, the force commander, received a remarkably inhibiting order, for a leader engaged on an offensive sweep with many unknown hazards waiting in the stormy darkness ahead. It was from Admiral Otto Klüber – the Flag Officer, Northern Waters – from whom Kummetz had personally received his orders just prior to departure. Klüber's message was: 'Contrary to the operational order regarding contact against the enemy, use caution even against enemy of equal strength because it is undesirable for the cruisers to take any great risks.'* Raeder, knowing Hitler's preoccupation with loss, had sent a cautionary signal to Group North, which had

* B. B. Schofield, *The Russian Convoys*, p 134.

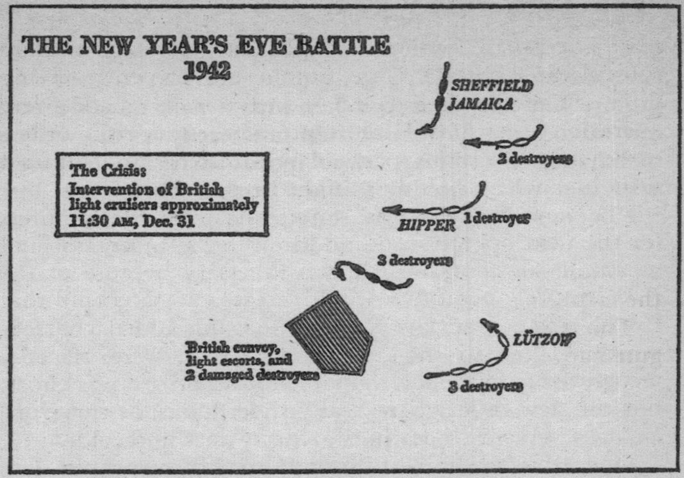

passed it to Klüber too late for the conference with Kummetz; so he in turn had protected himself by sending it on by radio.

Kummetz planned to come up astern of the convoy with his six destroyers spread ahead in a scouting line and the two heavy ships spread well apart so they could attack from different directions, each with three destroyers. Although division of forces was hazardous, it was designed to draw the escorts towards whichever heavy ship attacked first and leave the convoy open to attack by the other. At dawn Kummetz in the *Hipper* was in contact with the convoy, his ship coming at it from the north-west. His destroyers had lost touch in some manoeuvring designed to locate the convoy, and some of them had fired briefly at a British destroyer. The *Lützow* was in position south of the convoy, as intended.

The *Hipper* moved in through an unusually mild wind and sea. Visibility under the clouds was variable, reaching ten miles at times but closing in sharply as snow flurries moved across the sea. Ahead, the *Hipper*'s lookouts sighted a destroyer laying a smoke screen to cover the convoy. The *Hipper* tried to stop her with 8-inch gunfire but only damaged her with a near miss. After a few salvoes the *Hipper* shifted fire briefly to the nearest merchantmen. Then two more British destroyers appeared, blocking the *Hipper* from a direct dash into the convoy. They appeared to be launching torpedoes, the form of attack which German captains feared above all others since their grim experiences culminating with the crippling of the *Bismarck*.

The *Hipper* turned away and engaged in a sporadic gun battle, as visibility permitted, using her aft turrets. Kummetz hoped to lure the destroyers away from the convoy; but soon, failing in that, he ordered the *Hipper* to swing back towards the enemy. The destroyers feinted repeatedly but did not launch torpedoes, and the *Hipper* dodged but failed to close. Kummetz called for his destroyers to engage the British escorts while the *Hipper* continued the gun battle. As usual, German gunnery was good. The leading destroyer, the *Onslow*, was badly damaged by three 8-inch shells, one of which seriously wounded the gallant Commodore, Captain R. St Vincent Sherbrooke. The *Onslow* withdrew towards the convoy, covered by a snow squall which prevented the *Hipper* from hitting her or the remaining destroyer. The latter, in turn, made smoke to cover the *Onslow*.

The *Hipper*'s next target was a detached minesweeper, which blundered into the battle area and was promptly disabled. Kummetz ordered one of his three destroyers, which had just caught up with the battle, to sink the minesweeper. The destroyer *Achates*, which had been covering the convoy with a smoke screen, emerged from the smoke at an unlucky moment and was badly damaged by the *Hipper* before she disappeared again, but she continued to obscure the situation for Kummetz with her smoke screen. She sank after the battle.

The *Hipper* swung south and then west after three more British destroyers appeared – the last undamaged

British escorts. Had Kummetz known it, he could have ordered the *Lützow* and the destroyers in to annihilate the convoy out of hand while he continued to engage the destroyers. As it was, the *Lützow* and three destroyers had circled ahead of the convoy. In abominable visibility, the *Lützow*'s captain could not distinguish friend from foe and hesitated, waiting for better visibility. The three British destroyers played their deadly charade against the *Hipper*, not daring to fire their torpedoes because, had they fired and missed, their threat value would have been gone, leaving the *Hipper* free to close in on them and on the convoy. Instead they boldly fired their 4-inch and 4·7-inch guns at the heavy cruiser, which damaged one of the destroyers slightly with an 8-inch near miss, then turned away from the torpedo threat.

At that critical point, with the British facing annihilation the moment the *Lützow*'s captain decided to steer into the defenceless convoy, two British light cruisers, the *Sheffield* and *Jamaica*, raced into the arena at 31 knots and opened fire on the *Hipper* from the dark northern horizon. Their commander, Rear-Admiral Robert Burnett, had no doubts about his rôle. He had steered for the flash of the heaviest guns, and his ships quickly began straddling the surprised *Hipper* with two twelve-shell salvoes every twenty seconds. Theirs were 112-pound 6-inch shells, unlikely to cripple their armoured enemy, but the range was down to seven miles and closing rapidly to four miles. The *Hipper* was hit, hit again, and hit twice more, one of the shells penetrating the armour and flooding an engine room. The *Hipper*'s speed dropped from 31 to 28 knots as she swung in a circle towards the light cruisers, opened fire, and disappeared into a smoke screen. The *Hipper* reappeared briefly, then disappeared again. Two German destroyers, one of which had been detached to sink the disabled minesweeper, suddenly broke out of the murk and steered to join what they thought were their own ships two miles away. The *Sheffield* was so close to one of the German destroyers that she turned to ram – but she smashed her foe so hard with gunfire that the German quickly came to a blazing halt. The *Sheffield* swept by, firing every gun that would bear. The other destroyer dodged into her own smoke screen. The *Hipper* pulled out to the west in the thickening darkness.

Meanwhile, the *Lützow* sighted and ineffectively fired on a few ships of the convoy. The three British destroyers rushed in to draw the *Lützow*'s fire and successfully hid the convoy and themselves in another smoke screen.

Aboard the *Hipper*, Kummetz made his most difficult decision. He called his forces out of the battle and steered for port. The *Hipper* briefly exchanged fire with the three destroyers, broke off, and was chased at long range by the light cruisers. Then two German destroyers and the *Lützow* sighted the British cruisers. All four heavy ships exchanged fire, but the odds were too great and the British broke off as 8-inch salvoes straddled the *Sheffield*. They opened the range and shadowed the German force until its withdrawal was confirmed. The three-hour New Year's Eve battle was over.

The 'no unnecessary risks' orders, combined with the *Hipper*'s reduced speed and the worsening visibility, had caused Kummetz to abandon the attack on the far inferior foe, an action subsequently approved by Raeder. Captain Sherbrooke, whose forces had fought a brilliant defensive battle until aid arrived, won the Victoria Cross. Both sides had lost a destroyer, and the British a minesweeper – but the *Hipper* needed major dockyard work, which more than balanced the damage to the remaining British destroyers.

Meanwhile, German signals were to have an explosive effect on the German High Command. The first message was from the lone submarine present. She was too far from the action to intervene, but at its height she signalled: 'According to our observation, the battle has reached its climax. I see nothing but red.'* The next

* B. B. Schofield, *The Russian Convoys*, p 145.

radio message was from Kummetz: 'Break off engagement and retire to the westward.'* Hitler was harassed by the situation at Stalingrad, where a quarter-million men were surrounded and, following his orders not to retreat, were being decimated. He was quarrelling endlessly with his generals, accusing them of lying to him and failing to carry out their orders. In his East Prussia headquarters, he anxiously awaited the results of the convoy battle, hoping to be able to announce a glorious victory to usher in the New Year 1943. The two radio messages were taken as indications of success, and Hitler's expectations increased.

That evening, Hitler was shown a report from the British radio claiming the sinking of a German destroyer and the damaging of a cruiser. Hitler asked Vice-Admiral Theodor Krancke, the naval representative at his headquarters, why no information was available. Krancke explained the need for radio silence and then called the Naval Operations Staff in Berlin to suggest sending a query to Kummetz to clarify the situation. Raeder vetoed it, refusing to ask for even a one-letter response, despite the storm building up at Hitler's headquarters. There, Hitler chatted with New Year's Eve guests and checked with Krancke every half-hour until he went to bed shortly after 4.00 AM.

New Year's Day dawned over Hitler's headquarters; but no word had arrived from the far north. Krancke called Naval Headquarters and learned only that there had been a battle with the British escort and damage to the German force. Shortly afterwards, Raeder sent a message for Krancke to give Hitler. It merely said that information was delayed by telephone and radio breakdowns. No further news came in. By noon, Hitler was building up to a fury. He suspected the Navy was withholding information from him – something the Army sometimes tried to do. He demanded a report from the ships and then loosed a tirade against the big ships and

* Dudley Pope, *73 North*, p 242.

their timid officers, ignoring the fact that he was the author of the 'no unnecessary risks' orders.

All afternoon Krancke's demands for information went along the chain of command to Alten Fiord; all afternoon the victory or defeat message did not come in. At 5.00 PM Krancke was called into Hitler's presence. Hitler raged about the 'useless' ships. Then he announced that it was his unalterable decision to scrap the big ships, using their guns and armour in his 'Fortress Europe' scheme and their crews in more active units. Krancke could not even get a delay to await the action report. He left to send the news to Raeder.

The action report, which had been delayed by numerous mischances caused by weather and changed codes, was finally dictated to Krancke by Raeder at 7.25 PM. Hitler was sleeping, but when he awoke, Krancke gave him the report. It did nothing to cool Hitler's anger. He, who operated on deliberately developed emotional impulses, had no intention of backing off. The evening conference was a nightmare for Krancke. One accusation followed another: the ships were not fought to the end; the Air Force would accomplish what the ships had failed to do; the ships had no value, but demanded enormous resources for their protection. They were to be scrapped. Raeder was to be called to headquarters immediately to face Hitler.

Krancke arranged a delay which was stretched to five days, but when Raeder arrived on January 6th Hitler's attitude had not changed. Hitler began with a monologue on the German Navy's history, stressing its surface-ship failures and the failure of its leadership. He reiterated his stand on the comparative value of heavy ships, coastal guns, submarines, and aircraft. He tried to assure Raeder that scrapping the big ships was no degradation. Then he ordered Raeder to prepare answers on details of decommissioning the ships, utilizing the guns, rebuilding some ships as aircraft carriers, and speeding the submarine building programme. Raeder had little opportunity to reply, but when the tirade died down he asked to speak to Hitler alone, or 'under four eyes', as the German expression puts it. He realized that it was his only chance to talk rationally with Hitler, who often behaved quite differently when he had no audience. When the others had left, Raeder tendered his resignation. Hitler tried to dissuade him, but Raeder refused to reconsider. He accepted an honorary post and set January 30th, which marked the end of the tenth year of Raeder's service to Hitler, as the date of the change. Hitler asked for the names of two possible successors.

Vice-Admiral Krancke, who had been helpless to change events, went to Berlin to gather information about the battle. He returned and asked for a private conference with Hitler. Krancke had been the Captain of the *Scheer* on her long raiding voyage in 1940–41, and, some time before the New Year's Eve crisis, he had stood up to Hitler, correcting Hitler despite the rage that engendered and proving his point from earlier conference records. Hitler respected such men, so he paced up and down while Krancke told the whole story and corrected all Hitler's errors. Krancke feared that he was courting a concentration camp; but when he finished, Hitler suddenly thanked him and shook his hand!

Meanwhile, Raeder determined to make one last effort to reorient Hitler's thinking. His staff prepared a 5,000-word memorandum which was, in effect, a basic guide to sea power, emphasizing the deterrent effect on the Allies of the ships, the possibilities of British operations against Europe, and the possibilities for British redeployment in the Mediterranean or Orient should the German ships be withdrawn. He prefaced this with a letter describing a move to scrap the ships as a victory without effort to the British, which would cause joy in the enemy camp and disappointment to the allies of Germany, who would view it as a sign of weakness and lack of comprehension of naval war. Hitler, showing just that total lack of comprehension, ordered his ideas into effect, ignoring the memorandum.

As his possible replocements, Raeder selected General-Admiral Rolf Carls, a man much like himself in orientation, and Admiral Karl Dönitz, should Hitler decide to emphasize submarines. Hitler chose Dönitz; and on January 30th, 1943, he gave him the rank of Grand Admiral – a rank Raeder had held since April 1st, 1939. Raeder retired as Inspector-General of the Navy, an honorary position, with a request to Hitler to protect the Navy and his successor from Göring. To Dönitz he stressed the need for retention of the capital ships and the necessity for their operation without restriction or fear of losses.

The new Commander-in-Chief's personality was sharply different from Raeder's, although the same thorough professionalism dominated his outlook. He recognized the handicap the Navy was under in having no one close to Hitler to further its viewpoints and defend its interests against men such as Göring, whose influence was obvious in the January upheaval. Dönitz determined to meet frequently with Hitler, to impress him with the Navy viewpoints in both formal and informal contacts. Raeder had been formal and brief, often leaving studious memoranda for Hitler to read. Dönitz realized that Hitler operated by carefully nurtured bursts of enthusiasm, so he kept contacts at an informal, spoken level as much as possible. He accepted the risk of falling under Hitler's spell, a fault he had recognized in Raeder since long before the war.

Raeder had tried to maintain his independence from Hitler by distance and had failed; Dönitz would also fail – but he would gain Hitler's confidence and benefit the Navy. He was to protect it from Party interference and see that its needs were met, as much as that was possible in the last years of the war.

Some changes followed Dönitz's accession. He retained

command of the submarine arm, although Captain Eberhard Godt, who had been his Chief of Staff, took over the day-to-day operation of the submarines with the rank of Rear-Admiral. Some older men were pensioned, and others transferred, when the command structure was somewhat streamlined. Later in the year Dönitz was able to obtain an accelerated submarine building programme from Hitler. He arranged a faster construction system by turning over all naval construction to Albert Speer, the Armaments Minister. Speer created a very efficient Central Committee for Shipbuilding, which was able to make the best use of German industry for submarine construction. A Shipping Commissioner was appointed to give centralized control for economical use of merchant shipping.

Dönitz plunged into his new tasks with such energy and fearlessness that he wondered how long Hitler would keep him in his post. At an early conference with Hitler, Göring interrupted with one of his usual comments about the Navy. Dönitz told him quite sharply to stay out of naval affairs, just as he avoided Air Force matters. The silence which followed was broken by Hitler's chuckle. Hitler came to trust and listen to a man who ordered his officers to correct him in front of Hitler if necessary to avoid errors in his presentations. Such honesty was rare in Hitler's headquarters.

It was well for the Navy to be led by someone who could influence Hitler in the last two years of the war. Sometimes Dönitz's victories came in open conferences, sometimes in personal meetings and after violent, emotional attacks which Dönitz met with firmness and objectivity. To those outside his tiny trusted circle, Hitler became even more stubborn and distrustful. He insisted on taking more and more control into his own hands, especially over Army operations. A vicious cycle developed, with Hitler giving detailed orders, the generals on the scene finding them meaningless and acting on their own initiative, Hitler accusing them of cowardice and betrayal, and Hitler tightening his hold. That cycle, and the mounting defeats, eventually led to the plot of July 20th, 1944, in which Hitler barely escaped assassination, an event that merely added to his fanaticism. He believed that he had been preserved by the Almighty for his assigned task: to lead Germany to victory. To that end he became even more obstinate, inflexible, and ruthless.

Dönitz's first and most vital decision after he took command on January 30th was the disposition of the capital ships. Navy morale was suffering from rumours of radical changes and Dönitz was being blamed. At his first meeting with Hitler, Dönitz said nothing about the ships other than to submit the plans for laying them up and reassigning the crews. On February 9th, however, Krancke announced to Hitler that Dönitz considered it his duty to send the big ships to sea when favourable opportunities offered and that they required full operational freedom. Two weeks later Dönitz personally followed up Krancke's statements. By that time he had become well enough acquainted with the problems involved to be sure that the ships had a good chance of operating successfully and that laying them up or scrapping them would add practically nothing to the rest of the war effort. Their greatest strategic value was considered to be the threat inherent in their mere existence. The decision he asked Hitler to confirm was to decommission two ancient training battleships, two light cruisers, and the damaged *Hipper*; to use the *Lützow*, *Scheer*, *Prinz Eugen*, and one light cruiser for training in the Baltic (until they were needed for battle); and to deploy the *Tirpitz* and *Scharnhorst* with destroyer screens to defend Norway and attack Murmansk convoys. He also wanted more aerial reconnaissance. In a stormy session, Hitler agreed but assured Dönitz that time would show that *he*, Hitler, had been right.

So the *Scharnhorst* went to northernmost Norway to join the *Lützow* and the *Tirpitz* – the 'Lonesome Queen', as the Norwegians called her – in the only sea where German forces could still make themselves felt. They had operational orders permitting full tactical freedom, but their presence halted the convoys until the winter of 1943–4, so they could not use those orders. The freeing of the Sicilian Channel by the Allies made the Persian Gulf route to Russia much more economical, in terms of shipping turn-around time, than it had been before; so the Murmansk Run declined in importance.

Elsewhere the surface war slowly ended. The idea of completing the aircraft carrier was dropped in February 1943; the last disguised merchant raider attempted to get to sea in the same month but was unable to break through the Channel; and the last raider at sea was sunk in October.

The *Tirpitz* had been refitting during the New Year's Eve battle. Through the spring and summer she lay with her consorts at Alten Fiord, greatly affecting the war even though fuel was so short that she was able to sail for brief trials and gunnery practice only about twice a month. In her more southerly anchorage she had been the target of a series of attacks by long-range bombers, but the North Cape region was beyond their range. She had escaped a daring manned-torpedo attack without her crew's being aware of it. The short-range 'chariots' had been submerged and unmanned while being towed by a Norwegian fishing boat to within striking range of the battleship, but they had broken their tow lines and sunk only five miles from their goal.

On September 6th the *Tirpitz*, the *Scharnhorst*, and a destroyer screen sortied to bombard and destroy the Spitzbergen weather station and other installations – a minor task. They returned without incident. The *Lützow* returned to Germany for engine repair, and the *Scharnhorst* left her usual berth to anchor in a nearby fiord to confuse the British intelligence system. The *Tirpitz* lay deep in the fiord, surrounded by anti-torpedo nets. In broad daylight on September 22nd, 1943, a midget submarine surfaced briefly inside the torpedo nets, dove, surfaced again under small-arms fire, and disappeared again. Four men appeared on the surface and were immediately picked up by one of the *Tirpitz*'s boats. Another midget submarine surfaced within the nets. The *Tirpitz*'s light guns opened fire and the submarine disappeared. The British prisoners were questioned but refused to cooperate.

Captain Hans Meyer ordered watertight doors closed, shifted the battleship's bow 150 feet to starboard within her nets by having cables hauled in, began shifting the stern, ordered steam raised, and called for a tug. Then four 2-ton charges went off simultaneously. Three exploded off the bow; but one exploded under the engine rooms, heaving the ship bodily upwards, knocking out the lights, and leaving her with a list to port. The second submarine surfaced repeatedly beyond the nets, apparently damaged by the explosions, and was greeted with gunfire each time. She surfaced a final time; a hatch opened; and one man climbed out before she sank. Another man escaped from the sunken hull two hours later. Both submarine commanders received the Victoria Cross after the war for putting the world's most dangerous ship out of action.

The *Tirpitz* had all her main engines damaged, two turrets jammed, and her rudder twisted; and there were massive equipment failures, including damage to the main fire-control system. Instead of being moved to Germany, which would have exposed her to attack on the voyage and in the dockyard, she was repaired where she lay by a force of 700 men sent from Germany. They built caissons, which were lowered into the water to cover the holes so the damaged plates could be replaced. Slowly the machinery was repaired. The *Tirpitz*'s presence in the north and the uncertainty as to the extent of her damage permitted her to exercise continuing restraint on British sea power.

The damage to the *Tirpitz* meant that the *Scharnhorst*

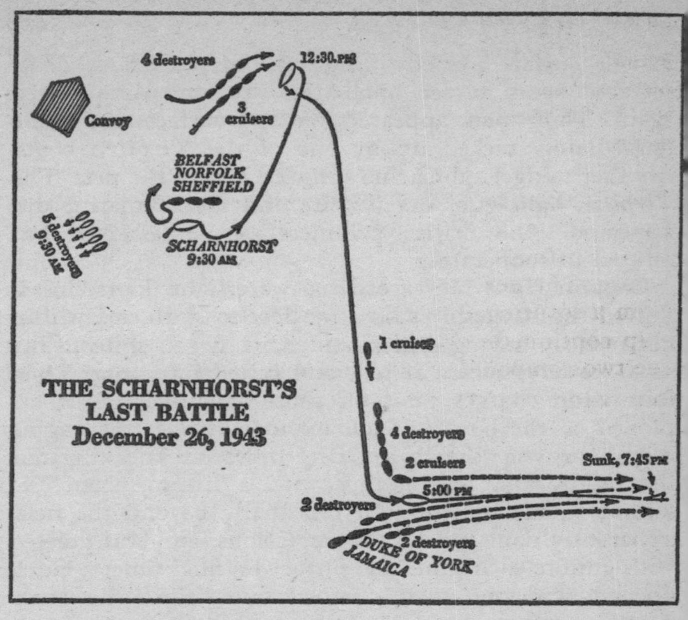

and a few destroyers were the only combat-ready ships in the north as the nights became longer and British convoy movements resumed. Three outward-bound convoys and two returning ones slipped through in November and December 1943. Despite unfavourable conditions of visibility, identical to those faced by the *Hipper-Lützow* group the preceding winter but aggravated by steadily increasing British radar superiority, the *Scharnhorst* and five destroyers were sent against a Murmansk convoy on Christmas Day 1943. The deteriorating situation on the Eastern Front, where the German forces were being pushed relentlessly back, encouraged the move, although the naval leadership was divided on its wisdom. For the sortie, the force commander, Rear-Admiral Erich Bey, was to enjoy tactical freedom wrung from Hitler for the surface forces. The battle was to be the only one in German naval history fought without restraints, and it was to be the last classic single-ship duel between battleships.

The six ships sailed into the storms normal for the North Cape region, leaving behind the peaceful moments of the Christmas which had been celebrated only hours before. The next morning, Bey ordered his destroyers to form a scouting line headed south-west while the battleship continued north for a while. That move separated the two components of his force. Violent weather slowed the destroyers to 10 knots.

The *Scharnhorst* was suddenly illuminated with a starshell from the light cruiser *Belfast*; and the heavy cruiser *Norfolk*, a veteran of the *Bismarck* action, opened fire, hitting the *Scharnhorst* and smashing her forward radar set. The light cruiser *Sheffield*, a participant in the New Year's Eve battle of the previous year, was also present but could not get close enough to open fire. The battleship was practically blind forward; Bey turned her south, out of the battle, but then swung her east and north to get around the cruisers towards the convoy's possible position. The cruisers, commanded by Vice-Admiral Robert Burnett, who had foiled the New Year's Eve attack and subsequently been promoted, disappeared to the north.

Bey called for his destroyers, but they were far away by that time. Aerial reconnaissance informed Bey that a group of ships was far south-west of him – that is, in a position to block his return to Alten Fiord – but Bey stood to the north. He ordered his destroyers to swing west again to find the convoy, whose position had been reported by a submarine. That again drew them farther away from the battleship.

A little after noon, the *Scharnhorst* was again attacked by the cruisers and again turned away. For twenty minutes, a gun battle raged in which the battleship hit the *Norfolk* with 11-inch shells, smashing a turret and all radar sets but one. Two cruisers fell back to shadow while the *Sheffield* dropped out with engine trouble as Bey took his ship south towards his base. He made no attempt to shake off pursuit, apparently considering himself little threatened by the slower cruisers, which had been joined by four destroyers. Bey ordered his destroyers to return to Alten Fiord, where he expected to join them.

Four hours after the second action with the cruisers, a starshell again illuminated the *Scharnhorst*. Then 14-inch shells from the battleship *Duke of York* and 6-inch shells from the cruiser *Jamaica*, another veteran of the New Year's Eve battle, began to straddle the German battleship from six miles to the south. Radar had made such remarkable shooting possible. The *Scharnhorst* had been surprised a third time – that time because her forward radar had been destroyed. She turned east to run and opened fire, swinging to starboard repeatedly to permit her six forward guns to bear, then back to the easterly escape course to try to outrun her pursuers. The *Norfolk* and *Belfast* opened fire briefly, but the cruisers could not keep within gun range as the *Scharnhorst* fled at full speed. The two battleships straddled each other again and again. The *Scharnhorst*, a 'lucky ship', finally ran out of luck. She was hit near the forward triple 11-inch gun turret, which jammed. The second forward turret ceased fire temporarily. Another shell struck amidships. Still she was opening the range, despite more 1,400-pound shell hits, until she was hit aft and flooding started, slowing her slightly. Twenty minutes after the battle began, the range was up to ten miles, so great that the *Scharnhorst* and then the *Duke of York* ceased fire.

For a few minutes there was a lull as the *Scharnhorst*'s lookouts tried to see beyond the eerie light of the starshells which hung over the ship. Then her secondary battery was turned on two destroyers which were trying to work their way up her port side; but two others, one of them a Norwegian, closed unseen to one mile off her starboard side. Suddenly the *Scharnhorst*'s lookouts sighted the threat and she turned – too late to avoid all the destroyers' torpedoes. One struck her. The port-side destroyers took advantage of her turn to hit her with three more torpedoes. One torpedo hit a boiler room, and her speed dropped to 8 knots. Furious work by the engineers quickly brought it up to 22 knots; but it was not enough.

After the torpedo hits, the end was inevitable. Heavy, close-range shell-fire from the *Duke of York* and the three cruisers was combined with torpedo attacks by two of the cruisers and four more destroyers. The final battle lasted thirty-six minutes. Explosions and fires ravaged the doomed ship, but each gun fired until it was shot out. The *Scharnhorst* settled, listed to starboard as more torpedoes struck, then rolled over and sank. British destroyers and cruisers rushed into the cloud of smoke that marked her passing; but the icy waters silenced those who gave one last cheer for the ship and started to sing, 'Over a seaman's grave no roses bloom.' Only thirty-six men survived of the 1,900 who had cheered their sailing less than a day before.

A few days later, when the *Duke of York* again passed the site of the battle, Admiral Sir Bruce Fraser paraded a guard of honour and had a wreath dropped over the side in honour of his late adversaries. The wreath marked more than the end of a ship: the German high-seas surface forces and an era of naval warfare were gone.

The sinking of the *Scharnhorst* ended effective German assaults on the Murmansk Run. In the rest of the war, losses to the heavily escorted convoys were well under 4 per cent of the ships dispatched.

The *Tirpitz* was missed by bombs from a Russian heavy-bomber raid in February, and she was ready for operations in March 1944. On April 3rd sixty-one carrier aircraft appeared without warning over the mountain tops and hurled themselves down along the fiord walls towards the battleship. Fighters machine-gunned the decks to hold down the anti-aircraft fire, and dive bombers followed them in. Within one minute, nine 500- and 1,600-pound bombs burst on her upper works, leaving them a shambles. An hour later, a second wave attacked through a smoke screen and scored five more hits. One hundred and twenty-two dead and 300 wounded lay scattered on the torn hull. Her engines and 15-inch gun turrets were intact behind their massive armour, but she was once again out of action, at a cost to the British of three aircraft.

In July another carrier-borne assault was launched against the giant ship, which had again been repaired. A smoke screen foiled that attempt. Bad weather frustrated one attack in August. Another raid hit her twice through a smoke screen: one bomb struck a turret without effect and the other penetrated eight decks, including eight inches of armour, but failed to explode. The third raid in the same month was unsuccessful. In September, British heavy bombers flying from Russian bases took a turn. Despite the smoke, two 6-ton bombs were near misses and a third smashed her bow. She was moved to Tromsö to escape the Russian advance and to be used as a floating coast-defence battery. There Bomber Command went for her again in October, scoring only a near miss because of weather.

Two weeks later, on November 12th, the heavy bombers finally had a clear shot at her in good weather and with the smoke screen incomplete. The German fighters had received muddled orders and did not appear. Six-ton bombs hit her amidships, tearing her hull open for a hundred feet. She listed sharply, a magazine exploded, and she turned over, drowning almost 1,000 men. The 'Lonesome Queen', which had so long haunted enemy strategy on the broad oceans she never sailed, was finally destroyed. Her fate echoed that of the German High Seas Fleet of World War I: both were potent threats contained by the British at great cost, and both were destroyed after their real usefulness had ended.

Ironically, the battleship had been named in honour of the creator of the High Seas Fleet – Grand Admiral Alfred von Tirpitz.

Long before the end of the *Tirpitz*, the Naval Staff had to consider a far broader problem than action in northern Norway. The Allies were massing strength for an invasion somewhere in western Europe. Points from Narvik to Spain had to be considered as vulnerable to raids, to secondary and feint assaults, or to major invasion. The long fronts to be protected, together with shortages of material, men, and weapons, made passive defence development slow and very incomplete. Command differences regarding strategy, both between the Services and within them, caused poorly integrated action before and during the invasion. The worst problem, from the Navy's point of view, was the inefficient use of mines, which were laid too late, in insufficient quantities, and often in the wrong places.

Against the Normandy invasion on June 6th, 1944, only a few destroyers, torpedo boats, motor torpedo boats, and submarines were used. Most of them were soon destroyed, at sea or by bombing their bases, while the survivors were driven out of France by capture of those bases.

Midget submarines and manned torpedoes were used soon after the invasion began and some had some successes until 1945. Only surprise could give them success, and their total effect was small, although Dönitz professed confidence in them to Hitler.

Defeat was obviously threatening Germany after the success of the Normandy landing. However, with the Allied goal being unconditional surrender, an idea unacceptable to any military organization, and with Hitler's fanatic leadership, there was little for the Navy to do but fight on.

The final tasks of the German Navy were in roles it had tried to outgrow: those of aide to the Army, protector of the Baltic shipping and training areas and evacuator of encircled coastal positions on the Baltic. The *Prinz Eugen*, a 'lucky ship', began the campaign in August 1944, and she was followed by all the remaining heavy ships. In September, when Finland capitulated, the Baltic was open to Russian incursions in spite of Dönitz's hopes, but the Russians did little. The German ships held up well and, until almost the end, had few losses. Eventually Allied air power destroyed all but the *Prinz Eugen* and a light cruiser.

Dönitz's last official act was to delay slightly an armistice after he had been made the head of the German nation by Hitler's final command. He did that to enable his Navy and the Army to move as many people as possible westwards out of Russian reach. That act was to foreshadow the attitude of the German people in the struggle among the victors which was to cloud the peace.

Chapter 9

THE NORTH ATLANTIC

The submarine defensive June 1943–May 1945

'Black May' of 1943 – the turning point in the Battle of the Atlantic – was the last of the decisive defeats that put the Axis on the defensive. The Battle of Midway in the Pacific, in June 1942, had been the first, followed by El Alamein and the North African invasions in November 1942, and Stalingrad in February 1943. For once, Hitler did not heap blame on the naval leaders involved in the submarine disaster. Dönitz had warned him of the rising British strength long before, and Hitler trusted that Dönitz was doing his best. The defeat on the convoy lanes lacked the drama of the *Bismarck*'s end and, as it was a naval matter, did not reflect on Hitler's view of himself as the 'greatest general of all times'.

The submarine disaster called for extremely difficult decisions. For some time, estimates of Allied shipbuilding had indicated that construction had topped sinkings; for some time, defensive concepts had been creeping into German naval thought – ideas such as sinking enough shipping to prevent Allied assaults on Europe or Africa. Finally the blow had fallen: the submarines had been forced out of the North Atlantic.

Despite the submarine fleet's heavy losses, even before new anti-aircraft, anti-radar, and anti-destroyer devices became available, Dönitz decided to continue sending the submarines to sea. They were still needed – were vital, in fact, to the entire German war effort. They tied down

Allied naval forces far more numerous than themselves; forced continued convoying, with its attendant delays; forced enormous production commitments for escort vessels and anti-submarine devices; and, most important of all, kept thousands of aircraft from attacking other targets. Any losses the submarines might still inflict were of course a valuable contribution, but secondary to the indirect drain of Allied resources that they caused by their mere presence in the Atlantic. They still affected the war directly when they destroyed specific targets such as the Murmansk convoys. Two other considerations were important: for the new submarines being constructed, experienced men would be needed; and, if the submarines were all recalled, inadequate bombproof shelter space assured destruction of large numbers in their ports.

Dönitz's conference with Hitler on May 31st, 1943, was devoted largely to the submarine problem. During the conference new Allied aerial search devices were correctly credited with major responsibility for the loss of an estimated thirty-six or thirty-seven submarines during the month.* The need for new radar search receivers for submarines was recognized, along with radar jammers, radar foxer buoys and balloons, and anti-radar covering for conning towers. Offensive radar for submarines was still inefficient, for it swept the whole horizon much too slowly, in very narrow beams. New aircraft to destroy Allied search aircraft in the Bay of Biscay were asked for, but the request was pessimistically dismissed by Hitler, who considered the aircraft unsuitable for the task. An acoustic anti-destroyer torpedo was expected soon, and anti-aircraft machine guns were being installed with dispatch. As soon as some of the new weapons were installed, attacks on North Atlantic convoys were to begin again.

Despite the grimness of the outlook, a new construction programme of forty submarines a month was approved by Hitler, and all submarine construction was put into

* The final total was forty-one; but Dönitz could not have had an accurate total at that date.

the hands of Speer, the Armaments Minister.

Hitler's secret-weapon dreams had already touched naval thinking with discussions of submarine-fired rockets to fight destroyers and the development of 16-inch-diameter submarine-fired rockets to use against cities. Hitler had warned against optimism regarding the former, and the latter were rejected by the Navy as impractical, although such a rocket had been test-fired from a submerged submarine. The Navy settled down to further development of less exotic weaponry. What a few rockets hitting New York would have done to Allied defensive distributions remains one of the many might-have-beens of World War II.

The first attempt to answer Allied air attacks in the Bay of Biscay was already in progress in May. A quadruple heavy machine gun and some lighter weapons were installed on an extra platform aft of each submarine's conning tower, and some submarines were armed even more heavily to serve as floating anti-aircraft traps. They were to fight it out with aircraft to engender future caution, a caution which could be used by submarines to escape on the surface or submerge as they saw fit. At first the tactics worked, with lone British aircraft falling victim to the traps. Encouraged, Dönitz ordered normal submarines to cross Biscay in groups for mutual support. The British met their firepower with massed aircraft firepower, and met grouped submarines with simultaneous group attacks from many directions. An air-to-surface rocket was thrown in, and casualties mounted in the short but vicious battles. By the end of the summer the submarines were traversing the Bay under water again, and the flak traps were dismantled.

For the rest of the year 1943 and into 1944 the battle raged – not for victory but for simple survival. The Germans introduced radar foxers. One type consisted of balloons dragging tinfoil strips across the water. Another type, used in the Bay of Biscay, was a buoy with reflective surfaces. New explosive shells with incendiary effect gave added sting to the anti-aircraft weapons mounted on all the submarines by early autumn and to the heavy anti-aircraft cannon available later in the year. An acoustic anti-destroyer torpedo came into use in August, along with a new radar search receiver to replace a device whose own telltale radiations, it was erroneously believed, were being detected by Allied instruments.

Continued heavy losses forced the dispersion of lone submarines into relatively unfrequented waters, a dispersion hampered by the loss of all but three of the twelve submarine tankers by August 1943. However, as soon as the new weapons were available, a new attempt was made in the North Atlantic. In mid-September, a submerged group attack was launched on a convoy with seeming success, especially with the acoustic torpedo used against the escorts; but by February 1944 that type of attack was ended because more submarines were lost than merchant ships sunk. From that point on, simple survival of lone submarines was the only operational idea. 'No unnecessary risks' was the new rule.

There was really little choice, for anti-submarine successes quickly became cumulative. As early as June 1943, fast Allied ships sailed without escort, releasing escorts to join hunter-killer groups centred around small aircraft carriers. Escort carriers were released from convoy duty by equipping large tankers and ore carriers with flight decks and a few aircraft. Escorts combined to track and attack single submarines, one keeping Sonar contact and the others attacking with a variety of weapons. One of the most effective new weapons was the 'hedge hog', a launcher which threw groups of small depth charges ahead of the attacking ships. The charges exploded only on contact, so hits registered clearly and Sonar contact was not disturbed. Heavier depth charges with $\frac{1}{2}$-ton explosive loads were also used. For defence against the German acoustic torpedoes, noise-making 'foxer' buoys were towed to 'fool' the torpedoes' guidance systems. Aircraft dropped buoys that listened for submarines' propellers, and contacts were pursued with airborne acoustic torpedoes. Noise-making buoys were reported by submariners who thought the buoys were designed to frighten them into thinking escort vessels were everywhere. A trawl used to find submarines in shallow water and explode charges against their sides was reported. Some of the efforts were minor, but cumulatively they reduced submarine successes to very small figures.

The radar mystery was finally solved in August 1943 when a British radar set assembled from parts found in shot-down aircraft was reconstructed and its characteristics revealed. That set, called the 'Rotterdam apparatus' by the Germans, after the place where the first fragmentary set was found, showed that German radar technology had fallen hopelessly behind the Allies'. Even possessing the British set helped little. While radar search receivers and search radars could be built and aircraft used to lead submarines to targets, the submarines were still forced to operate too often below the surface, where they were slow, blind, and clumsy and had very limited endurance. The last submarine tanker was sunk in April 1944, and experiments with underwater refuelling never came to much. Anti-radar covering for submarines showed some promise, but its use was never extensive either.

The only solution to the problem was a completely new type of craft – a 'true submarine', with long endurance and high underwater speed. Before the war began, an engineer named Hellmuth Walter had suggested a propulsion plant for such a submarine, combining a gas turbine and a non-air-using fuel system. Development of that idea, and incidentally that of radar, was held up first by conservative thinking, then by war exigencies and by Hitler's order of mid-1940 cancelling research that could not be completed within a year.

As early as September 1942 Dönitz had realized that a new submarine type, which he had always advocated, would be needed very soon, and he pressed the point in an interview with Hitler to which he had been invited by

Raeder. Hitler approved building two experimental Walter submarines; and months later he approved building twenty-four small and two large ones.

The entirely new craft developed from those ideas had a submerged speed of 24 knots – well above the top speed of most escorts – and was extremely manoeuvrable, with the ability to change depth and speed rapidly to confuse escorts. The large craft had ten forward-firing torpedo tubes. Unfortunately for Dönitz, the first production-run deliveries were not made until December of 1944. The long development needed for such a radically new weapon prevented its use in the war.

Complete novelty was not a bar to the other submarine concept developed, however. When, in November 1942, Dönitz had held a conference with Walter and the two top submarine designers and found that development work on the Walter submarines would be slow, he expressed his feelings of urgency and asked for ideas. Walter suggested the development of a captured Dutch device, a collapsible air mast which would allow conventional submarines to use diesels under water to recharge batteries. That became the snorkel (*schnorchel*), or 'snort'. The second idea, thus, was for a large submarine with the streamline form of the Walter boat, enormous battery capacity for high speed and underwater endurance, and the snorkel for battery charging. Dönitz approved prompt action.

Speed, essential that late in the submarine war, was the hallmark of the entire programme. In mid-June 1943 the first plans were shown to Dönitz. They were for two submarine types of similar characteristics: one, quite small at 200 tons, was given the number XXIII; the other, a long-range, deep-sea type of 1,500 tons, was numbered XXI. The first was designed with a short-time underwater speed of 13 knots, and the second with a 17-knot underwater speed. Dönitz ordered immediate production planning; when he found that the Navy's production time was too slow, he turned the problem over to Speer. Speer assigned a civilian construction specialist, who designed a sectional mass-production building system and set April–May 1944 as the target date for delivery of the first submarine, with production of thirty-three per month to be reached by September 1944. No prototype was to be built. Parts were to be manufactured at many carefully dispersed factories; sections were to be assembled at eleven inland sites; and three shipyards were to assemble the craft.

On July 8th, 1943, Dönitz presented the ideas to Hitler and obtained his full approval. A remarkable record of production was then set, beginning with one large submarine delivered in April 1944 and eight by August. Technical difficulties slowed production somewhat and bombings hampered it in the spring of 1945, yet mass production of both types was achieved and maintained through the 1944–5 winter and spring.

During the months that the submarines were waiting for the installation of the new protective devices and weapons which would enable them to re-enter the Atlantic battle, they continued to fulfil various functions. In the Far East, the group that had gone to Penang in May 1943 was kept reinforced throughout that year and the next. The group lost its tanker in January 1945. As diversions were feasible with the collapse of North Atlantic operations, and as surface blockade runners could no longer get through, fifteen German submarines and some Japanese and Italian ones were converted for carrying low-bulk, high-value cargoes to and from the Orient. Most of them were lost, however. A submarine was sent to the Japanese as a present, but the Japanese considered it too complicated to copy.

The German submarines also reinforced the Mediterranean operations in late 1943 and early 1944, but by autumn of 1944 the last submarine there had been sunk. The Arctic theatre was also reinforced again, both against invasion and against Murmansk convoys, but successes were very rare. There was an eight-month series of discussions in 1944 about British aircraft carriers sailing with Murmansk convoys and ruining submarine opportunities, but Dönitz insisted his submarines could not eliminate them, even though he finally did agree to send submarines to the Scapa Flow approaches. Göring insisted that his aircraft strength was too low to attack the carriers, although he agreed to send some torpedo planes to Norway. None of those operations could have seriously affected the war.

In March 1944 Allied pressure had mounted to the point that the commander of *U852*, fearful of discovery after sinking the merchantman *Peleus*, machine-gunned the survivors and the wreckage to destroy the evidence of his attack. Later in the same cruise his submarine was destroyed and he was captured. Three of the *Peleus*' crew had survived the massacre. They testified in the trial which ended in death sentences for the commander and his gunner. Dönitz did not learn about the case until the war was over. To the credit of the German submariners is the fact that the *Peleus* case is the only deliberate atrocity on record. Dönitz's resolute leadership blocked Hitler's ideas of attacking shipwrecked crews, and the *Laconia* Order was neither intended nor generally interpreted to mean destruction of survivors. Despite the somewhat ambiguous sentence, 'Rescue runs counter to the primary demands of warfare for the destruction of enemy ships and their crews,'* it was a 'no rescue' order based entirely on the need to protect submarines from air attack.

In June 1944 a carefully planned operation gave the Allies another direct view of submarine capabilities. *U505* was located and depth-charged by the American destroyer escort *Chatelain*, a member of a hunting group. As the damaged submarine broke surface, her decks were swept by small-calibre gunfire from three ships while aircraft from the escort carrier *Guadalcanal* flew menacingly overhead. The submarine's crew jumped overboard after

* Léonce Peillard, *The Laconia Affair*, p 190.

removing a large-diameter pipe cover to speed her sinking. Aboard the American ships, the ancient cry, 'Boarders!' rang out; and a courageous group from the destroyer escort *Pillsbury* boarded *U505* from a small boat, stopped the flooding, and secured the US Navy's first warship prize in over a century. The value of the capture was enhanced by the discovery that the submarine's code books were still on board.

Still the submarines fought on. Despite continuing losses, more than fifty submarines were on operation each month in late 1943 and early 1944. In the spring of 1944 the snorkel came into operational use. It did not enhance the attack capability of the existing submarines, but it did allow them to operate without surfacing for battery charges, thus increasing their opportunities for survival. The head of the snorkel was covered with foam rubber to absorb radar impulses, and a radar search receiver aerial was fitted to the head to reduce the submarine's blindness. A submarine at snorkelling depth was hard to find from a distance by Asdic; but the head made a large wake, and a submarine could sometimes be seen at shallow depths by aircraft, so snorkelling had to be done at night. A submarine with diesels going was unable to use its listening gear, so the device, while a great advantage, was not a cure-all.

Dönitz saw in it an opportunity, though, to strike once more at Britain's supply lines. In May 1944 a group of snorkel-equipped submarines was sent to the shallow-water areas right off the British coast to lie in wait among the wrecks and reefs. Surprise was achieved to some extent, and after June 1st no submarine was permitted to operate without a snorkel. When on station, in the Atlantic or close to shore, they did moderately well; but time consumed in transit drastically cut their effectiveness.

In March submarines were grouped in each possible sector in readiness for invasion. When it came at Normandy in June, sixteen Biscay submarines attacked in the

Channel, with the idea that any losses at sea might hurt the Allied build-up in the critical beachhead period. A group of nineteen submarines operated in the Bay of Biscay, and a few from Norway joined the battle in the Channel. Losses to the submarines were high, fifteen of them being sunk in two months as against twenty-one Allied ships sunk; but the snorkelling submarines could continue to operate. Some submarines from other areas were sent to the North Atlantic to force dispersion of the invasion escorts. When the Allies became firmly entrenched on land and submarine losses equalled supply-ship sinkings in the invasion area, the submarines were withdrawn, in August. A few were used to bring supplies to beleaguered ports; but as the Allies took their bases from the land side, the submarines were shifted to Norwegian and to German ports.

That the submarines continued the struggle in the two nearly hopeless years from May 1943 to May 1945 is a remarkable comment on Dönitz's leadership. Of 1,170 submarines, 784 were eventually destroyed, many with their entire crews. Well over half that total were sunk in the last two years; yet the submarines continued to sail, almost defiantly, as late as April 1945 – as if to blot out the stain of the High Seas mutinies of 1918.

Despite continued losses for small gain and ever-increasing Allied countermeasures, Dönitz waited hopefully for the time when the new submarine types would be ready to put to sea. In February 1945 the first small Type XXIII submarines sailed to the British Isles, where they operated very successfully in the war's end, with no loss among the eight that finally participated. With only two torpedoes apiece, their effect was small, however. Given more time, the sixty-one Type XXIII's ready in May plus the eight small Walter-type submarines had much potential menace.

For the large Type XXI submarines, on which Dönitz's hopes were based, his staff made radically new plans, which matched the craft's remarkable capabilities. They carried an anti-radar-coated snorkel head with radar search receiver aerials attached; ultrasensitive hydrophones with fifty-mile range for locating ships while submerged; a supersonic echo device to give the course, range, speed, number, and type of targets; acoustic torpedoes that could not be fooled by foxers or by ships turning off their main engines; zigzag torpedoes and torpedoes which could be fired at targets at any angle from the submarine; and propellers that were noiseless when moving at a speed of five knots, driven by a soundless motor with belt drive. The submarines were to sail boldly under the convoys, where they could not be detected or attacked, and then to launch torpedoes from a depth of 150 feet without so much as a glimpse of their opponents.

The new submarines' features effectively countered the most potent Allied anti-submarine methods. Aircraft visual and radar sightings were practically eliminated by the submarines' tactics of remaining submerged and using the snorkel at night. Asdic, depth charges, and hedge hogs became far less effective when the submarines' underwater speed and attack depth were increased sharply. The designers of Type XXI and Dönitz's experienced tacticians had overtaken the Allies in the technological race: the Battle of the Atlantic was about to begin again, with German tactical superiority assured and the Allied lifelines in dire jeopardy.

Over a hundred of those formidable submarines were completed, and many crews had finished training, when the first one went to sea on April 30th, 1945. She easily escaped a hunter-killer group, cruised for days, located a cruiser with a destroyer screen, lined up for the attack, broke off without arousing suspicion, then surfaced while the cruiser group went on its way. The new attack method was perfect; the new weapon which was to reverse the war at sea was ready; but Hitler had killed himself the week before, and the submarine was but the spoils of war.

EPILOGUE

Implications of World War II German naval strategy for the Cold War era

German strategy failed to prevent World War II, to win it, or to end it short of total defeat. That statement, however, should not be the epitaph for German strategic thought or for its value to history. German naval strategy, in particular, deserves most thoughtful analysis; for the problems inherent in the position of the Western maritime community in the Cold War period have many parallels in the problems faced by Germany's enemies from 1919 to 1945.

German naval strategy included a number of bold and imaginative plans. The surface forces' Dispersion Strategy functioned well early in the war until the complementary Tonnage War Strategy could be used effectively through a large-scale increase in the submarine fleet. Both correctly sought decision on the Atlantic trade routes. The Mediterranean Strategy was equally sound so long as it supplemented the Battle of the Atlantic.

Strategic thinking, however, tended to lag behind events. Committing submarines to the Mediterranean was an attempt to salvage one campaign at the expense of the far more important North Atlantic campaign. In the Murmansk Run battles, rules for reducing risk, which had been useful in the Atlantic, were still enforced even though a policy of taking calculated risks in an aggressive and daring manner would have been more appropriate where units were more numerous and more expendable.

Tactically, it would appear that more than the urge to caution was involved in German failures. The German Navy had not had time or opportunity to develop the type of naval tradition that in the moment of crisis could create a Drake, a Nelson, or a Spruance – men who were able to plan carefully, marshal their forces, and then strike through to decision, believing that when all that was humanly possible had been done, 'fortune favours the brave'. Admittedly, conditions were not favourable. German commanders were pinned to their ports by fuel shortages. They lacked air coordination, they were short of destroyers and light cruisers as anti-submarine and anti-destroyer screens, and they struggled with constantly rotating, inexperienced personnel. Those factors, however, do not account entirely for a philosophy which made scuttling an honourable tradition rather than a last resort. Nor do they explain either the lack of initiative of six large destroyers which failed to close the enemy in the New Year's Eve battle or the argument on the *Bismarck*'s bridge as the *Prince of Wales* retreated. Certainly there was nothing wrong with personal courage; rather, some subtle doctrinal poison seems to blame.

On the level of grand strategy, the tendency to blame Hitler for every disaster and to credit military men for most successes detracts from a fair appraisal of military events. Hitler's faults as a leader were numerous, and his understanding of naval strategy was always weak; but he had strengths in his political insights and in his daring, which was based on a sometimes remarkable grasp of his enemies' habits of thought and action. In the long run, flashes of brilliance were not enough, however. He did not make detailed, long-term plans, and when hostile sea power faced him he was not able to improvise a counter to it. He could neither bring himself to accept a long campaign of attrition nor muster the power to bring about outright destruction of the enemy at sea.

Hitler's failures clearly illustrate the importance of a series of unities which are essential to national success in an international arena dominated by power politics. Those unities include armed might and diplomacy, economics and strategy, and Armed Forces plans and grand strategy. The need for unity of military and diplomatic moves is shown in Hitler's failure to use his victories in France and Norway to create a basis for a negotiated settlement with Britain or for the application of military power to force Britain to terms. The need for unity of economics and strategy is illustrated in the over-extension of German military efforts, which made the economy so inflexible that first, research on such critical programmes as submarine propulsion systems was curtailed and then, as the war demanded more resources, normal military requirements began to go unfulfilled. The importance of unity of the individual Armed Services' war plans and the national strategy is shown, again in the negative, in the divisive tendencies among the High Commands of Hitler's Armed Forces – schisms such as that over the use of air power at sea – which eventually became fatal liabilities to the state the Armed Forces were expected to support. In the application of all those principles, the measure of Germany's failure to deny the sea lanes to the Allies is the measure of her defeat in the West in World War II.

The application of the lessons of German strategic failure need not lead to more warfare, although if there must be war it is to be hoped that it can be directed in as rational a manner as possible. Strategic thought can be a limiting factor in the search for solutions or accommodations to international tensions. If the implications of the Wegener thesis regarding the strength of sea power had been worked out and applied to the 1930s, or if the British political position and military resiliency had been fully evaluated by the Nazi leadership in 1939, there would have been no World War II.

West Germany's post-war decisions have shown a clear grasp of world power relationships. The West Germans have become active partners in the Atlantic system, a recognition not only of the strength of the Russian Empire but also of the effectiveness of Western sea power. German military forces have been integrated into the Atlantic community's forces, rather than organized independently in a new search for means to create a separate power system for strictly national goals. The new German Federal Navy is prepared to hold the Baltic entrances to protect the Atlantic sea routes from Russia's threat from the east, rather than to hold the Baltic as a base against the Atlantic system.

In the broader power structure, while some have been seeking Utopia and others retreating to cynical nationalism in the frustrating deadlock of the Cold War, a remarkable consensus has been tacitly established to enable the feuding great powers to coexist for over twenty years without a world war. The atomic threat is not enough of an explanation. A grasp by all sides of the strength of the Western maritime community has established limits to various power blocs, just as the Red Army has stabilized the power relationships of central Europe. The carefully maintained balance of strength implies a world of some tension, although less tension can be said to exist than in 1939, when Hitler's inner drives dominated the world scene. The balance is not perfect, nor is it sure to survive; but it is noteworthy that large parts of the world have been without war for nearly a quarter-century, and that wars have occurred only in regions outside the areas where a rationally understood balance exists.

In the grand strategies of the future, the influence of Western sea power will continue to be a determining factor in the world power picture. Nothing has displaced or threatens soon to displace the seaways as the indispensable routes for the movements of goods and military forces for the Western alliance. Understanding that fact, the United States deploys part of its 'ultimate threat' in atomic-powered missile-carrying submarines; builds aircraft carriers for both atomic and small-scalt warfare; and improves its amphibious capability. Russia, meanwhile, has built the world's greatest submarine fleet as a threat to Western sea lanes. All those forces contribute to the balance of terror, as well as to a stability based on relatively rational analyses of the world power balance.

Weapons systems change, but the Atlantic alliance has maintained its ability to project its military strength against land targets by way of the sea. On the other hand, the sea powers will clearly be in a defensive posture on the ocean trade routes in the event of any major war, including a 'total' one if it should last beyond the stage of initial holocaust. Once more, numerically inferior fleets, of whatever composition and with whatever integrated aerial forces, may threaten Western lifelines. Once more the sea powers must be ready to counter such threats – now, however, by effective methods developed in peacetime; for time is compressed, technologies are increasingly complex, and any signs of weakness are likely to be exploited by Russian strategists, who will apply pressure at any level of confrontation, from border incident to the edge of major conflict.

Once more the hegemony which the Western maritime powers have maintained since the sixteenth century is in jeopardy. How well will the understanding of their maritime heritage, the development of imaginative strategies, and the simple determination to victory serve their future? The threat posed to Western sea power by the German Navy of 1939–45 may well serve as a grim warning to the Atlantic community now.

APPENDICES

GERMAN SUBMARINES

	Produced to date*	Sunk to date	Sunk per quarter	At sea in Atlantic per month (average)
1939				
Sept–Nov	55	8	8	16
1940				
Dec (1939)–Feb	60	15	7	11
Mar–May	70	24	9	15
Jun–Aug	80	29	5	14
Sept–Nov	100	33	4	12
1941				
Dec (1940)–Feb	125	33	0	10
Mar–May	150	41	8	19
Jun–Aug	200	49	8	32
Sept–Nov	250	58	9	37
1942				
Dec (1941)–Feb	310	73	15	39
Mar–May	350	86	13	53
Jun–Aug	425	110	24	72
Sept–Nov	500	150	40	100
1943				
Dec (1942)–Feb	575	180	30	102
Mar–May	650	251	71	115
Jun–Aug	725	330	79	76
Sept–Nov	800	384	54	75
1944				
Dec (1943)–Feb	875	427	43	67
Mar–May	925	495	68	56
Jun–Aug	975	578	83	44
Sept–Nov	1,050	619	41	51
1945				
Dec (1944)–Feb	1,100	669	50	46
Mar–May	1,170	784	115	52
TOTAL (where applicable)	1,170	784	784	

* *See note on p 264*

APPENDIX I

The Battle of the Atlantic 1939–45

ALLIED MERCHANT VESSELS				GERMAN RAIDERS	
New construction per quarter (thousand tons)	*Losses to subs in North Atlantic per quarter (thousand tons)*	*Losses to subs in all oceans per quarter (thousand tons)*	*Losses to all causses in all oceans per quarter (thousand tons)*	*Major raiders at sea per month (average)*	*Minor raiders at sea per month (average)*
300	322	421	800	2	0
300	240	465	1,000	0	0
300	112	161	800	0	3
300	815	834	1,800	0	6
300	764	784	1,500	1	6
300	502	536	1,500	3	6
400	510	846	2,300	2	6
600	336	435	1,800	0	4
700	378	483	1,500	0	3
800	286	789	2,000	0	1
1,200	125	1,426	2,800	0	2
1,700	350	1,589	3,300	0	3
2,200	518	1,801	3,150	0	2
2,500	475	915	1,800	0	1
3,100	620	1,093	2,200	0	1
4,000	0	421	1,600	0	1
4,100	52	220	700	0	1
3,900	23	213	500	0	0
3,500	26	186	500	0	0
2,900	83	227	900	0	0
2,800	37	68	300	0	0
2,600	142	225	900	0	0
—	129	179	—	0	0
	6,846	14,316			

APPENDIX 1

NOTE: Statistical tables about the battle of the Atlantic rarely agree because of the large number of variables involved. These include such problems as whether auxiliary-cruiser losses should be included in Allied merchant-ship losses, whether ships near coasts fell victim to mines or torpedoes, and whether incomplete submarines destroyed in port should be counted among submarine losses. The statistics in Appendix I give a reasonably accurate picture without claiming to be exact. Many numbers are rounded for convenience in reading.

Columns 1, 5, and 8 are derived from Karl Kurzak, 'German U-Boat Construction', *USNIP*, LXXXI (April 1955), pp 374–89. Columns 2 and 3 are derived from Captain S. W. Roskill, DSC, RN, *The War at Sea* (London. Her Majesty's Stationery Office, 1954–61), Vol I, pp 599–600; Vol II. pp 467–71; Vol III, part 1, pp 365–72; and Vol III, Part 2, pp 463–9. Column 4 is derived from Harald Busch, *U-Boats at War* (New York, Ballantine Books, Inc, 1955), p 176. Columns 6 and 7 are derived from Jürgen Rohwer, *U-Boote* (Oldenburg/Hamburg, Gerhard Stalling Verlag, 1962), pp 93–5. Columns 9 and 10 are derived from David Woodward, *The Secret Raiders* (New York, W. W. Norton & Company, Inc, 1955).

* To June 1944 most production was Type VIII. After June 1944 most production was Type XXI.

APPENDIX II

German naval chronology
Major events 1919–45

1919 June 21st Imperial High Seas Fleet scuttled at Scapa Flow
1928 *Deutschland* class designed
September 15th Admiral Erich Raeder became Commander-in-Chief of the Navy
1933 January 30th Adolf Hitler became Reichs Chancellor
Hermann Göring became Air Minister
1935 March 16th Air Force established under Göring
Scharnhorst and *Gneisenau* construction began
June 17th Anglo-German Naval Treaty
June 28th *U1* commissioned
September 27th Captain Karl Dönitz became commander of Weddigen Submarine Flotilla
October 3rd Italy attacked Ethiopia
1936 *Bismarck* and *Tirpitz* construction began
March 7th Rhineland remilitarized
July 18th Spanish Civil War began
September 3rd London Submarine Protocol
1937 May American Neutrality Act
1938 March 12th–13th Anschluss of Austria.
September Z-Plan development began
September 29th Munich Agreement to partition Czechoslovakia
December German submarine tonnage increase approved by British
1939 January 27th Z-Plan given highest priority by Hitler
March 15th–16th Remainder of Czechoslovakia occupied
March 23rd Memel seized from Lithuania
March 28th Spanish Civil War ended
April 7th Italy invaded Albania
April 27th Anglo-German Naval Treaty abrogated by Hitler
August 23rd Nazi-Soviet Non-Aggression Pact
September 1st Poland invaded

September 3rd France and Britain declared war
September 4th *Athenia* sunk west of British Isles
September 17th *Courageous* sunk in Western Approaches
September 26th British announced arming of merchant ships
October 13th *Royal Oak* sunk at Scapa Flow
November 23rd *Rawalpindi* sunk by *Scharnhorst* and *Gneisenau* in Iceland-Faeroes Passage
November 30th Russo-Finnish War began
December 13th Battle of the River Plate
1940 February 16th *Altmark* incident
March 12th Russo-Finnish War ended
March 31st *Atlantis*, first auxiliary cruiser, sailed
April 8th *Glowworm* sunk by *Hipper* off Norway
April 9th Invasion of Norway and Denmark began
April 9th *Blücher* sunk off Oslo
April 10th *Königsberg* and *Karlsruhe* sunk in Norwegian campaign
April 10th First Battle of Narvik
April 13th Second Battle of Narvik
May 10th Blitzkrieg began
May 27th–June 5th Dunkirk evacuation
June 8th British withdrew from Norway
June 8th *Glorious* sunk by *Scharnhorst* and *Gneisenau* off Norway
June 10th Italy entered war
June 25th French armistice
July 3rd Battle of Oran
July 16th 'Sea Lion' Directive
August 15th Day of Eagles
September 7th Blitz of London began
September 15th Battle of Britain Day
September 17th 'Sea Lion' postponed indefinitely
September 23rd–25th Battle of Dakar
September 27th Tripartite Alliance: Germany, Japan, Italy
October 28th Italy invaded Greece
October 29th *Scheer* sailed for Atlantic
November 11th Taranto Night
November 30th *Hipper* sailed for Atlantic
December 9th O'Connor's desert offensive against Italians began
December 11th Mediterranean Plan cancelled
December 18th 'Barbarossa' Directive for war against Russia
1941 January 23rd *Scharnhorst* and *Gneisenau* sailed for Atlantic
February 7th O'Connor's desert offensive ended
March 22nd *Scharnhorst* and *Gneisenau* reached Brest
March 28th *Hipper* returned from Atlantic

March 30th Battle of Cape Matapan
March 31st Rommel's first desert offensive began
April 1st *Scheer* returned from Atlantic
April 6th Balkan campaigns began
April 13th Russo-Japanese Non-Aggression Pact
April 30th Balkan campaigns ended
May 18th *Bismarck* and *Prinz Eugen* sailed for Atlantic
May 20th Battle of Crete began
May 27th *Bismarck* sunk
May 30th Rommel's first offensive ended
May 31st Battle of Crete ended
June 1st *Prinz Eugen* reached Brest
June 8th British campaign in Syria and Lebanon began
June 22nd Russian campaign began
July 11th British campaign in Syria and Lebanon ended
September Submarines began deployment to Mediterranean
November 14th *Ark Royal* sank in Mediterranean
November 25th *Barham* sunk in Mediterranean
December 7th Pearl Harbor attacked
December 9th *Prince of Wales* and *Repulse* sunk off Malay Peninsula
December 11th Germany and Italy declared war on United States
December 18th *Valiant* and *Queen Elizabeth* crippled at Alexandria

1942 January 13th Submarines' American campaign began
January 21st Rommel's deep drive into Egypt began
February 11th–13th Channel dash
March 6th Murmansk Run battles began
March 27th–28th St-Nazaire raid
June 4th–7th Battle of Midway
July Submarines concentrated in North Atlantic
July 1st–17th First Battle of El Alamein
July 5th *PQ 17* scattered off North Cape
August 11th *Eagle* sunk in Mediterranean
August 31st–September 6th Second Battle of El Alamein
September 12th *Laconia* sunk in South Atlantic
October 23rd–November 4th Third Battle of El Alamein
November Submarine sinkings reached highest point: 118 ships (743,321 tons)
November 8th Anglo-American landings in French North and West Africa began
November 19th Russian counter-attack at Stalingrad began
December 31st New Year's Eve battle off North Cape

1943 January 30th Raeder retired; Grand Admiral Karl Dönitz became Commander-in-chief of the Navy

February 2nd Stalingrad fell to Russians
March 16th–20th Largest convoy battle in history in North Atlantic
May Submarines lost Battle of Atlantic
May 13th Tunisia fell to Allies
July 10th Sicily invaded by Allies
September 9th Italy invaded at Salerno by Allies
September 22nd *Tirpitz* damaged by midget submarines at Alten Fiord
October 18th *Michel,* last auxiliary cruiser, sunk off Japan
December 26th *Scharnhorst* sunk off North Cape

1944 April 3rd *Tirpitz* damaged by carrier planes at Alten Fiord
May Snorkel came into widespread use
June 6th Normandy invasion
July 20th Bomb plot wounded Hitler
August Surface ships began gunfire support of Eastern Front
August 15th Allied landings in southern France
September 15th *Tirpitz* crippled by heavy bombers at Alten Fiord
November 12th *Tirpitz* sunk by heavy bombers at Tromsö

1945 February First Type XXIII submarines entered combat
April 30th First Type XXI submarine entered combat
April 30th Hitler committed suicide
April 30th Dönitz became Chief of State
May 8th German surrender

BIBLIOGRAPHY

Readers interested in the German Navy will find a wide variety of English-language books available, so this listing is restricted, with a few exceptions, to such books and to articles in the *United States Naval Institute Proceedings* (abbreviated to *USNIP*), a journal available in most major libraries. Articles in the *Proceedings* are often followed in later issues by interesting commentary.

GENERAL SOURCES

The most important single book about the German Navy is the annotated collection of notes on meetings with Hitler prepared for the use of a few staff officers by Raeder and later by Dönitz. These are the 'Führer Conferences on Naval Affairs', *Brassey's Naval Annual, 1948* (London, William Clowes & Sons, Limited). The documents are biased in the direction of the Navy's strategic concepts as opposed to Hitler's. Two other books of prime importance are Grand Admiral Erich Raeder, *My Life* (Annapolis, The US Naval Institute, 1960); and Grand Admiral Karl Dönitz, *Memoirs: Ten Years and Twenty Days* (London, Weidenfeld and Nicolson, 1959). The first consists of rather personal and often enlightening memoirs, while the second is a carefully checked strategic and tactical study based largely on Dönitz's war diary.

Trial of the Major War Criminals before the International Military Tribunal (Nuremberg, 1948) is useful for its intensive look at a limited number of events.

A fine general history is by Vice-Admiral Friedrich Ruge, *Der Seekrieg* (Annapolis, The US Naval Institute, 1957). More anecdotal in format is C. D. Bekker, *Defeat at Sea* (New York, Henry Holt and Company, Inc, 1955).

Strategic studies include Vice-Admiral Friedrich Ruge, 'German Naval Strategy across Two Wars', *USNIP*, LXXXI (February 1955), pp 152–66; Captain H. J. Reinicke, 'German Surface Force Strategy in World War II', *USNIP*, LXXXIII (February 1957), pp 181–7; and Commander D. L. Kauffman, USN, 'German Naval Strategy in World War II', *USNIP*, LXXX (January 1954), pp 1–12.

Another approach is seen in a fine anthology which contains a number of studies of naval interest: Hans-Adolf Jacobsen and Jürgen Rohwer, eds, *Decisive Battles of World War II* (London, Deutsch, 1965).

Submarines are dealt with in many works in addition to Dönitz's. Among them are Wolfgang Frank, *The Sea Wolves* (New York, Rinehart & Company, Inc, 1955); Harald Busch, *U-Boats at War* (London, Pan/Ballantine, 1972); Jochen Brennecke, *The Hunters and the Hunted* (New York, W. W. Norton & Company, Inc, 1958); and David Mason, *U-Boat: The Secret Menace* (New York, Ballantine Books, Inc, 1968). Submarine construction is covered in Karl Heinz Kurzak, 'German U-Boat Construction', *USNIP*, LXXXI (April 1955), pp 374–89. A German-language pictorial submarine history, Jürgen Rohwer's *U-Boote* (Oldenburg/Hamburg, Gerhard Stalling Verlag, 1962), includes very detailed tables of submarine losses and Allied ship losses by month and area.

The histories of individual ships which affected more than one period of the war include that of David Woodward, *The Tirpitz* (New York, W. W. Norton & Company, Inc, 1954), a fine book with a broad view; Commander Burke Wilkinson, USNR, '*Tirpitz* Tale', *USNIP*, LXXX (April 1954), pp 374–83; Corvette-Captain Fritz-Otto Busch, *Holocaust at Sea: The Drama of the Scharnhorst* (New York, Rinehart & Company, Inc, 1956); and Albert Vulliez and Jacques Mordal, *Battleship Scharnhorst* (Fair Lawn, NJ, Essential Books, 1958).

The German High Command structure can be viewed from many sides. The standard work on the Army is by Walter Goerlitz, *History of the German General Staff* (New York, Frederick A. Praeger, Inc, 1959). A look at the Army command in action is found in B. H. Liddell Hart, *The German Generals Talk* (New York, William Morrow and Company, Inc, 1948). Other materials are in Vice-Admiral Kurt Assman, 'Hitler and the German Officer Corps', *USNIP*, LXXXII (May 1956), pp 508–20; and Captain Roland E. Krause, USN, 'The German Navy under Joint Command in World War II', *USNIP*, LXXIII (September 1947), pp 1029–43.

The standard biography of Hitler is by Alan L. Bullock, *Hitler: A Study in Tyranny* (London, Penguin, 1969). Other materials on Hitler include Felix Gilbert, ed, *Hitler Directs His War* (New York, Oxford University Press, 1951); Captain Heinz Assmann, 'Some Personal Recollections of Adolf Hitler', *USNIP*, LXXIX (December 1953), pp 1288–95; F. H. Hinsley, *Hitler's Strategy* (Cambridge, University Press, 1951); and Walter Warlimont, *Inside Hitler's Headquarters* (New York, Frederick A. Praeger, Inc, 1964).

Naval aviation is dealt with by Lieutenant-Commander Edward L. Barker, USNR, in 'German Naval Aviation', *USNIP*, LXXVI (July 1950), pp 730–41, and, by the same author, in 'War without Aircraft Carriers', *USNIP*, LXXX (March 1954), pp 280–89; and in Clark G. Reynolds, 'Hitler's Flattop – The End of the Beginning', *USNIP*, XCIII (January 1967), pp 40–49. The last-mentioned does not agree with the generally accepted views of Hitler's ideas and of German strategy in general.

The standard British source is the three-volume series by Captain S. W. Roskill, DSC, RN, *The War at Sea* (London, Her Majesty's Stationery Office, 1954-61). That set is indispensable for detailed study of the naval war. A smaller work by the same author is *White Ensign* (Annapolis, The US Naval Institute, 1960). Winston S. Churchill, *The Second World War*, Vols I–VI (London, Cassell, 1960) is especially useful for presenting Churchill's views about events.

The American side of the conflict is dealt with quite differently in two works. A scholarly approach is E. B. Potter and Fleet Admiral Chester W. Nimitz, USN, eds, *Sea Power* (Englewood Cliffs, NJ, Prentice-Hall, Inc, 1960), while a colourful work, subject to serious error regarding foreign attitudes and actions because of its closeness to the events, is the fifteen-volume series by Samuel Eliot Morison, *History of the United States Naval Operations in World War II* (Boston, Little, Brown and Company, 1947–62). A shorter book by the same author is *The Two-Ocean War* (Boston, Little, Brown and Company, 1963).

The French Navy's history is recorded, with obvious bias, in Rear-Admiral Paul Auphan and Jacques Mordal, *The French Navy in World War II* (Annapolis, The US Naval Institute, 1959).

CHAPTER ONE

Few books deal in detail with the period between the wars, although some of the general sources, most notably Raeder's autobiography, devote one or more chapters to the subject.

The development of German naval thought in the early Tirpitz era is covered in Jonathan Steinberg, *Yesterday's Deterrent* (New York, The Macmillan Company, 1965).

The inter-war years are dealt with by Commander William A. Wiedersheim III, USNR, 'Factors in the Growth of the Reichsmarine (1919–39)', *USNIP*, LXXIV (March 1948), pp 317–24, and, by the same author, in 'Officer Personnel Selection in the German Navy, 1925–45', *USNIP*, LXXIII (April 1947), pp 444–9.

Material in English is scant on the personalities in the German Navy, strategic ideas such as the Wegener thesis, and critiques of such German ideas as the Z-Plan. One brief article is Vice-Admiral Friedrich Ruge, 'Dönitz – The Last Führer', *USNIP*, LXXX (October 1954), pp 1156–9.

CHAPTER TWO

Heavy surface ships are dealt with in a number of works, of which the compendium by Sir Eugene Millington-Drake, compiler, *The Drama of the Graf Spee and the Battle of the River Plate* (London, Peter Davies, 1964), is outstanding. Another of the good books on the subject is Dudley Pope, *Graf Spee* (Philadelphia, J. B. Lippincott Company, 1957). An article from the British viewpoint is by A. Cecil Hampshire, 'British Strategy in the River Plate Battle', *USNIP*, LXXXIV (December 1958), pp 85–91, while Willie Frischauer and Robert Jackson, *The Altmark Affair* (New York, The Macmillan Company, 1955), deals with a significant sequel to the *Graf Spee*'s cruise. Lieutenant Theodore Taylor, USNR, 'A Matter of Judgment', *USNIP*, LXXXIV (July 1958), pp 70–75, deals with the *Deutschland*'s seizure of the American ship *City of Flint.*

For raider references, see the listings for Chapter Six.

For the dramatic story of *U47* sinking the *Royal Oak*, the generally accepted German and British versions have been followed. Alexander McKee, in *Black Saturday* (New York, Holt, Rinehart & Winston, Inc, 1959), points out many inaccuracies in the propaganda 'memoirs' of the raid and some errors in Prien's log, but he goes on to build an essentially unsubstantiated story of sabotage covered by a fictitious submarine attack which seems highly imaginative. A restudy, utilizing all British and German sources, would be useful to clarify the details of the event.

CHAPTER THREE

The Norway operation is well covered in English. Besides the coverage in the general sources, the German side is dealt with by Vice-Admiral Kurt Assman, in 'The Invasion of Norway', *USNIP*, LXXVIII (April 1952), pp 400–13.

The official British history of the campaign is T. K. Derry, *The Campaign in Norway* (London, Her Majesty's Stationery Office, 1952).

An article about the Sea Lion operation by Dr Stefan T. Possony, 'Decision without Battle', *USNIP*, LXXII (June 1946), pp 762–4, sees Norway as a German loss – an acquisition of a base at the cost of the Fleet which would use it. That seems too severe an indictment, for few major ships were lost; and even if more had been lost, the basic German reasons for the operation included far more than a move to acquire naval bases. In addition, most high-ranking Army and Navy officers did not expect French bases to become available, so arguments from that point of view cite information acquired after the fact.

CHAPTER FOUR

Three good books deal with Sea Lion in different ways. Peter Fleming, *Operation Sea Lion* (New York, Simon and Schuster, Inc, 1957), emphasizes the British view; Ronald Wheatley, *Operation Sea Lion* (Oxford, Clarendon Press, 1958), is strong regarding German planning; and Walter Ansel, *Hitler Confronts England* (Durham, NC, Duke University Press, 1960), is an extremely fine study of the German view, especially of the thinking and methods of planning of Hitler, Raeder, and Göring both before and during the 1940 confrontation. His unusual conclusion is that the Germans could have carried out an invasion if they had planned differently, particularly if they had concentrated on sea control in the Channel rather than on absolute air control.

Two shorter studies contribute to the picture: Vice-Admiral Kurt Assmann, 'Operation Sea Lion', *USNIP*, LXXVI (January 1950), pp 1–13; and Dr Stefan T. Possony, 'Decision without Battle', *USNIP*, LXXII (June 1946), pp 761–72.

A dramatic incident from the French Fleet's retreat to North Africa is recounted by Captain Isaiah Olch, USN, in 'The *Jean Bart*'s Escape to Safety', *USNIP*, LXXXII (October 1956), pp 1054–65.

CHAPTER FIVE

The relationships between Stalin and Hitler are dealt with by Vice-Admiral Kurt Assmann in 'Stalin and Hitler', *USNIP*, LXXV: Part I, 'The Pact with Moscow' (June 1949), pp 638–51, and Part II, 'The Road to Stalingrad' (July 1949), pp 758–73.

Mediterranean studies include Rear Admiral Raymond de Belot, French Navy, *The Struggle for the Mediterranean* (Princeton, Princeton University Press, 1951); and Wyatt E. Barnes, 'Changing Trends in the Mediterranean Balance of Power, 1935–1957', *USNIP*, LXXXIV (March 1958), pp 52–61.

The Italian side is presented by Commander Marc' Antonio Bragadin, Italian Navy, *The Italian Navy in World War II* (Annapolis, The US Naval Institute, 1957); Admiral Romeo Bernotti, Italian Navy, 'Italian Naval Policy under Fascism', *USNIP*, LXXXII (July 1956), pp 722–31; and Vice-Admiral Giuseppe Fioravanzo, Italian Navy, 'Italian Strategy in the Mediterranean, 1940–1943', *USNIP*, LXXXIV (September 1958), pp 64–72.

Cooperation among the Axis powers is discussed by Professor John W. Masland, 'Japanese-German Naval Collaboration in World War II', *USNIP*, LXXV (February 1949), pp 178–87; Assistant Professor Robert M. Langdon, 'And Your Task, Dear Partner', *USNIP*, LXXVII (April 195[illegible]), pp 564–9; and Vice-Admiral Giuseppe

Fioravanzo, Italian Navy, 'The Japanese Military Mission to Italy in 1941', *USNIP*, LXXXII (January 1956), pp 24–31.

Individual events are covered by A. Cecil Hampshire, in 'Triumph at Taranto', *USNIP*, LXXXV (March 1959), pp 70–79; and Commander Luigi Durand de la Penne, Italian Navy, 'The Italian Attack on the Alexandria Naval Base', *USNIP*, LXXXII (February 1956), pp 124–35.

A very controversial person's role is analysed by American Consul General Russell Brooks in 'The Unknown Darlan', *USNIP*, LXXXI (August 1955), pp 878–92. The same author deals with the neutralization of the French Alexandria Fleet in 'A Gentlemen's Agreement', *USNIP*, LXXVIII (July 1952), pp 701–11.

Among the many books on the desert war, two of the best are Correlli Barnett, *The Desert Generals* (New York, The Viking Press, 1961); and Desmond Young, *Rommel* (London, Fontana, 1969).

The decisive Battle of Midway is described by eyewitnesses from both sides by Captain Mitsuo Fuchida, Imperial Japanese Navy, and Commander Masatake Okumiya, Imperial Japanese Navy, in *Midway* (Annapolis, The US Naval Institute, 1955); and by Vice-Admiral William Ward Smith, USN, in *Midway* (New York, Thomas Y. Crowell Company, 1966).

CHAPTER SIX

Heavy-ship histories include Admiral Theodor Krancke and H. J. Brennecke, *The Battleship Scheer* (London, William Kimber and Co Ltd, 1956); and Lieutenant-Commander Peter Handel-Mazzetti, 'The *Scharnhorst-Gneisenau* Team at Its Peak', *USNIP*, LXXXII (August 1956, pp 852–60.

Many writers have dealt with the *Bismarck* story, but no complete account exists in English. The following two works do not comprise a complete list of *Bismarck* materials, but both have value in conjunction with the accounts in the more general books. A crisp account of the voyage is that of Commander T. Gerhard F. Bidlingmaier, 'Exploits and End of the Battleship *Bismarck*', *USNIP*, LXXXIV (July 1958), pp 76–87. A fine study from the British side is by Captain Russell Grenfell, RN, *The Bismarck Episode* (London, Faber & Faber, 1968). Mention must also be made of Will Berthold, *The Sinking of the Bismarck* (London, New York, and Toronto, Longmans, Green and Company, 1958). That miserably organized book contains much material unavailable elsewhere in English, apparently derived from interviews with survivors; but it is so propagandistic, fictionalized, and in places obviously false that none of its information can be accepted without independent confirmation.

A fine survey of the auxiliary cruisers' careers is David Woodward, *The Secret Raiders* (New York, W. W. Norton & Company, Inc,

1955). Among the individual ship histories are those of Wolfgang Frank and Bernhard Rogge, *The German Raider Atlantis* (New York, Ballantine Books, Inc, 1956); Captain Theodor Detmers, *The Raider Kormoran* (London, William Kimber and Co Ltd, 1959); Richard S. Pattee, 'The Cruise of the German Raider *Atlantis*, 1940–41', *USNIP*, LXXV (December 1949), pp 1322–33; and Anthony E. Sokol, 'The Cruise of "Schiff 45" ', *USNIP*, LXXVII (May 1951), pp 476–89.

The logistics problems of all the raiders are covered by Commander Roy O. Stratton, USN, in 'German Naval Support Techniques in World War II', *USNIP*, LXXX (March 1954), pp 256–63, and, by the same author, in 'Germany's Secret Naval Supply Service', *USNIP*, LXXIX (October 1953), pp 1084–90.

CHAPTER SEVEN

The Italian effort in the Atlantic is described by Rear-Admiral Aldo Cocchia, Italian Navy, in 'Italian Submarines and Their Bordeaux Base', *USNIP*, LXXXIV (June 1958), pp 37–45.

Two studies of large-scale convoy battles are by Ronald Seth, *The Fiercest Battle* (New York, W. W. Norton & Company, Inc, 1962); and by Captain John M. Waters, Jr, USCG, 'Stay Tough', *USNIP*, XCII (December 1966), pp 95–105. A rather uncritical biography of Otto Kretschmer is Terence Robertson, *Night Raider of the Atlantic* (New York, E. P. Dutton & Co, Inc, 1956).

Radar development is outlined in Captain Donald Macintyre, RN, 'Shipbourne Radar', *USNIP*, XCIII (September 1967), pp 70–83.

The *Laconia* story is thoroughly dealt with in Léonce Peillard, *The Laconia Affair* (New York, G. P. Putnam's Sons, 1963); but vital information not available earlier is in Dr Maurer Maurer and Lawrence J. Paszek, 'Origin of the *Laconia* Order', *Air University Review*, XV (March–April 1964), pp 26–37.

An American contribution to the Atlantic contest is discussed in John Forney Rudy, 'The American Merchant Marine in World War II', *USNIP*, LXXV (December 1949), pp 1402–11.

CHAPTER EIGHT

The Channel dash of 1942 is dealt with by Captain H. J. Reinicke in 'The German Side of the Channel Dash', *USNIP*, LXXXI (June 1955), pp 636–46; and by Terence Robertson in *Channel Dash* (New York, E. P. Dutton & Co, Inc, 1958). The latter also includes a description of the *Victorious*' torpedo-plane attack on the *Bismarck*. Air cover for the sortie is described in Adolf Galland, *The First and Last* (London, Methuen, 1970).

The Murmansk convoys are dealt with in Anthony E. Sokol, 'German Attacks on the Murmansk Run', *USNIP*, LXXVIII (December 1952), pp 1326–41; and the thorough B. B. Schofield, *The Russian Convoys*, (London, Pan, 1971). The New Year's Eve battle of 1942 is covered in Dudley Pope, *73 North* (Philadelphia, J. B. Lippincott Company, 1958); and the *Scharnhorst*'s last battle a year later is detailed in Karl-Hinrich Peter, 'The Sinking of the *Scharnhorst*', *USNIP*, LXXXII (January 1956), pp 48–53.

Attacks in the *Tirpitz* are covered by T. J. Waldron and James Gleason in *The Frogmen* (London, Pan, 1954); and by Paul Brickhill in *The Dam Busters* (London, Pan, 1954).

Normandy-invasion planning is covered by Vice-Admiral Friedrich Ruge in 'With Rommel before Normandy', *USNIP*, LXXX (June 1954), pp 612–19; and by Captain Martin Blumenson, USA, and Major James Hodgson, USAR, in 'Hitler versus His Generals in the West', *USNIP*, LXXXII (December 1956), pp 1281–7.

The St-Nazaire raid is seen from the British side in *Combined Operations* (New York, The Macmillan Company, 1943); and C. E. Lucas Phillips, *The Greatest Raid of All* (London, Pan, 1961).

CHAPTER NINE

Two submarine histories are Hans Joachin Decker, '404 Days! The War Patrol of the German *U505*', *USNIP*, LXXXVI (March 1960), pp 33–45, about a submarine which was eventually captured at sea; and Heinz Schaeffer, *U-Boat 977* (New York, W. W. Norton & Company, Inc, 1952), about one which sailed to Argentina at the end of the war.

The *Peleus* case is covered in Assistant Professor Robert M. Langdon, 'Live Men Do Tell Tales', *USNIP*, LXXVII (January 1952), pp 16–21.

An effort with few results is seen in Franz Selinger, 'German Midget Submarines', *USNIP*, LXXXIV (March 1958), pp 102–3.

INDEX